GOLD

first

g coursebook

NEW EDITION
with 2015 exam specifications

Jan Bell

Amanda Thomas

CONTENTS

Exam information

The *Cambridge English: First* examination is made up of four papers, each testing a different area of ability in English. The Reading and Use of English paper is worth 40 percent of the marks (80 marks), and each of the other papers is worth 20 percent (40 marks each). There are five grades. A, B and C are pass grades; D and E are fail grades.

Reading and Use of English (1 hour 15 minutes)

The Reading & Use of English paper has seven parts. Parts 1–4 contain grammar and vocabulary tasks within texts or as discrete items. Parts 5–7 contain texts and accompanying reading comprehension tasks. You write your answers on an answer sheet during the test.

Part 1 **Multiple-choice cloze**	*Focus*	Vocabulary/Lexico-grammatical
	Task	You read a text with eight gaps. You choose the best word or phrase to fit in each gap from a set of four options (A, B, C or D).
Part 2 **Open cloze**	*Focus*	Grammar/Lexico-grammatical
	Task	You read a text with eight gaps. You have to think of the most appropriate word to fill each gap. You must use one word only. No options are provided.
Part 3 **Word formation**	*Focus*	Vocabulary/Lexico-grammatical
	Task	You read a text with eight gaps. You are given the stems of the missing words in capitals at the ends of the lines with gaps. You have to change the form of each word to fit the context.
Part 4 **Key word transformations**	*Focus*	Grammar and vocabulary
	Task	There are six items. You are given a sentence and a 'key word'. You have to complete a second, gapped sentence using the key word. The second sentence has a different grammatical structure but must have a similar meaning to the original.
Part 5 **Multiple-choice questions**	*Focus*	Detail, opinion, attitude, text organisation features (e.g. exemplification, reference), tone, purpose, main idea, implication
	Task	There are six four-option multiple-choice questions. You have to choose the correct option (A, B, C or D) based on the information in the text.
Part 6 **Gapped text**	*Focus*	Understanding text structure, cohesion, coherence, global meaning
	Task	You read a text from which six sentences have been removed and placed in jumbled order after the text. There is one extra sentence that you do not need to use. You must decide from where in the text the sentences have been removed.
Part 7 **Multiple matching**	*Focus*	Specific information, detail, opinion and attitude
	Task	You read ten questions or statements about a text which has been divided into sections, or several short texts. You have to decide which section or text contains the information relating to each question or statement.

Writing (1 hour 20 minutes)

The Writing paper is divided into two parts, and you have to complete one task from each part. Each answer carries equal marks, so you should not spend longer on one than another.

Part 1	*Focus*	Outlining and discussing issues on a particular topic
	Task	Part 1 is compulsory, and there is no choice of questions. You have to write an essay based on a title and notes. You have to write 140–190 words.
Part 2	*Focus*	Writing a task for a particular purpose based on a specific topic, context and target reader.
	Task	Part 2 has three tasks to choose from which may include: •a letter or email •an article •a report •a review. You have to write 140–190 words for Part 2.

Listening (approximately 40 minutes)

There are four parts in the Listening paper, with a total of thirty questions. You write your answers on the question paper and then you have five minutes at the end of the exam to transfer them to an answer sheet. In each part you will hear the text(s) twice. The texts may be monologues or conversations between interacting speakers. There will be a variety of accents.

Part 1 Extracts with multiple-choice questions	Focus	Each extract will have a different focus, which could be: main point, detail, purpose or location of speech, relationship between the speakers, attitude or opinion of the speakers.
	Task	You hear eight short, unrelated extracts of about thirty seconds each. They may be monologues or conversations. You have to answer one three-option multiple-choice question (A, B or C) for each extract.
Part 2 Sentence completion	Focus	Specific information, detail, stated opinion
	Task	You hear a monologue lasting about three minutes. You complete ten sentences with information heard on the recording.
Part 3 Multiple matching	Focus	Gist, detail, function, attitude, purpose, opinion
	Task	You hear a series of five monologues, lasting about thirty seconds each. The speakers in each extract are different, but the situations or topics are all related to each other. You have to match each speaker to one of eight statements or questions (A–H). There are three extra options that you do not need to use.
Part 4 Multiple-choice questions	Focus	Specific information, opinion, attitude, gist, main idea
	Task	You hear an interview or conversation which lasts about three minutes. There are seven questions. You have to choose the correct option (A, B or C).

Speaking (approximately 14 minutes)

You take the Speaking test with a partner. There are two examiners. One is the 'interlocutor', who speaks to you, and the other is the 'assessor', who just listens. There are four different parts in the test.

Part 1 Interview (2 minutes)	Focus	General interactional and social language
	Task	The interlocutor asks each of you questions about yourself, such as where you come from or what you do in your free time.
Part 2 Individual long turn (4 minutes)	Focus	Organising your ideas, comparing, describing, expressing opinions
	Task	The interlocutor gives you a pair of photographs to compare, and to give a personal reaction to. You speak by yourself for about a minute while your partner listens. Then the interlocutor asks your partner a question related to the topic. Only a short answer is expected. You then change roles.
Part 3 Collaborative task (4 minutes)	Focus	Interacting with your partner, exchanging ideas, expressing and justifying opinions, agreeing and/or disagreeing, suggesting, speculating, evaluating, reaching a decision through negotiation
	Task	You are given a task to discuss together for 1–2 minutes, based on a written instruction and prompts. You then have a minute to try and reach a decision together. There is no right or wrong answer to the task and you don't have to agree with each other. It is the interaction between you that is important.
Part 4 Discussion (4 minutes)	Focus	Expressing and justifying opinions, agreeing and disagreeing
	Task	The interlocutor asks you both general questions related to the topic of Part 3, and gives you the chance to give your opinions on other aspects of the same topic.

For more information see the **Writing reference** (page 179), the **General marking guidelines** (page 194) and the **Exam focus** (page 200).

Bands and fans

Speaking

1 **Discuss the questions.**

1 Why do people like listening to different kinds of live music?

2 What do you enjoy doing most: playing a musical instrument, listening to music at home or going to a live gig?

3 Are you a fan of a particular band or musical artist? What makes someone a 'fan'?

Vocabulary

free time activities: verb/noun collocations

2 **Match the verbs in A with the activities in B. There may be more than one possibility.**

Example: *go to/watch a film*

A	do	go (to/out for/on)	have	play	watch

B	the computer	computer games	a DVD	a film	football
	friends round	a gig	the guitar	a pizza	running
	shopping	the theatre	television	yoga	

3 **Add any other free time activities you can think of to list B. Put the verb it goes with in list A.**

Listening and speaking

asking and answering questions

4 **▶ 01** **Read and listen to the questions about free time. Underline the words which are stressed.**

1 How do you usually relax when you have some free time?

2 What do you do when you stay in? Where do you go when you go out?

3 Do you like being in a large group or would you rather be with a few close friends?

LANGUAGE TIP

Adverbs of frequency (*usually, never, hardly ever*, etc.) come before a main verb and after auxiliary verbs such as *be*.
*I **hardly ever** go shopping.*
*I'm **always** busy.*

Longer adverbials (*from time to time, every day, now and again*, etc.) can come at the beginning or end of a sentence.
*I go running **every evening**. **Now and again** I play squash.*

5 ▶ 02 **Listen to the students' answers and complete the gaps.**

1 I usually find .... quite relaxing but it depends on ....

2 I tend to .... on weekdays though I sometimes ....

3 .... is good fun.

4 .... helps me to switch off.

5 I'm really into ....

6 I go out .... now and again.

6 Work in pairs. Ask and answer the questions in Activity 4.

Interview (Part 1)

listening to and answering questions

▶ **EXAM** FOCUS p.206

7 **In Part 1 of the Speaking paper, you answer some questions in which you give personal information and opinions. Match questions 1–7 to topics A–E.**

1 What kind of music do you enjoy listening to?

2 Do you have any brothers or sisters?

3 What do you like about the place where you were brought up?

4 What subject did you enjoy most at school?

5 What do you think you'll be doing in five years' time?

6 Where do you think you'll go on holiday this year?

7 Tell us about your closest friend.

A your personal relationships

B your home town

C your job or studies

D your free time activities

E your future plans

EXAM TIP

Answer in full, giving reasons. Avoid one-word answers and don't move away from the question.

8 **Add two more questions to each topic A–E. Use question words such as *what* (*kind*), *when*, *how* (*many*), *who*, *why*, *where*.**

9 ▶ 03 **Listen to Julia and Stefan and answer the questions.**

1 Which of the questions in Activity 7 were they each asked?

2 Did they answer them in enough detail?

3 Did they vary their tone of voice?

4 What did Stefan say when he didn't understand the question?

10 Choose one question from each topic in Activities 7 and 8 and ask your partner.

▶ **GRAMMAR** REFERENCE p.162

Speaking

1 Look at the photos and discuss the questions.

1 When do you think these photos were taken?
2 What kind of music do you think the people were into?
3 Why do groups of young people get together like this?

Gapped text (Part 6)

▶ **EXAM** FOCUS p.202

2 You are going to read a magazine article about music sub-cultures. Read the text quickly. How does the writer answer the question in the title?

ARE MUSIC 'TRIBES' A THING OF THE PAST?

Like-minded music fans have been bonding together for half a century. But is this on its way out?

There was a time when the average person formed their opinions about pop music not just on what they heard, but also on their reaction to the many groups of young people who followed the very different kinds of music. *These impressions* were based on the clothes *they* wore as much as their behaviour in general. The style-conscious mods of the 1960s would <u>roam around</u> on their scooters all day, getting off only for an occasional fight with passing rockers, identified by their powerful motorbikes, greased hair and leather jackets. And in the 70s and 80s, punks would dye their hair pink and terrorise grannies, or at least that is how *they* <u>came across</u> in the media. But when was the last time a new kind of music was associated with a particular group of youths in the same way?

These days you can't always tell what music someone likes just by looking at them. People now seem less likely to hold on tight to their cultural identity, which means that, although tribes still exist, they are looser and broader than before. This change is probably due to the fact that music is now accessed in very different ways, with people able to listen to it at any time. Hardly any young people remember pop culture before the internet, when records were bought rather than streamed or downloaded. **1** *E*

19-year-old Bianca Munyankore agrees that the excitement of listening to a song you waited to buy has probably gone. **2** In any case, saving up to buy a CD means you wouldn't be exploring any other music, and she believes an openness to music is now a natural part of being young.

Music writer and teacher Neil Kulkarni observes that although sub-cultures still exist, they are no longer participated in with pride or any form of aggression. 'These days, rather than making any kind of statement, it's just a way for kids to say what kind of music they're into. **3** The internet has made them more prepared to listen to things that they wouldn't necessarily have expected to like and, as a result, there are more connections between sub-cultures.'

4 Author Paul Hodkinson thinks so; he believes the fact that pop tribes have changed over the years means that they've succeeded rather than failed. 'If other people find you odd, and if that makes you unpopular, it's important to connect with other people like you,' he says. He rejects the claim that angry mods and rockers and rebellious punks were driven by a spirit of protest, explaining, 'The desire to be part of a group is often about far less exciting things, such as trying to make friends or having something to do.'

Mass communication has meant that sharing music is now easy. **5** The most underground metal or hip-hop can be found not just on the internet, but even on TV; many musicians make their money from TV or adverts rather than from fans buying music or concert tickets.

Perhaps the biggest change to pop tribes, though, is that they are no longer restricted to young people. Today, audiences for punk gigs or metal nights range in age from 16–60 and mix well together. **6**

3 **Read the first two paragraphs again and answer the questions.**

1 In the first paragraph, what do *these impressions* and *they* in line 5 refer back to? What does *they* refer to in line 12?

2 In the second paragraph, which words in the answer (sentence E) link to the topic and vocabulary? How does *neither* link back? What does *they* refer to?

4 **Six sentences have been removed from the article. Choose from sentences A–G the one which fits each gap. There is one extra sentence which you do not need to use.**

EXAM TIP

Look for linking words and phrases in the options which link to the ideas and language (e.g. connecting words, synonyms, pronouns which link to nouns) in the sentences before and after each gap.

A So does that mean that tribes are, in fact, expanding rather than dying?

B Another consequence of this is that all kinds of music are now found much more in the mainstream.

C However, the freedom of simply listening to whatever you want, whenever you want more than makes up for that feeling.

D Which appears to show that, if a pop tribe means anything these days, it seems to be about a set of tastes, rather than a stage of life you go through before reaching adulthood.

E Neither have *they* experienced a time when they were limited to tracks they could hear on the radio or get on a cassette from friends.

F Does the lack of very visible teenage tribes matter for the health of pop culture?

G And a lot of youngsters are now finding that their taste overlaps with other groups.

5 **Compare your answers and give reasons for your choices.**

6 **What sub-cultures exist in your country? In what ways can you identify people in these sub-cultures by the way they dress and the music they like?**

Vocabulary
deducing words in context

7 **Look at these words and phrases and choose the correct meaning. Which clues in the text helped you?**

Example: *'scooters' and 'all day' might help you to understand 'roam around'.*

1 *roam around* (para 1)
   A cause trouble
   B travel with no real purpose

2 *come across* (para 1)
   A appear to be
   B find by chance

3 *track* (option E)
   A a narrow path or road
   B a piece of music or a song from a CD

4 *make up for* (option C)
   A improve a bad situation
   B do something to show you are sorry

5 *in the mainstream* (option B)
   A conventional
   B respected

6 *tastes* (option D)
   A experiences of something
   B things you like

Present simple and continuous

▶ **GRAMMAR** REFERENCE p.176

1 **Look at the sentences and decide whether they should be in the simple or continuous form. Then discuss why.**

1 My son's *always downloading/always downloads* music instead of getting on with his work.

2 I *work/'m working* overtime this month while the music editor is on sick leave.

3 Someone *plays/'s playing* the piano. Can you hear it?

4 Did you know that band *comes/'s coming* from my home town?

5 I *get/'m getting* better at recognising classical music.

6 I *take/'m taking* my iPod everywhere.

2 **Match the uses of the present simple and present continuous with the examples in Activity 1.**

A a repeated action/habit

B a permanent situation/fact

C an activity happening at the moment of speaking

D an activity in progress but not at this exact moment

E a changing or developing situation

F emphasises repetition of typical (often annoying or surprising) behaviour

LANGUAGE TIP

Verbs such as *believe, own, belong, like, understand, know, hear* are not usually used in the continuous form because they describe states, not actions.

Some verbs can be used in both the simple and continuous form with different meanings.

*I **see** what you mean. (see = understand)*

*I**'m seeing** her next week. (see = meet)*

3 **Look at the pairs of sentences and say why the speaker has used the present simple or continuous in each case.**

1 A I <u>have</u> a ticket to see Lady Gaga.

  B I'<u>m having</u> a shower.

2 A That singer <u>appears</u> to be doing well.

  B Eminem'<u>s appearing</u> at the V Festival.

3 A He'<u>s being</u> really kind.

  B He'<u>s</u> really kind.

4 A He'<u>s thinking</u> about joining a band.

  B I <u>think</u> that band is really good.

5 A It <u>depends</u> on how much money I've got.

  B I'<u>m depending</u> on her to organise everything.

6 A This soup <u>tastes</u> good.

  B Joe'<u>s tasting</u> the soup.

4 **Complete the sentences with the present simple or present continuous form of the verbs in brackets.**

1 I .... (*not like*) pop music.

2 The band .... (*appear*) in Manchester all week.

3 I can't hear what you .... (*say*). It's too loud.

4 I .... (*think*) it's dangerous to listen to your iPod when you're riding a bike.

5 You can never have a conversation with her – she .... (*always check*) her phone for messages.

6 That band .... (*get*) more and more popular.

7 We .... (*often go*) to a jazz club on Friday nights.

8 You .... (*be*) very difficult today!

5 **Write sentences about three things that**

1 you do on a regular basis.

2 you are doing now (but not at this exact moment).

6 **Compare your sentences in pairs. Do you have anything in common?**

Vocabulary

phrasal verbs with *take*

1 Match the phrasal verbs in 1–5 with meanings A–E.

1 His career *took off* as soon as he won the prize: he's so talented.
2 He *takes after* his father, who's also really musical.
3 I *took up* the saxophone last year.
4 Tom *took over* as the band's manager when Sam left.
5 I made him *take back* what he said about my taste in music.

A have similar characteristics
B become responsible for something
C start an activity
D admit you are wrong
E become successful

Multiple-choice cloze (Part 1)

▶ **EXAM** FOCUS p.200

2 Read the text about a musician quickly and say what is different about Josh Freese's relationship with his fans. Don't worry about the gaps yet.

3 Look at the example. Why are options A, B and D wrong?

4 Now look at the options for gap 1 and answer the questions.

1 Which of the verbs A–D can be followed by *of*?
2 Choose the phrase which means *familiar with*.

5 For questions 2–8, decide which answer (A, B, C or D) best fits each gap.

EXAM TIP

Think about which word might fit the gap before looking at the options. Check each side of the gap to make sure that the option you choose goes with the other words.

---

6 Look at questions 4 and 8 again and check you have chosen the correct phrasal verb.

7 Discuss the questions.

1 Do you think this is a good way for artists to promote their music?
2 Would any of these offers attract you?

Drumming up business

Josh Freese is a very successful session drummer **(0)** ..*C. based*.... in Los Angeles. You probably won't have **(1)** .... of him but he's played with some very successful bands. When Freese **(2)** .... his first solo album, called *Since 1972*, he decided to set up a system where fans could buy something unique. By **(3)** .... with fans directly, he hoped to sell more of his music.

The CD didn't cost much but if you paid $50 for it, you would also get a personal five-minute 'thank you' phone call. Sales of the album quickly took **(4)** .... But there were other limited options which gave fans the opportunity to meet Freese in **(5)** .... The option to have lunch with Freese for $250 **(6)** .... out in about a week. Fans could also **(7)** .... an individual drum lesson from Freese for $2,500. There were other offers ranging from $10,000 to $75,000. Not all of these were taken **(8)** .... by fans, but a teenager from Florida actually purchased the $20,000 option and spent a week on tour with Freese.

0	**A** situated	**B** located	**C** based	**D** lived
1	**A** recognised	**B** noticed	**C** heard	**D** known
2	**A** released	**B** sent	**C** presented	**D** brought
3	**A** joining	**B** discussing	**C** contacting	**D** communicating
4	**A** after	**B** back	**C** off	**D** up
5	**A** person	**B** front	**C** life	**D** face
6	**A** stayed	**B** gave	**C** sold	**D** let
7	**A** achieve	**B** receive	**C** collect	**D** gain
8	**A** over	**B** back	**C** off	**D** up

Multiple matching (Part 3)

▶ **EXAM** FOCUS p.205

1 **Tick the statements which are true for you. Then compare with a partner.**

A I like following band members on Facebook and Twitter.

B These days I only download music that's free.

C I think the videos a band makes are just as important as their music.

D Most people haven't heard of the music I like.

E My music tastes are quite varied.

F I spend a lot of time listening to music at home with friends.

G I often discover new bands through personal recommendations.

H I prefer listening to live music.

2 ▶ 04 **You will hear five people talking about listening to music. Listen to Speaker 1. Which things does he mention?**

his taste in music   new bands   Twitter   video

3 **Look at extracts from Speaker 1 (1–4). Which one matches one of the statements A–H in Activity 1?**

1 Now I'm just into the same stuff as my friends – hip hop mainly.

2 I don't usually bother with Twitter or Facebook.

3 My group of friends are always sharing music files and telling each other about new discoveries. I've found a lot of new bands that way.

4 They'll only listen to new bands that no one's heard of. It's just a way of showing off, I think.

4 ▶ 05 **Now listen to Speakers 2–5. Match statements from the list A–H in Activity 1 with what each speaker says. Use the letters only once. There are three extra letters which you do not need to use.**

EXAM TIP

Listen for words and phrases that are synonyms or paraphrases of the key words in the statements.

5 **Compare your answers in pairs. Then listen again to check.**

Speaking

6 **Work in pairs and discuss the questions.**

1 Which speaker's opinions are the most similar to yours?

2 How are your listening habits and attitudes to music similar to or different from your partner's?

Habit in the past
used to/would

▶ **GRAMMAR** REFERENCE p.168

1 **Look at the sentences and answer the questions.**

I <u>used to be obsessed</u> with music videos.

When I was growing up, my mum <u>would play</u> 1970s' music and dance around the kitchen.

1 Is she still obsessed with music videos?
2 Did her mother often listen to 1970s' music?
3 Which underlined verb describes a past state?
4 Which underlined verb describes a past habit?
5 Which of the underlined verbs can you use to describe <u>both</u> past states and habits?

LANGUAGE TIP

Be careful not to confuse *used to do* (describing past habit) with *be/get used to doing* (be accustomed to something in the present).

*I **used to** hate classical music.* (= but now I like it)

*I **am used to** being alone.* (= It's something that happens a lot and I don't mind it)

---

2 **Look at sentences 1–4. Is it possible to use both *would* and *used to*?**

1 My parents would always listen to classical music while we were having dinner.
2 My parents used to go to a jazz festival every year.
3 My dad used to have a really old radio.
4 My mum used to know all the words to every song by Madonna.

3 **Complete the text with the present simple, present continuous, *used to* or *would* forms of the verbs in brackets. Sometimes more than one answer is possible.**

Speaking

4 **Discuss the questions with a partner.**

1 How do you think the writer's children feel about her taste in music?
2 What kind of music did you use to listen to when you were younger? What did your parents think of it?
3 How do you think your taste in music will change as you get older?

My life as a punk

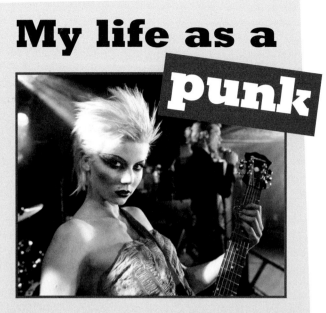

Insurance broker Sarah Collins might have a boring day job, but she's a punk at heart.

I always say that the best time of my life was when I **(1)** .... (*be*) a punk. It's a time that I look back on fondly and I still **(2)** .... (*smile*) when I think of those wonderful people, their fantastic haircuts and clothes and their great personalities.

On Saturdays I **(3)** .... (*go*) down the Kings Road in London.
I **(4)** .... (*meet*) punks from all over and we **(5)** .... (*just walk around*), sit in the pubs, look in the shops and get searched by the police. That was a very good way to spend a Saturday.

Now I'm in my fifties. I **(6)** .... (*work*) in insurance and I've got three children. But just recently I've started to return to my punk roots. Although I **(7)** .... (*get*) older, I've realised I still **(8)** .... (*love*) going to gigs and hanging around with punks.
I **(9)** .... (*discover*) fantastic new bands and I **(10)** .... (*enjoy*) myself so much!

Informal email (Part 2)

using informal language

▶ **WRITING** REFERENCE p.182

1 **Discuss the questions with a partner.**

1 How easy is it to see live music where you live?

2 Would you travel abroad to go to a music festival or concert?

3 What advice would you give to someone who is visiting your country about where to see live music?

2 **Read the exam task and answer the questions.**

1 Who do you have to write to?

2 Why are you writing?

3 What kind of style do you have to write in?

> You've received an email from your English friend Josh. Read this part of the email and write your email to Josh.
>
> > I'm really looking forward to visiting you this summer. If possible, I'd really like to see some live music. Can you tell me what kind of music is popular with you and your friends? How easy is it to get tickets for concerts?
> > Thanks
> > Josh
>
> Write your **email** in **140–190** words in an appropriate style.

3 **Look at the model email and choose the word or phrase which is most appropriate for an informal email.**

Hi Josh

Yes, I'm really looking forward to your visit too! It's good you want to see some live music while you're here because in my town **(1)** *there's a music festival every summer/an annual music festival takes place* and **(2)** *you will have the opportunity/you'll be able to* see lots of local bands play. None of them is very famous but there's a fantastic atmosphere there and I always **(3)** *find it very enjoyable/ enjoy going a lot.* The tickets are very reasonable and you can spend the whole day there. Of course, like all my friends, I'm **(4)** *mainly interested in/have a preference for* rock bands but you can find reggae and traditional music there too **(5)** *– you won't be disappointed because there's something for everyone/; it offers something for everyone, which means no one will be disappointed.*

There aren't any large music venues near where I live, so it's not that easy for me to go to big concerts very often. **(6)** *But/However,* one of my favourite bands, Mystery Jets, is playing in the nearest city on 22 August, so **(7)** *if you like, I could/if you're interested, I'd be willing to* get tickets for us to go to that.

(8) *Let me know what you think./Please reply as soon as possible.*

Alice

4 **Which of the expressions 1–4 could you use to end the email to Josh?**

1 Hope to hear from you soon.

2 I look forward to hearing from you.

3 Can't wait to see you in the summer.

4 Don't hesitate to get in touch if you have any more questions.

5 **Read the exam task and tick the information you could include in your email to Max.**

> You have received an email from a student called Max. Read this part of the email and write your email to Max.
>
> > I'm moving to your town soon to go to college. Can you tell me what kind of things there are to do in the evening for students and what you like doing best?
> > Thanks
> > Max
>
> Write your **email** in **140–190** words in an appropriate style.

1 recommend some places to go

2 offer to take Max out one evening

3 tell him about the most expensive restaurants in your town

4 complain about the lack of entertainment venues

5 describe a typical evening out in detail

6 describe your favourite kind of evening out and why you like it

6 **Write I (informal) or F (formal) next to the phrases 1–6.**

1 I would advise you to …

2 The best place to eat is …

3 You really must go to …

4 If you feel like dancing, there's a good club in …

5 You should definitely try …

6 I'd highly recommend visiting …

7 **Write your email, using some of the language from Activities 3 and 6. Then check your work using the writing checklist on page 179.**

1 Complete the second sentence so that it has a similar meaning to the first sentence. Use between two and five words, including the word given.

Example:
I was given responsibility for booking gigs for our band.
OVER
Last month I _took over booking gigs_ for our band.

1 I enjoyed learning to play the guitar and I'd like to take it up again one day.
USED
I .... learning to play the guitar and I'd like to take it up again one day.

2 We always went to the jazz festival every July.
WOULD
We .... to the jazz festival every July.

3 I perform in front of people all the time, so I don't mind doing it.
USED
I .... in front of people, so I don't mind doing it.

4 Her career was an instant success as soon as she appeared on a TV advert.
TOOK
Her career .... as soon as she appeared on a TV advert.

5 Unfortunately, I'm not like my grandfather, who could play the piano really well.
AFTER
Unfortunately, I .... my grandfather, who could play the piano really well.

6 When we started going out, I hated my boyfriend's taste in music but it's becoming less of a problem.
USED
I .... my boyfriend's taste in music but it's becoming less of a problem.

2 Complete the sentences with the present simple or present continuous form of the verbs in brackets.

1 I .... (*not like*) classical music.

2 I don't understand what you .... (*say*). Can you say it again, please?

3 I .... (*not think*) it's a good idea to learn an instrument when you're too young.

4 She's never at home. She .... (*always do*) something in the evening.

5 Traditional music .... (*get*) more and more popular.

6 You .... (*play*) really well today.

3 Choose the correct word to complete the sentences.

1 I try and .... running as often as I can.
A go   **B** do   **C** doing   **D** going

2 I often have friends .... in the evening.
A in   **B** round   **C** along   **D** down

3 Let's go .... the theatre soon.
A out   **B** for   **C** to   **D** at

4 He's always .... on the computer to check his messages.
A doing   **B** having   **C** going   **D** watching

4 Complete the text with the words in the box.

available	collection	concerts	downloaded
fans	once	released	tastes

mp3s have ruined our listening habits
Sometimes I feel the rise of mp3s has made music too easy to obtain. Instead of taking time to appreciate good music, most **(1)** .... now consume as much music as they possibly can. My music **(2)** .... feels increasingly impersonal, to the point where I don't even know if I've **(3)** .... an album or not. Sometimes I'll listen to an album I like only **(4)** .... The problem is there's just not enough time to give every album the same attention because there's always a new band that's just **(5)** .... their first album that I want to listen to.
And another problem is that, despite the huge variety of music **(6)** .... , I feel like people's **(7)** .... are actually narrowing because they generally only go to **(8)** .... where bands sound exactly like all the others they enjoy listening to.

Relative values

Speaking

1 **Discuss the questions.**

1 How do you think your friends would describe your personality?

2 What personality characteristics do you share with other members of your family?

2 **Do the personality quiz.**

PERSONALITY QUIZ

	How likely are you to ...	Very likely	Quite likely	Neither likely nor unlikely	Quite unlikely	Very unlikely
1	start a conversation with a stranger?					
2	give advice to other people?					
3	use difficult words?					
4	change your mind about things?					
5	organise social events?					
6	worry about being late?					

3 **Turn to page 157 to get your results. Then complete sentences 1–4 so they're true for you.**

1 I'm (very/quite) (un)likely to …

2 I tend to …

3 I'm good at … *-ing*.

4 I find it difficult to …

4 **Compare your sentences with a partner's and discuss the questions.**

1 How much do you have in common?

2 What did you learn from your results?

3 Do you think this is an accurate test of personality?

Vocabulary

formation of adjectives

5 Copy and complete the table with the adjective forms of the nouns in the box.

caution	comfort	drama	emotion	generosity	harm	hope
love	meaning	person	pessimist	prediction	reliability	sympathy

-able	-ous	-ic	-al	-ful
sociable	adventurous	realistic	practical	thoughtful

-ent

6 ▶ 06 Mark the stress on each adjective, then listen and check. Practise saying the words. Which ones stress different syllables from the noun form?

7 Which adjectives use the suffix *-less* or the prefix *un-* to form the negative?

Examples: *hopeless, uncomfortable*

Word formation (Part 3)

▶ **EXAM** FOCUS p.201

▶ **EXAM** FOCUS p.201

8 Read the text quickly without worrying about the gaps. What problem with describing people's personalities is mentioned?

How well do you know yourself?

When trying to understand our own or other people's
(0) *behaviour* , we tend to over-simplify things. We use one or   **BEHAVE**
two adjectives to sum each other up. We think of one friend as
having a generally **(1)** .... and positive outlook, while   **HOPE**
another friend is considered **(2)** .... and negative.   **PESSIMIST**
Of course, in **(3)** ...., none of us is so easily defined.   **REAL**

The truth is that we are all made up of inconsistent and
contradictory **(4)** .... ; we can be serious and reliable with   **CHARACTER**
our colleagues at work but in our personal relationships at home
we are more **(5)** .... and emotional. With some friends we   **PREDICT**
can be very cautious, while we are **(6)** .... thrill-seekers   **ADVENTURE**
with other friends.

So can people be neatly divided into personality types? Or do
we alter our personality according to the **(7)** .... in our   **DIFFERENT**
changing moods and situations? Perhaps the idea of a fixed
personality is just a **(8)** .... misconception. Maybe we can   **MEANING**
never truly understand ourselves or other people.

9 What part of speech goes in each gap? If it's a noun, is it singular or plural?

10 Use the word given in capitals at the end of some of the lines to form a word that fits in the gap in the same line.

Multiple choice (Part 4)

▶ **EXAM** FOCUS p.205

1 **Discuss the questions.**

1 What do you think is the ideal number of children in a family? Why?

2 Are older children more or less independent than their younger siblings? Why?

2 **You're going to listen to a radio interview with a psychologist called Max about birth order. Read the first question in Activity 4 and underline the key words in the statement and the options.**

3 ▶ 07 **Listen to the first part of the interview.**

1 Which key words, or words with a similar meaning to the statement and options, did you hear?

2 Which option correctly completes the statement?

4 ▶ 08 **Read through questions 1–7 and underline the key words. Then listen and choose the best answer, A, B or C.**

EXAM TIP

The radio presenter's questions will help you to follow the discussion, so you know which question you should be listening for.

1 Max says that people mistakenly believe that oldest children

    A are likely to do well in the future.
    B will be happier than their siblings.
    C are often very independent at a young age.

2 According to Max, what is the reason for oldest children's results in intelligence tests?

    A Parents expect more from the oldest child.
    B Oldest children spend more time alone.
    C The oldest child benefits from teaching younger siblings.

3 What typical characteristic of oldest children does Max share?

    A He is very competitive.
    B He experienced jealousy of a sibling.
    C He always wanted to please his parents.

4 Max says that youngest children can often be

    A confident.
    B creative.
    C cautious.

5 What do some psychologists believe is likely to increase the 'birth order effect'?

    A a large age gap between siblings
    B families with three or more siblings
    C having siblings of the same sex

6 Max suggests that the best combination for a successful marriage is between people who are both

    A oldest children.
    B middle children.
    C third-born children.

7 According to Max, why should we be cautious about the 'birth order effect'?

    A Personality can also be affected by other things.
    B Personality can change when people are away from their families.
    C Personality is too complicated to define simply.

5 **Compare your answers with a partner. Then listen again to check.**

Speaking

6 **Work in pairs. How well do you get on with your siblings? What impact has the 'birth order effect' had on your family?**

Adverbs

▶ **GRAMMAR** REFERENCE p.161

1 **Underline the adverbs in sentences A–D. Then answer the questions.**

A   They will have to work very hard to make their marriage work.

B   It could be difficult for them to get on well.

C   They are allowed to grow up more slowly.

D   It can have hardly any impact on large families.

1   Which adverbs are irregular?

2   Which words can be both an adverb and an adjective?

2 **Choose the correct adverb.**

1   I *hardly/hard* know my brother because he's so much older than me.

2   I try *hard/hardly* to get on with my brothers and sisters.

3   He's been feeling depressed *late/lately*.

4   My mother had children *lately/late* in life.

5   My parents live *closely/close* to me.

6   We studied the results of the test *close/closely*.

Vocabulary

extreme adjectives

3 **Match adjectives 1–6 with extreme versions A–F.**

1   difficult
2   intelligent
3   angry
4   frightened
5   tired
6   big

A   enormous
B   terrified
C   exhausted
D   impossible
E   brilliant
F   furious

4 **Which adverbs in the box give the sentence a similar meaning?**

absolutely   a bit   completely   fairly   very

1   He's *quite* intelligent.
2   He's *really* cautious.
3   She's *really* impossible to get on with.
4   She's a *really* good person.
5   He's a *really* amazing person.
6   He can be *quite* difficult.

5 **Choose the correct adverb(s) to form the rules.**

1   *Really/Very* can be used with any adjective in order to intensify meaning.

2   *Completely* and *absolutely/Really* and *very* are only used with extreme adjectives.

3   *Quite/A bit* is only used when making a criticism with adjectives with a negative meaning.

Speaking

6 **Complete sentences 1–3 with phrases A–C to make statements you agree with. Discuss your sentences with a partner. Do you agree?**

1   It's fairly easy …
2   It's quite hard …
3   It's absolutely impossible …

A   … to judge a person's character from their appearance.
B   … to get on with everyone in your family.
C   … for parents to treat all their children equally.

Colin Firth in *The King's Speech*

Speaking

1 How would you feel if you had a brother or sister who was gifted or famous?

Multiple matching (Part 7)

▶ **EXAM** FOCUS p.203

2 You are going to read an article in which four people talk about their relationship with their brother or sister. Read the text quickly and find out which person is

1 a twin.
2 the oldest.
3 a middle child.
4 the youngest of four.

3 Look at the underlined words in Activity 4, question 1. What information would you expect to find in the text? Check your answer in extract A.

EXAM TIP

Underline the key words in the options and then read through the texts quickly to find a similar word or expression which says the same thing in a different way.

---

4 For questions 2–10, choose from the people (A–D). The people may be chosen more than once.

Which person

remembers having <u>mixed feelings</u> about the <u>success of a sibling</u>?	1	*A*
used to try not to get involved when a sibling was badly behaved?	2	
once stopped doing something because of sibling rivalry?	3	
now finally appreciates the value of a sibling relationship ?	4	
felt rather irritated on the birth of a sibling?	5	
could depend on a sibling for practical advice as a child?	6	
thinks people can get labelled too easily?	7	
noticed how a sibling was treated differently as a child?	8	
was too cautious to take up a much-wanted career?	9	
regards a sibling as the most efficient person in the family?	10	

5 Which sibling relationship in the article did you find most interesting? Why?

Vocabulary

phrasal verbs

6 Match the underlined phrasal verbs in the article with meanings 1–8.

1 organise something
2 escape
3 succeed
4 make (someone) leave
5 be determined
6 suddenly become successful
7 admire
8 arrive unexpectedly

7 Work in pairs and discuss the questions.

1 Who do you look up to?
2 Have you ever set your heart on something?
3 Do you sort out your possessions regularly and get rid of things you don't need?
4 Where would you like to get away to?

RELATIONSHIPS

Friend or enemy?

Can siblings ever really be friends?

A Kate Firth, voice coach; sister to film star Colin

As the older brother, Colin was protective of me. As a teenager, I looked up to him because he was much more capable and confident than I was. I was jealous of his arty friends because I felt I had to be safe and conventional and go to university as our parents expected us to. Colin could have gone but he had set his heart on drama school. I desperately wanted to act too but never had his courage, although I did act for a while, as did my younger brother, Jonathan. Our parents didn't think that success as an actor was a real possibility but Colin and I shared a strong belief that one day we would make it. In my first year at university he did *Hamlet* and I sat there feeling terribly proud and jealous at the same time because he was doing exactly what I wanted to do. After that his career took off.

B Jonathan Self, journalist and author; brother to novelist and broadcaster Will

When Will was three, he packed a suitcase with toys and ran away from home. I think he only got about four kilometres down the road before he was found but I remember feeling delighted that we had finally got rid of him. I hadn't been at all pleased, at the age of two, when a new child turned up. Even so, we played a lot together as kids and I remember finding him very lovable. But I saw how he became the favourite as soon as my parents, who valued intellect enormously, discovered what an incredible brain he had. When I started working on my first book, I found out that he was doing the same. I felt very competitive and when I read his, I thought 'I'll never be as good as that' and gave up. Now I've established myself as a writer, I don't feel like that any more and I'm pleased with Will's success.

C Zoë Heller, author and journalist; sister to headhunter, Emily

Unlike me, Emily has always been grown up for her age. She's only three years older than me but she looked after me a lot when we were growing up. She taught me how to write a cheque and would rescue me when I got lost on the underground. And even today, if I or my two other older siblings need a document or a family photograph, she's the one you'll call. When she visits me, she still tidies my flat and sorts out my filing system. I've come to understand the importance of family rather late in life. During my twenties I just wanted to get away. I've lived in New York for years, yet now the first thing I do when I get back to London is have dinner with Emily.

D Will Young, singer-songwriter and actor; brother to Rupert, founder of a charity which helps people with depression

The problem with being twins is that you constantly get compared, and one twin can suffer. I remember when we went to school, it was decided that I was the clever one and Rupert was the sporty one. But we ended up getting more or less the same exam results – it's just that people put you in a certain box and it's difficult to get away from that. Rupert was more of a tearaway than me and I'd get annoyed by teachers who tried to make me responsible for him. As we got older, Rupert was more sociable. He'd get on the dance floor, whereas I was very self-conscious. It's funny that I'm now the performer. ■

Listening

1 **Work in pairs and discuss the questions.**

1 Do you have a lot of relations?

2 Which ones do you get on well/badly with?

2 ▶ 09 **Listen to five people talking about one of their relations. Match Speakers 1–5 with comments A–E.**

A We'd like him to move house. ....

B It's a waste of time saying anything to him. ....

C I once felt worried about being alone with him. ....

D We enjoy doing the same things. ....

E I've offered to teach him a sport. ....

Verb patterns: -ing/infinitive

▶ **GRAMMAR** REFERENCE p.178

3 **Match examples A–E in Activity 2 with rules 1–5.**

Use -ing

1 after some verbs (___D___)

2 after prepositions (..............)

3 after some expressions (..............)

Use infinitive

4 after some verbs (..............)

5 after some verbs + object (..............)

LANGUAGE TIP

Some verbs (e.g. *make, let*) are followed by object + infinitive without *to*: I **made her tidy up**.

Some verbs (e.g. *love*) can be followed by *-ing* or infinitive with little or no change in meaning:
I love **riding/to ride**.

To form a negative, use *not* before the verb:
I hate **not going**./He told me **not** to go.

---

verbs with -ing or infinitive with a change of meaning

4 **For sentence pairs 1–5, choose the correct options and explain the difference in meaning between each pair.**

1 A My mother stopped *making/to make* lunch because the phone rang.

   B My mother stopped *making/to make* lunch because we were hungry.

2 A Dad tried *phoning/to phone* but nobody answered.

   B Dad tried *phoning/to phone* but he couldn't remember the number, so he gave up.

3 A The kids remembered *buying/to buy* Grandma a present and write a card for her.

   B The kids remembered *buying/to buy* Grandma a present but couldn't find it again later.

4 A My father went on *having/to have* children until he was in his sixties.

   B My father went on *having/to have* children with my stepmother.

5 A I regret *telling/to tell* you that all train services have been cancelled.

   B I regret *telling/to tell* you because now you're upset.

5 **Read the article quickly. What did Ben like and dislike about having famous parents?**

6 **Complete the text with the -ing or the infinitive form of the verbs in brackets.**

7 **Work in pairs. Imagine you have become a celebrity. Talk about what you love, can afford, regret, don't mind, can't stand, etc.**

Ben Taylor: My famous parents

The son of singers James Taylor and Carly Simon talks about his childhood.

As a child, I remember **(1)** .... (*go*) on tour with my dad. It was awesome and I particularly loved **(2)** .... (*sleep*) on the tour bus. He encouraged me **(3)** .... (*travel*) with him on holiday too – we've been everywhere together.

I didn't mind my parents **(4)** .... (*split up*) because, although I lived with my mother, I still saw my dad a lot. I never regretted **(5)** .... (*have*) celebrity parents because there are lots of advantages too, although I didn't like people **(6)** .... (*introduce*) me as their son.

I started **(7)** .... (*play*) the guitar myself when I was about ten, just because I wanted **(8)** .... (*know*) if I could do it. I asked my father **(9)** .... (*teach*) me. If he thinks I'm keen on **(10)** .... (*do*) something, he's always very supportive.

Now I'm an adult, I still try **(11)** .... (*go*) on holiday with my dad whenever I can. Sometimes my sister comes with us but I prefer **(12)** .... (*be*) on my own with him. There's always been a lot of rivalry between us for my father's attention.

2 ▶ 10 **Listen to Alana and Federico. Which of the relationships do they discuss? Why do they think they're important?**

3 **Copy and complete the table with the phrases in the box. Which of the expressions of agreement are uncertain?**

So do I./Neither do I.   I'm not convinced.
That's very true.   Good point.
I'm not sure about that.
I see what you mean, but …   I suppose so
OK, but …
What about you?   What's your view on that?
I hadn't thought of that.   Exactly!
Well, actually …

Agreeing	Disagreeing politely	Asking opinions

4 **Work in pairs and decide which person might have the most influence on a young person's life. You have a minute to do this.**

EXAM TIP

Give your opinions but make sure you also listen to your partner. Ask about their opinions and respond to what they say.

5 **Discuss the following questions.**

1   Which people do you think have had the most influence on different stages of your life?

2   Do families sometimes get closer as they get older? Why/Why not?

3   What are the advantages and disadvantages of belonging to a big family?

Collaborative task (Part 3)
agreeing and disagreeing

▶ **EXAM** FOCUS p.207

1 **Look at the photos and the exam task and discuss the question.**

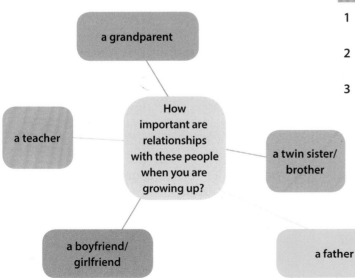

a grandparent

a teacher

How important are relationships with these people when you are growing up?

a twin sister/brother

a boyfriend/girlfriend

a father

Essay (Part 1)

using linkers for contrast

▶ **WRITING** REFERENCE p.180

1 Work in pairs. Read the exam task and essay title and think of some advantages and disadvantages of both situations.

> In your English class you have been discussing family relationships. Now your teacher has asked you to write an essay.
>
> Write an essay using **all** the notes and give reasons for your point of view. Write **140–190** words.
>
> Is it better to have a small or a large age difference between siblings?
>
> **Notes**
> Write about:
>
> 1 competition
> 2 friendship
> 3 learning to share (your own idea)

2 Match 1–6 with A–F to make sentences. Then decide with a partner which sentences you agree with.

1 Even though siblings who are close in age may argue,

2 Despite being born eight years apart,

3 I wish I had a much older brother to give me advice. On the other hand,

4 A small age gap between sisters can be a good thing, whereas

5 There is likely to be less competition between siblings born several years apart. However,

6 While having a sibling of a similar age may seem desirable,

A in my experience, boys may become too competitive.

B my younger brothers are happy to share a bedroom.

C they are more likely to grow up with many shared memories.

D forming a close bond depends much more on personality than age.

E they may find it difficult to develop a lasting relationship.

F I expect I'd get tired of him telling me what to do all the time.

3 In which of the sentences in Activity 2 is it also possible to use *although*?

4 Read the essay and find where the three points from Activity 1 are mentioned.

Is it better to have a small or a large age difference between siblings? I think it's hard to say whether it's better to have siblings of a similar age or much older or younger because all families are different. We can't judge properly what it would be like to be in a different situation. (1) *However/Even though* we might like the idea of having a baby brother or sister, we can't judge what that would be like in reality.

But I think the greatest advantage of having a small age gap is that when you're a child, you have someone to play with. As well as this, you have to learn to share your toys, instead of just keeping them to yourself. This makes playing with other children outside the family easier. (2) *Although/However*, there's likely to be much more competition with a sibling who's close in age because they may be jealous of each other.

The danger with having a large age gap is that you may not have a close relationship when you're grown up because you don't have the same shared memories. (3) *On the other hand,/While* the age gap becomes less important as you get older, so it's always possible to make friends with your sibling as adults. Speaking from my own experience, having a sister who's only two years younger has been ideal. (4) *Whereas/Despite* being quite different, we've always got on and we're good friends now we're adults.

5 Underline the reasons the student gives for her point of view. Decide whether you agree and compare with a partner.

6 Read the essay again and choose the correct linking word or phrase.

LANGUAGE TIP

Some linking words can be used at the beginning or in the middle of a sentence, e.g, *although, though, even though, while.*

James is good friends with his brother, **although** *there's a big age difference between them.*

Although *there's a big age difference between them, James is good friends with his brother.*

However usually comes at the beginning of a sentence and is followed by a comma.

7 Work in pairs. Turn to page 157 and do the exam task.

EXAM TIP

There are no right or wrong answers to the question. The important thing is to make sure you include all three points in your essay and explain your point of view.

1 Complete the second sentence so that it has a similar meaning to the first sentence. You must use between two and five words, including the word given.

1 I'm going to throw away all those old newspapers tomorrow.
RID
I'm going to .... all those old newspapers tomorrow.

2 Peter has always admired his uncle for everything he has achieved.
LOOKED
Peter has always .... his uncle for everything he has achieved.

3 She didn't know I was coming – I just arrived unexpectedly on her doorstep.
TURNED
She didn't know I was coming – I just .... on her doorstep.

4 After fifteen years , the company suddenly became successful.
TOOK
The company suddenly .... after it had been running for fifteen years.

5 Not many people become successful in the world of acting.
MAKE
Not many people .... in the world of acting.

6 Olivia has told me she wants to escape to a hot country this summer.
GET
Olivia has told me she wants to .... to a hot country this summer.

2 Correct the mistake in each of the sentences.

1 He's tried really hardly to get tickets for you.
2 The cinema is fairly closely to the station.
3 The football results were absolutely close.
4 She finished late and I was very furious with her.
5 They spoke free about their difficult childhood.
6 It was hardly dark but he was completely frightened.
7 It would be a bit brilliant if we won the Cup Final.
8 She's been working very hardly lately.

3 Complete the sentences with the adjectives in the box.

cautious   confident   creative
independent   practical   sociable

1 Whereas I'm quite shy about speaking in public, my brother's always been ....
2 Even at the age of eighty-five, my gran never likes relying on other people. She's very ....
3 My husband's not very good at doing things with his hands. He's not at all ....
4 I prefer my own company but my sisters are the opposite; they're all really ....
5 My father paints and writes really well. He's always been really ....
6 I am not prepared to take risks any more. I'm getting more and more ....

4 Complete the sentences using the correct form of the word in capitals.

1 My new car isn't as .... as I hoped it would be.   **RELY**
2 Molly's story is very .... I don't know where she gets her ideas from.   **IMAGINE**
3 My children will never try any new food. They aren't very ....   **ADVENTURE**
4 I don't think you're being very .... about how much we can finish.   **REAL**
5 I'm absolutely .... at languages. I just can't do them.   **HOPE**
6 I explained I'd been ill but the boss wasn't at all ....   **SYMPATHY**

5 Complete the sentences with the correct alternative.

1 I regretted not *having/to have* a car to drive.
2 He'd like us *working/to work* late this evening.
3 I'm not very good at *running/to run*.
4 Have you remembered *locking/to lock* the door?
5 Melanie has promised *inviting/to invite* us to stay.
6 She stopped *working/to work* and had a rest.
7 The teacher made me *to finish/finish* my work before I left.
8 Jim asked me *not to/to not* speak.

Things that matter

Multiple choice (Part 5)

▶ **EXAM** FOCUS p.202

1 What matters to you? Put the things in the box in order of importance.

education/career   family   friends   interests   possessions

EXAM TIP

Read the question stems and highlight the part of the text which answers each question. Then read the four options very carefully and decide on the answer.

2 Read the title and first paragraph of the newspaper article and guess what it will be about. Then read the rest of the article and check.

3 Read the article again. For questions 1–6, choose the answer (A, B, C or D) which you think fits best according to the text.

1 What is the writer's attitude towards football fans at matches?

A She's impressed by their behaviour.

B She's astonished by how they can afford tickets.

C She's embarrassed by how irresponsible they are.

D She's sympathetic towards the strength of their emotions.

2 What does *it* refer to in line 14?

A an ugly side

B passion

C football

D a penalty shoot-out

3 The writer thinks everyone should have a passion because

A it puts them in touch with their basic emotions.

B it encourages affectionate behaviour.

C it gives them an excuse to take time off work.

D it makes everything else in life seem unimportant.

4 What does *thin on the ground* mean in line 77?

A unimpressive

B infrequent

C inflexible

D unexpected

5 The writer mentions Wimbledon to show that

    A it's not only football which inspires strong feelings.

    B a wide range of people enjoy this kind of event.

    C sports spectators can behave uncharacteristically.

    D people often behave badly to get on TV.

6 The writer's main purpose is to encourage her readers to

    A become sports fans.

    B have an enthusiasm for something.

    C show their emotions openly.

    D enjoy themselves more.

4 **Work in pairs. Do you know anybody who has a passion for something? Have you ever had a passion in common with a member of your family?**

Vocabulary

-ed adjectives and prepositions

5 **Choose the correct preposition. Then ask your partner these questions.**

1 What are you interested *in/at*? What do you find boring?

2 Who are you frightened *with/of*? What do you find frightening?

3 What do you sometimes feel worried *about/in*?

4 Who or what do you get annoyed *of/by*?

5 What do you sometimes feel embarrassed *in/by*? Who do you find embarrassing?

6 What do you get excited *with/about*?

LANGUAGE TIP

-ed adjectives describe how you feel about something.
*I'm **bored** with this TV programme.*

-ing adjectives describe the noun.
*This programme's so **boring**.*

All you need is love (and a scarf)

Grown men with their heads buried in each other's shoulders or hidden behind shaking hands. Young mothers shouting with joy. This is what last Saturday's penalty shoot-out for the European Cup produced. If you missed the semi-final, then try and catch the European Cup Final on television tomorrow. Then you'll see what passion does to people. And, while having an ugly side, it is, in fact, more likely to enrich our lives and make us better people. *(line 14)*

Today, supporters are gathering for the big match. Fans who could not afford the fare to travel abroad have sold their car. Others have borrowed from relatives they once promised themselves they would never borrow from again. And many will turn up without any accommodation or even a match ticket. Despite this, they will be relieved just to be there, to be part of it all. It might sound like madness but, as one who is going and is incredibly excited about it, I can tell you I feel extremely fortunate.

Passion should not be confused with obsession. There are those who live in a dream state, madly in love with someone they will never meet – because he is a dead singer or a famous actor who is unlikely ever to visit their hometown – and therefore unable to form real relationships. However, there are also ordinary people – sensible parents, husbands, employees and employers – whose interests are much more healthy and straightforward. Their emotions are also linked to forces they cannot control, but they are to be admired for it.

Maybe some people are incapable of finding a passion, but if so, they are missing out. Passions are deep, full of joy and pain, teaching you how to sob when you feel hurt, how to deal with disappointment, how to sing with enthusiasm in public (not easy). Because of them you might end up hugging a complete stranger or making new friends. They help you to feel part of a community and have something to tease your neighbour about. They are a great way for families to bond together; many dads insist that they are spending their time fishing or playing chess because their child is keen, when, actually, they are delighted to become absorbed by something outside home, job or money worries.

Explosions of joy are normally thin on the ground. *(line 77)* The birth of your child, your wedding day, a pay rise are all lovely and a reason to do something special, but they do not happen every week. If you happen to follow a football or rugby team, there are celebrations all the time.

For some, a passion can be switched on and off – which is better than not having a passion at all, I suppose. Witness the behaviour that tennis brings about at the annual two-week UK tennis tournament at Wimbledon. Calm, controlled middle-aged women are suddenly prepared to camp overnight on damp pavements in London and squeal encouragement. Otherwise cool, fashionable students are happy to wave at the TV cameras while wearing silly hats and sunglasses that spurt water.

In the end, what defines us as human is not only language. It is the ability to care about something that does not directly affect our health or wealth or importance. Passions are a rehearsal for life, a distraction from boredom and, most of all, they are fun – even when they let you down.

Present perfect and past simple

▶ **GRAMMAR** REFERENCE p.176

I've been mad about horses for most of my life. I've never owned one, but my friend and I used to help out every weekend at the local riding stables and then the owner would let us ride the ponies. But I haven't been back there since I left home to go to college five years ago. Last month a colleague at work persuaded me to take up riding again so I've been having lessons with her. I've only had four so far but I've just got my confidence back, so I'll definitely keep it up.

Home	Archive	News	Members	Search

1 **Read Anna's blog, in which she talks about her passion. Answer questions 1–5.**

1 How long has Anna loved horses?
2 Does she still help out at the stables?
3 When did she start riding again? Why?
4 How long has she been riding again?
5 How many lessons has she had?

2 **Look at the underlined verb forms in the text. Which ones describe**

1 completed actions in the past?
2 past habits which are now finished?

3 **Look at the highlighted example of the present perfect simple in the blog. Circle four more examples.**

4 **Match examples 1–3 with uses of the present perfect described in A–C.**

1 I've just got my confidence back.
2 I've never owned one.
3 I've been mad about horses for most of my life.

A began in the past and is still continuing
B has recently happened and is relevant to the present
C refers to indefinite time in the past

5 **Look at the sentences. Which of the time expressions underlined refers to a period of time and which to a point in time?**

1 I've been mad about horses <u>for</u> most of my life.
2 I haven't been back there <u>since</u> I left home to go to college five years ago.

6 **Divide these time expressions into those which are usually used with**

1 the past simple.
2 the present perfect.

yet	so far	already	in 2010
never	once	just	last month
ago	this month		at lunchtime

present perfect simple or continuous?

7 **Match the sentences from the blog (1 and 2) with the uses of the present perfect (A and B).**

1 I've been having lessons.
2 I've had four lessons.

A a completed activity
B an activity over a period of time (which may or may not be finished)

8 **Complete the sentences below with the past simple, present perfect simple or present perfect continuous form of the verbs and phrases in brackets. There may be more than one possibility.**

1 I .... (ride) a motorbike since I was seventeen.
2 I .... (once witness) a crime.
3 I .... (live) abroad when I was a child.
4 I .... (have) an operation a few years ago.
5 I .... (never go) camping.
6 I .... (just win) a competition.

9 **Work in pairs. Ask and answer questions with *Have you ever …?* and *How long …?* Use the ideas in Activity 8 to help you. If appropriate, ask for more details, using *When? Why?* etc.**

Grammar

as and *like*

▶ **GRAMMAR** REFERENCE p.164

1 **Complete sentences 1–6 with *as* or *like*.**

1 Was that film .... all his other ones?

2 Shall we still have lunch together, ... we said yesterday?

3 I've always regarded you .... a friend.

4 A job .... that one takes a long time to finish.

5 He's working .... a waiter in the holidays.

6 Please do it carefully, ... I asked you.

LANGUAGE TIP

as + noun, for a role or purpose:
*She works **as a musician**. I use that room **as a study**.*

as + noun clause, for manner: *I treated him **as my son**.*

like + noun, for comparison:
*You're just **like Tony**.; **Like Jane**, I love jazz.*

like + noun for informal examples:
*Food **like that risotto** is worth waiting for.*

Open cloze (Part 2)

▶ **EXAM** FOCUS p.201

2 **Work in pairs and discuss the questions.**

1 What do you do to cheer yourself up when you're depressed?

2 What makes you really happy?

3 **Read the text quickly. Underline three things that make Pixie happy. Are you like her?**

4 **Look at the example (0). What part of speech is it? Now look at gaps 1–8. What kind of word is missing?**

5 **Read the text again and think of the word which best fits each gap. Use only one word in each gap.**

EXAM TIP

Read the whole sentence, especially the words before and after each gap. Think about what kind of word is missing (e.g. a preposition, a pronoun).

6 **Compare your answers with a partner.**

Pixie Lott: What makes me happy

The London-based singer tells us about the things that make her smile.

I'm at my happiest when I'm **(0)** ....*on*.... stage or writing music. Music, for me, is medicine and writing songs is a kind of therapy. And, **(1)** .... lots of people, even just listening to music makes me happy. If I'm fed up or worried **(2)** .... my family or something, I just put my iPod on loud. I use music **(3)** .... a way of relaxing and there's always a song that matches my mood. But the song I like best is a 1980s tune, **(4)** .... my friends and I play at full volume **(5)** .... we're getting ready to go out. I've got some very happy memories associated with that song. When I **(6)** .... had a bad day or feel unhappy, I usually go to the piano and write a song. Sometimes I'm almost crying at the time but I always feel much **(7)** .... cheerful afterwards. The emotion is real and it really helps me. I'm not really sure why music connects so strongly with me but it always **(8)** .... these days.

LIFE-OF-LUXURY.CO.UK

Sign in | Email updates | Shopping basket

WHAT'S NEW   BOUTIQUE   GIFTS   ACCESSORIES   MAGAZINE   DESIGNERS   CONTACT

VIEW DETAILS ►   ADD TO BASKET ►

VIEW DETAILS ►   ADD TO BASKET ►

VIEW DETAILS ►   ADD TO BASKET ►

VIEW DETAILS ►   ADD TO BASKET ►

VIEW DETAILS ►   ADD TO BASKET ►

Speaking and vocabulary

money

1   Match the price tags with the things in the pictures. Then see if your partner agrees. Decide whether each thing is

1   worth the money.
2   good value for money.
3   a waste of money.

£675	$102.3 million	$158,500
£35,000	€4,200	

2   Match the two halves of the expressions. Then discuss what they mean with a partner. Do you have similar expressions in your language?

1	He's got more money	A	to burn.
2	Put your money where	B	not made of money.
3	I'm a bit short	C	a fortune.
4	Money's a bit	D	your mouth is.
5	She's got money	E	tight at the moment.
6	He's worth	F	to make ends meet.
7	My mum always says she's	G	of money this month.
8	It's sometimes hard	H	than sense.

3   Complete the sentences with the prepositions in the box. Which of the statements do you agree with and why?

away	in	of	on	to	within

1   It's difficult to live .... your means when you're a student.
2   You should always avoid being .... debt.
3   Having to live .... a tight budget is boring.
4   Very rich people should give most of their money ....
5   It's not a good idea to lend your credit card .... a friend.
6   Young people today have a higher standard .... living than their grandparents' generation.

Sentence completion (Part 2)

▶ **EXAM** FOCUS p.204

4 You're going to hear a multi-millionaire called Gavin Norris talking about his life. Read the gapped sentences. Which of A–E do you expect to hear?

A how he made his fortune
B his attitude to money
C his typical working day
D what he spends his money on
E where he lives

5 ▶11 **Listen and check.**

6 **Look at the gap in each sentence. Where do you think you can put**

1 a number?
2 a noun?
3 a plural form?
4 only one word?

EXAM TIP

Usually, you only have to write one or two words or a number in the gap. Occasionally, you may need to write three words.

7 **Listen again and complete the gapped sentences.**

8 **Compare your answers in pairs. Then listen again to check. Make sure you have spelt the words correctly.**

9 **Work in pairs and discuss the questions.**

1 How do you think Gavin's children feel about his decision to give all his money away?
2 What problems can people have if they inherit a lot of money?

CD 1 Track 11

31 **BUSINESS**

giving it all away

Gavin Norris started his business career by selling (1) .... in a market in 1984.

Before Gavin sold his first company in 1998, he had 250 (2) ....

Gavin became interested in helping (3) .... learn about business.

In 2004 Gavin decided to lend money to (4) .... in Africa who needed help.

Gavin realised that as little as (5) £ .... was enough to change a person's life.

The project to build a (6) .... was very special for Gavin.

Being involved in charity work has helped Gavin to value his (7) .... more.

Now Gavin gives the profits from his (8) .... companies to development projects.

Gavin believes money can't bring happiness but it can bring (9) ....

Gavin intends to give his children money for a (10) ....

Comparing

▶ **GRAMMAR** REFERENCE p.165

1 ▶ 12 **Look at sentences 1–3 taken from the listening on page 31 and complete them with the correct comparative or superlative form of the adjectives in brackets. Then listen and check.**

1 I'm .... (*interested*) I used to be in holidays.
2 Building the hospital was .... (*satisfying*) experience of my life.
3 I'm .... (*happy*) I was twenty years ago.

2 **Decide which pairs of sentences have a similar meaning, and which have a different meaning.**

1 **A** I've never been as happy as I am now.
  B I'm just as happy now as I ever was.
2 **A** My car was by far the most expensive thing I've ever bought.
  B My car was a lot more expensive than anything else I've ever bought.
3 **A** My grandfather is one of the most generous people I know.
  B There aren't many people who are as generous as my grandfather.

3 **Complete the second sentence so that it has a similar meaning to the first, using the word in bold.**

Example: *A scooter isn't nearly as expensive as a sports car.* **LOT**
A sports car is **a lot more expensive than** *a scooter.*

1 Our standard of living is a bit lower than it was. **QUITE**
 Our standard of living is not .... it was.
2 There aren't many cities which are as exciting as Rio de Janeiro. **ONE**
 Rio de Janeiro is .... exciting cities.
3 She doesn't have nearly as much free time now. **LESS**
 She has .... free time than before.
4 Not many people earn such a high salary as he does. **THAN**
 His salary is .... most people's.
5 He's almost as wealthy as she is. **BIT**
 She's .... him.
6 It's getting much more difficult to get a bank loan. **AS**
 It is .... to get a bank loan now.

Speaking comparing quantities

4 **Use the table to make six sentences that are true about you.**

I spend	most	of my money on… of my time -*ing*.
	a large amount	
	quite a lot	
	hardly any	
I don't spend	much	
	any	

5 **Compare your answers in groups and write a paragraph about how your group spends time and money.**

Example: *The thing we spend most/least time/money on is … More/Less than half of us spend a large amount on …*

Long turn (Part 2)
comparing

▶ **EXAM** FOCUS p.206

1 **What do these photographs have in common? Choose A or B.**

A They show things which are important to people.

B They show people in unusual situations.

2 **Make a list of the similarities and differences between the two photographs.**

3 ▶ 13 **Listen to a student comparing the two photographs. Does she mention any of the points on your list?**

4 **Complete the sentences with *like* or *as if/as though*. In which sentences is it only possible to use *like*? Why?**

1 It looks .... a graduation ceremony.

2 The man looks .... he's very proud of his car.

3 It looks .... hard work.

4 He looks .... he's a bit obsessive.

5 She looks .... she's having more fun than the man.

▶ **GRAMMAR** REFERENCE p.164

5 **Look at sentences A and B and answer questions 1–3 about *whereas* and *while*.**

A *While* the man may have a passion for his car, it's probably not something that will last for his whole life.

B The first picture is celebrating an achievement *whereas* the second picture shows someone who values an important possession.

1 Which sentence is making a comparison and showing how the two things are different?

2 In which sentence is it possible to use both *whereas* and *while*?

3 In which sentence could you use *although* instead of *while/whereas*?

6 **Make sentences with *both*, *too* or *also*. Where can you put these words in the sentence? There may be more than one possibility.**

1 the pictures show an achievement (*both*)

2 the man looks happy (*also*)

3 the man seems to be enjoying himself (*too*)

7 **Work in pairs.**
Student A, look at the photos on page 152. Student B, look at the photos on page 154. Take turns to compare your photos. Try to use expressions with *whereas, while, both, also, too, like, as if/as though*.

EXAM TIP

Don't describe what's in the pictures. Focus on the main topic and compare the main similarity and any differences between the pictures.

8 **Work in pairs. Do you agree with this statement?**

Happiness is not having what you want but wanting what you have.

Article (Part 2)
engaging the reader

▶ **WRITING** REFERENCE p.185

1 **Look at the exam task and answer the questions.**

1 What kind of style will you write it in? How do you know?

2 What information do you need to include?

> You see this advertisement in a magazine for young people.
>
> > **What I'd save in a fire**
> > Write us an article describing something you own and explaining why it's important to you.
> > The best article will be published in the magazine next month.
>
> Write your **article** in **140–190** words.

2 **Look at opening paragraphs A and B. Which one is most effective? Think about**

1 how appropriate the style is.

2 how varied the language is.

3 whether it engages the reader.

EXAM TIP

Try to 'speak' directly to the reader for maximum impact.

A | **What I'd save in a fire**
Have you ever thought about which possession you'd choose to save if your house was on fire? Well, for me it would definitely be my laptop. Obviously, I'd rescue my family and pets first but after that it would be my precious computer.

B | **What I'd save in a fire**
My laptop is very important to me and I would be very upset if it got lost or damaged. I spend hours every day using my laptop and I would be lost without it. I think most people feel the same way about their laptops.

3 **Look at notes A–H and choose whether to include them in paragraph two (a simple description of the object) or paragraph three (the reasons why it's special to you).**

A | eighteenth birthday present from parents
B | not expensive and very ordinary to look at
C | two years old
D | used to have to share my brother's computer
E | all my photographs are on it
F | made by Toshiba
G | user-friendly
H | contains friends' details

4 **Work in pairs. Write paragraphs two and three, using the ideas in Activity 3.**

5 **Look at possible concluding sentences A and B. Which one would have the most positive effect on a reader?**

A | So for all these reasons, the first thing I would think of taking with me is my laptop.

B | The main reason I'd grab my laptop first in a fire is because I'd be heartbroken to lose all my photos, which have so many happy memories for me.

6 **Make notes on your own response to the advert. Choose a favourite possession and divide your notes into four paragraphs:**

1 Introduction (an introduction to get the readers' attention)

2 Background (a description of the object)

3 Opinion (the reasons why it is important to you)

4 Conclusion (a brief conclusion)

LANGUAGE TIP

Use extreme adjectives such as *amazing*, and extreme adverbs such as *absolutely* and *incredibly* for emphasis.

7 **Write your article in 140–190 words. Then check it for spelling and punctuation. Write another draft if necessary.**

8 **Read other students' articles and choose which ones to include in the magazine.**

1 **Choose the correct word to complete the sentences.**

1 A .... standard of living is important to me.

   A tall **B** big **C** great **D** high

2 The house they live in must be worth a ....

   A treasure **B** fortune **C** resource **D** wealth

3 When I was at college I had to learn to live .... a budget.

   A on **B** in **C** from **D** at

4 I'm afraid I can't come because I'm .... of money.

   A low **B** lacking **C** short **D** tight

5 She is always .... debt at the end of the term.

   A on **B** at **C** with **D** in

6 I'm still learning to live .... my means.

   A between **B** within **C** under **D** at

2 **Complete the second sentence so that it means the same as the first sentence using the word given. Use between two and five words, including the word given.**

1 Rebecca started living here five years ago. **FOR**
   Rebecca .... five years.

2 I last saw Mike in 2006. **SINCE**
   I .... 2006.

3 This is my first visit to India. **TIME**
   This is the first .... to India.

4 It's kind of you but I had a coffee earlier. **ALREADY**
   It's kind of you but I .... a coffee.

5 I don't spend much money on clothes these days. **ANY**
   I .... money on clothes these days.

6 This hotel isn't nearly as expensive as the other one. **FAR**
   The other hotel is .... this one.

7 Both Tom and Zak are equally friendly. **JUST**
   Tom is .... Zak.

8 There aren't many fashion designers that are as expensive as Prada. **ONE**
   Prada is .... fashion designers.

3 **Complete the sentences with a word formed from the word in capitals.**

1 I haven't got much money but I'm not .... about it. **WORRY**

2 Golf is not a very .... sport to watch on TV. **INTEREST**

3 Having a passion can make life more .... **EXCITE**

4 I'm really .... by my obsession with that actor. **EMBARRASS**

5 What is the most .... film you have ever seen? **FRIGHTEN**

6 I'm .... that the Cup Final is over at last. **RELIEF**

4 **Complete the gaps with one word.**

Letting go

When I was younger, I used to worry **(1)** .... all kinds of things. I knew I would never look **(2)** .... my sister, who was **(3)** .... more attractive than me and just **(4)** .... intelligent as me, but I still felt jealous. I was also embarrassed **(5)** .... my father, who worked **(6)** .... an actor, instead of having a 'normal' job. However, I have always **(7)** .... very close to **(8)** .... of my parents and know I am very lucky to have them.

Battling nature

Speaking

1 **How much do you know about Antarctica? Do the quiz. Then turn to page 160 and check your answers.**

1 Antarctica has the world's largest

    A volcano.   **B** desert.   **C** mountain range.

2 Has Antarctica always been cold?

    A No, it used to be tropical.

    B Yes, it's always been covered in thick ice.

    C Yes, but the ice used to be a lot thinner.

3 Which of these animals do you NOT get in Antarctica?

    A penguins   **B** seals   **C** polar bears

4 Who led the first team to reach the South Pole in 1911?

    A Roald Amundsen

    B Robert Falcon Scott

    C Ernest Shackleton

5 Why is Ernest Shackleton's 1908 expedition famous?

    A Everyone except Shackleton survived the trip.

    B The men survived but they didn't get to the South Pole.

    C All the men died on the way back from the South Pole.

Multiple choice (Part 4)

▶ **EXAM** FOCUS p.205

2 You are going to hear an interview in which an explorer called Leo Stone is talking about a book by Henry Worsley on his expedition to the South Pole. Before you listen, read the questions and underline the key words.

1 What does Leo say about Henry Worsley's team?

A They had never considered doing a trip to the South Pole before.

B They had personal reasons for wanting to complete the journey.

C They were trying to break a world record.

2 What does Leo say was the hardest thing for Worsley's team before the expedition?

A organising the finance

B preparing mentally

C getting physically fit

3 What does Leo say was easier for the twenty-first century expedition than for Shackleton's expedition?

A planning their daily route

B doing the cooking

C carrying their equipment

4 What problem did both expeditions experience?

A running out of food

B a serious illness

C bad weather

5 How did Worsley feel when he was crossing the Antarctic plateau?

A He hadn't expected it to be so difficult.

B He was worried they wouldn't reach the South Pole.

C He doubted his skills as a leader.

6 The part of the book Leo enjoyed most was when Worsley

A reached the South Pole.

B arrived at the point Shackleton had got to.

C completed the trip.

7 What does Leo admire about Shackleton?

A his determination

B his ambition

C his bravery

EXAM TIP

The information on the recording will be in the same order as questions 1–7.

3 ▶ 14 **Listen to the review and answer questions 1–7.**

4 Check your answers in pairs. Then listen again. What words or phrases did you hear to justify choosing A, B or C for each question?

5 Discuss the questions.

1 What would you find hard about a trip like this?

2 Shackleton is considered a hero and a role model by many people. Who are your heroes and role models?

3 Where would you most like to travel to? Why?

Vocabulary

idioms: the body

6 Match the underlined idioms 1–10 with meanings A–J.

1 The hardest part was getting their heads around doing a 900-mile journey.

2 When he came face to face with conditions there, Shackleton began to doubt he'd ever reach the Pole.

3 He's always putting his foot in it. He just doesn't know when to keep his mouth shut.

4 My father and I don't see eye to eye. Perhaps our relationship will improve when I leave home.

5 Something in the distance caught my eye.

6 I must keep an eye on the time. I don't want to be late.

7 It was really difficult to keep a straight face; he looked so silly.

8 I'm beginning to get cold feet about the whole idea.

9 I can't face going to work. I feel terrible.

10 You need to put your foot down. Don't agree to working late every evening.

A pay attention to

B look serious

C attract your attention

D change your mind

E get on with each other

F feel unable to

G very close to

H say the wrong thing

I say no to something

J understand/accept an idea

7 When was the last time you

1 put your foot in it?

2 couldn't face doing something?

3 put your foot down?

4 couldn't keep a straight face?

Narrative forms
past simple, past continuous and past perfect

▶ **GRAMMAR** REFERENCE p.177

1 You are going to read a story about a man who was shipwrecked on a desert island. Read paragraph 1 and predict what happens next.

Last October, 79-year-old Mark Richards <u>set off</u> from Florida in his cabin cruiser. He <u>had planned</u> to sail to Nassau in the Bahamas in twelve hours. However, while he <u>was sailing</u> there, a storm blew up and he was shipwrecked on a small island.

2 Read paragraph 1 again. Which of the underlined forms is

1 past simple?   2 past continuous?   3 past perfect?

3 Which one

1 refers to a finished event?

2 describes a situation which happened before another past action?

3 describes an action already in progress when something else happened?

4 Read the rest of the story quickly. Don't worry about the gaps yet. How well did you predict the ending?

5 Now complete the story with the correct form of the verbs in brackets.

His family realised he **(1)** .... (*miss*) and a massive search was launched. But they **(2)** .... (*have to*) wait for three long days before they finally **(3)** .... (*hear*) that some fishermen **(4)** .... (*rescue*) him.
Mr Richards survived for three days on a mixture of dried noodles and snack bars which **(5)** .... (*float*) ashore from his boat. Mr Richards knew he would be rescued eventually because there were a lot of boats in the area. 'I wasn't frightened but I was pleased to be rescued on the third day because I **(6)** .... (*start*) to feel quite hungry,' he said.

past perfect simple and past perfect continuous

6 Complete the sentences with the past perfect simple or past perfect continuous form of the verbs in brackets. Then match the examples with one of the statements, A or B.

1 He .... (*work*) as a lifeguard for ten years but .... (*never need*) to rescue anyone until last week.

2 Andy's leg .... (*hurt*) for ages before he went to the doctor.

3 We .... (*never see*) a glacier before.

4 I .... (*not hear*) the news until Sophie rang me.

A Only the simple form is possible here.

B It is more natural to use the continuous form here because the action continues over a period of time (although it isn't wrong to use the simple form).

7 Complete the sentences so that B has the same meaning as A. Sometimes more than one form is possible.

1 **A** Jack was hoping to compete in the Olympics. Then he hurt his back.
   B Before he .... (*hurt*) his back, Jack .... (*hope*) to compete in the Olympics.

2 **A** Luke spent six months in hospital. He studied to be a lawyer during this time.
   B While Luke .... (*recover*) in hospital, he .... (*study*) to be a lawyer.

3 **A** During his swim to the island, Lewis cut his knee badly on a rock.
   B Lewis .... (*swim*) to the island when he .... (*cut*) his knee on a rock.

4 **A** Fauzia didn't feel well all day, so she decided not to go to Zhara's party last night.
   B Because she .... (*feel*) well all day, Fauzia .... (*decide*) not to go to Zhara's party last night.

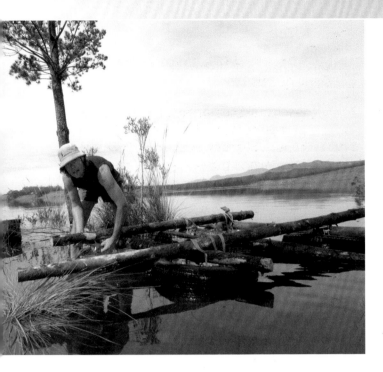

Collaborative task (Part 3)
ranking

▶ **EXAM** FOCUS p.207

1 **Work in pairs. Look at the examiner's instructions and underline the two things you have to discuss.**

> I'd like you to imagine that you are going on a college expedition to a desert island. Here are some survival skills you might need on the island. Talk to each other about how difficult it would be to learn these survival skills.
>
> (after a two-minute discussion) Thank you.
>
> Now you have about a minute to decide which two survival skills would be the most useful on the island.

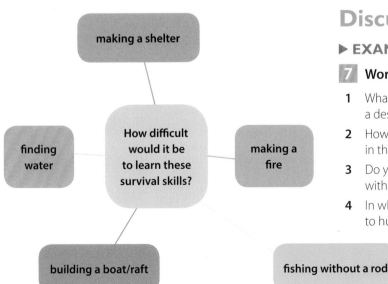

making a shelter

finding water

How difficult would it be to learn these survival skills?

making a fire

building a boat/raft

fishing without a rod

2 **Look at the exam task in Activity 1 and discuss the question with a partner. Talk about:**

- what in particular you think would be easy/difficult about each skill.
- why you personally might find a particular skill difficult.

3 ▶ **15** **Look at Activity 1 and listen to two students doing the second part of the task. Do you agree with their opinions?**

4 **Complete the sentences and then listen again to check your answers.**

1 .... of the .... for me would be finding water.
2 I'd .... making a fire .... making a shelter.
3 I think learning how to make a fire would be the .... for me.
4 So .... five skills, making a fire and finding water would be the most useful.

5 **Change the sentences in Activity 4 so that they have the opposite meaning.**

6 **Decide with a partner which two survival skills you think would be the *least* useful on the island. Include some of the expressions from Activity 5.**

EXAM TIP
Use all of the time (about one minute) you have to decide something together – don't reach a decision too quickly.

Discussion (Part 4)

▶ **EXAM** FOCUS p.207

7 **Work in pairs and discuss the questions.**

1 What kind of person do you need to be to survive on a desert island?
2 How essential is it for people to know how to survive in the wild?
3 Do you think most people today have lost touch with nature?
4 In what ways can the natural world be a threat to humans?

Speaking

1 **Look at the paragraph headings in the article. Discuss questions 1–4 with a partner.**

1 Which of these experiences do you think would be the most frightening?

2 Which of these experiences might give you shock, frostbite or hypothermia?

3 Which could give you injuries such as broken bones?

4 What other kinds of extreme weather conditions can you think of?

Multiple matching (Part 7)

▶ **EXAM** FOCUS p.203

2 **Read the article. Did anyone have serious injuries as a result of their experiences?**

3 **Read the questions in Activity 4 and underline the key words and phrases. Then scan the texts for words and expressions which have the same meaning. The first one is done for you.**

EXAM TIP

Be careful! There might seem to be similar information in more than one text. Make sure the word or expression you choose has the same meaning as in the question.

4 **For questions 2–10, choose from the people A–D. The people may be chosen more than once.**

Which person

remembers panicking about the situation he was in? | 1 | *A*

describes his efforts to stay awake? | 2 |

mentions being in pain all over after the incident? | 3 |

assumes he must have been thrown up into the air? | 4 |

believes that crying helped him to survive? | 5 |

describes the multiple injuries he received? | 6 |

remembers the long wait before being rescued? | 7 |

mentions the temporary deafness he suffered? | 8 |

says he was unable to relate to his rescuers? | 9 |

talks about experiencing big variations in body temperature? | 10 |

5 **Work in pairs and discuss the questions.**

1 Which person do you think had the luckiest escape?

2 How do you think you would react in these situations?

3 Do you know of any disaster films connected to the weather? What happens?

Vocabulary

collocations and idioms: weather

6 **Match the words in column A with their collocations in column B.**

Column A		Column B	
1	freezing	A	wet
2	boiling	B	black
3	soaking	C	frozen
4	pitch	D	cold
5	absolutely	E	hot
6	thick/dense	F	wind/sun
7	torrential/heavy	G	sea
8	strong	H	frost
9	a rough	I	rain
10	a hard	J	fog

7 **Work in pairs and discuss the questions.**

1 Which of the weather conditions in Activity 6 have you experienced?

2 Where were you and how did you feel?

8 **How would someone be feeling if**

1 they froze when they saw something?

2 they stormed out of somewhere?

3 they moved like lightning?

4 they were icy with someone?

5 their face clouded over?

6 their face was like thunder?

Battling with nature

FOUR PEOPLE TALK ABOUT THEIR STORIES OF SURVIVAL

A **Lester Morlang was buried in an avalanche in Colorado.**

There was no warning. It was instant. All of a sudden I was curled up in a ball. Then it was over and I was buried under about fifty feet of snow. It was totally dark. My mouth was packed with snow and the pressure was enormous. It was hard to breathe and I didn't know which direction was up. I thought I was already dead. Luckily I had my hands over my face so I cleared the snow out of my mouth and then I started screaming. I absolutely lost it – I was out of my mind, and then I noticed my tears were running across my face so I realised I must be lying kind of upside down. Now I felt determined to get out. I dug for twenty-two hours, and when I finally saw the first little bit of light I was over the moon, although it was fourteen hours before anyone found me. ■

B **Rod Herd was on a boat with the New Zealand Police Search and Rescue team when he nearly drowned.**

When we hit the wave, I was thrown against the window, which smashed and let in a tremendous volume of water. There was no air, just pitch darkness, noise and violent movement. I had no idea the boat had overturned. I felt sad, anxious and despairing, and the fear of drowning was unbearable. I couldn't hold my breath any longer and at this point I had a vision of my wife and sons waving me goodbye, and I felt at peace. But then I grabbed a stair rail and found myself back in the real world. I managed to pull myself up to the surface and then had to deal with the shock and hypothermia. Trying to stay afloat kept my mind off it, although I had to fight the desire to go to sleep. When the helicopter arrived soon afterwards, I vividly remember feeling disconnected from the people who were there to save me. ■

C **John Neidigh survived a tornado in Mississippi.**

I heard the warning on the television and had just enough time to lie down and cover my head with my arms. The feel of a twister approaching is like a goods train – that low, ever-louder howl and the shuddering ground. First, a sheet of rain sprayed against the side of my trailer like machine-gun fire. I could hear trees snapping, and the roof began to come off as the trailer started moving up and down. Just as I felt the entire trailer lift off the ground, I lost consciousness and woke up twenty minutes later face-down outside. The evening was completely quiet, no wind, no cars, no insect noises. I had gone through the trailer wall, ended up thirty feet up in a tree, and then dropped to the ground. I had concussion, a collapsed lung, cracked ribs and a shattered leg. These things should have killed me but the surgeons sewed me back together again. ■

D **Max Dearing was on the golf course in North Carolina when lightning struck.**

It happened on a lovely July afternoon while I was playing golf with friends from work. When it started to drizzle, we decided to get under a shelter. We were standing there teasing each other and I remember the air had an unusual sweet smell. When the lightning struck, I felt absolutely frozen but then part of me was boiling hot too. I saw these flashing lights and there was such an incredibly loud noise that I couldn't hear anything for a while. My arms and legs felt heavy. Every bit of my body – including my hair, my eyelashes – hurt. It was a dull ache and yet so sharp at the same time, like a bad headache and needles being stuck in every part of your body. ■

Articles

definite, indefinite and zero articles

▶ **GRAMMAR** REFERENCE p.163

1 Choose the correct option *a/an, the* or (-) for no article to complete rules 1–8. Use the text on page 41 to help you.

1 We use *a/an/the/*(-) when there is only one of something in existence.

2 We use *a/an/the/*(-) when there is only one of something in this context.

3 We use *a/an/the/*(-) to talk about plural countable nouns in general.

4 We use *a/an/the/*(-) to refer back to nouns mentioned before (or where the meaning is clear from the context).

5 We use *a/an/the/*(-) with superlative forms.

6 We use *a/an/the/*(-) with many common expressions such as *home, school,* etc.

7 We use *a/an/the/*(-) with singular countable nouns when mentioned for the first time, or when it is not important which one.

8 We use *a/an/the/*(-) with uncountable and abstract nouns.

2 Match rules 1–8 from Activity 1 with extracts A–F from the text on page 41.

A I grabbed *a stair rail* and found myself…

B I could hear *trees* snapping.

C … and *the roof* began to come off.

D My mouth was packed with *snow* and the pressure was enormous.

E I cleared *the snow* out of my mouth.

F I was playing *golf* with friends from *work*.

LANGUAGE TIP

We normally use possessives, not articles for parts of the body, e.g. **my** face NOT **the** face.

---

3 Complete the gaps in the story with *a/an, the* or (-).

Speaking

4 Work in groups. Find somebody who has had one of the following experiences. Tell the class about it.

Have you ever

1 been afraid of a storm?

2 been snowed in?

3 had heatstroke?

4 been in a flood?

5 skidded on a patch of ice?

6 seen lightning strike?

7 lost your way in fog?

8 been in or on a rough sea?

A pilot's story

As pilots, we have to get used to **(1)** .... storms and **(2)** .... severe weather, and we are obviously prepared for **(3)** .... emergencies. However, sometimes they can take you by **(4)** .... surprise. A year ago, I was flying to **(5)** .... USA and we were over **(6)** .... Atlantic Ocean when a ball of lightning struck **(7)** .... aircraft I was flying. Within seconds, **(8)** .... bright blue ball of light with **(9)** .... yellow tail filled **(10)** .... windscreen and there was **(11)** .... loud bang. My colleague said it felt as if **(12)** .... cat had brushed against his leg as **(13)** .... lightning struck. Fortunately, after a lot of violent shaking, **(14)** .... things soon returned to **(15)** .... normal.

Vocabulary
negative prefixes

1 In each sentence, underline the prefix which makes a word negative.

1 The first expedition was unsuccessful.
2 The Antarctic is the most incredible place I have been to.
3 The group on the expedition felt discouraged at times.
4 It's impossible to think of living in such freezing conditions.
5 They misunderstood our instructions and went the wrong way.
6 Some people thought it was irresponsible to go in such icy conditions.

2 Add a negative prefix to the underlined words in sentences 1–6.

1 One advantage of winter is how much we spend on heating our homes.
2 I read how severe the weather conditions would be so was not prepared.
3 It's likely that we'll be able to have a barbecue unless it gets much warmer.
4 I've noticed that people get patient when they're driving during hot weather.
5 It was a great job despite the regular working hours.
6 I'd be capable of surviving in low temperatures even if I had the right equipment.

3 Work in pairs. Discuss something

1 which is unusual about you.
2 incredible that has happened to you.
3 that makes you impatient.

Word formation (Part 3)

▶ **EXAM** FOCUS p.201

4 Look at the photo and the title of the article. What kind of place do you think Death Valley is? How do you think it got its name?

5 Look at each gap and decide what part of speech is missing.

6 Use the word given in capitals at the end of some of the lines to form a word that fits in the gap in the same line. Which words need a negative prefix?

DEATH VALLEY

The **(0)** ...*hottest*... place in North America got its name when a very **(1)** .... group of miners crossed it on their way to California in 1849. Having no idea that temperatures could get above 120 degrees Fahrenheit, they nearly died there, which is why it was named Death Valley. — HEAT / LUCK

Despite its name, more than 1.3 million **(2)** .... still go there every year. It is likely, however, that many of them have absolutely no idea how **(3)** .... being in such a hot dry climate can be. Also, **(4)** .... walkers often do not drink nearly enough water or wear the **(5)** .... clothes that are required in this extreme heat. — VISIT / DANGER / EXPERIENCE / SENSE

Heatstroke often occurs when the body is unable to control its temperature. **(6)** .... signs of this are high body temperature, red dry skin, very bad headaches and feeling dizzy. All this is also often accompanied by **(7)** .... If heatstroke is suspected, the person should get out of the sun at once and receive urgent medical **(8)** .... , otherwise they have only a 20 percent chance of surviving. — WARN / SICK / ASSIST

7 What advice would you give to someone going to a very hot or cold climate?

Examples:
You should (drink)… Make sure you (wear)… Avoid (sitting in the sun). Don't (ignore) warning signs.

(FCE Gold, Pearson, 2014)

Essay (Part 1)
expressing and supporting ideas

▶ **WRITING** REFERENCE p.180

1 Would you like the chance to explore an extreme environment such as Antarctica? What would you like to do if you had the opportunity?

2 Work in pairs. Read the essay title and discuss whether you agree or disagree with the idea of adventure tourism.

> In your English class you have been talking about extreme environments. Now your English teacher has asked you to write an essay.
>
> Write an essay using **all** the points and give reasons for your point of view. Write **140–190** words.
>
> Do you think 'adventure tourism' in unexplored parts of the world should be encouraged?
>
> **Notes**
> Write about:
>
> 1 negative effects of tourism
> 2 personal risk
> 3 _deculturation_ (your own idea)

3 Match the ideas 1–4 with notes 1 and 2 in Activity 2. Decide whether the writer is agreeing or disagreeing with the essay title in each case.

1 If people train and prepare for expeditions, there's a good chance they'll be safe.
2 The problem is that beautiful places will get spoilt if too many people go there.
3 As long as people respect the environment, there should be very little damage.
4 In my view, anything too dangerous should be left to the professionals.

4 Match the reasons A–D with the points 1–4 in Activity 3.

A An increased number of tourists will lead to more building development.
B If people don't know what they're doing, it can endanger their lives and the lives of others.
C It requires people to be responsible and avoid leaving rubbish around.
D These days, there is a lot of equipment to help people.

5 Think of some more points and supporting information (examples or reasons) for notes 1 and 2 in Activity 2. Compare your ideas with a partner.

> **EXAM TIP**
>
> Remember to clearly state your main point in the form of a topic sentence for each note. Support it with a reason or example if there is space.

6 Think about what your own point will be for note 3 in Activity 2 and compare your idea with a partner. There are some suggestions below. Remember to give a reason for the point you choose.

local job opportunities   personal development
cost of rescuing people
knowledge about the world

7 Read the essay title and task and plan how you will answer it. Use the guidelines 1–4 below.

> In your English class you have been discussing the importance of nature. Now your teacher has asked you to write an essay.
>
> Write an essay using **all** the notes and give reasons for your point of view. Write **140–190** words.
>
> Many people think living in the countryside provides a better way of life. To what extent do you agree?
>
> **Notes**
> Write about:
>
> 1 health benefits
> 2 day to day life
> 3 _____ (your own idea)

1 Read the question and underline the key points.
2 Brainstorm ideas around the topic. What will your own idea be?
3 Make notes on the positive and negative points. Do you agree or disagree, or can you see both sides?
4 Plan how many paragraphs you will have and decide which notes you will include in each one.

1 Complete the gaps in the article with *a/an*, *the* or *(-)* for no article.

Record-breaking walk

After **(1)** .... incredible 859 days and 6,000 miles, British explorer Ed Stafford became **(2)** .... first man to walk **(3)** .... entire length of **(4)** .... Amazon. He finally reached **(5)** .... Atlantic in **(6)** .... Brazil – two and a half years after he started his epic adventure in **(7)** .... jungles of Peru.

The final leg proved one of **(8)** .... most challenging, with Mr Stafford collapsing **(9)** .... few hours before reaching his final destination.

Mr Stafford fell out with his original walking partner Luke Collyer, 37, **(10)** .... outdoor activities instructor, and after only three months, Mr Collyer returned to **(11)** .... UK. Mr Stafford advertised for **(12)** .... new walking partner and was joined by Sanchez Rivera, **(13)** .... Peruvian forestry worker. Living off **(14)** .... piranha and rice, they made their way through Peru, Colombia and Brazil. Mr Stafford said on Monday, 'All I want now is **(15)** .... portion of fish and chips and **(16)** .... nice cold beer.'

2 Use the word given in capitals at the end of the sentence to form a word that fits the space.

1 I am .... of skiing. I'm too scared.　**CAPABLE**

2 I .... his explanation and went the wrong way.
UNDERSTANDING

3 He is a very .... worker. He never arrives on time.
RELY

4 My mother is .... with my younger brother. She never explains things properly.　**PATIENCE**

5 That is an extremely .... way to behave. You should be trying to set a good example.
RESPONSIBILITY

6 If you're .... , speak to the manager and I'm sure he'll be able to help.　**SATISFACTION**

3 Match the first part of sentences 1–6 with their endings A–F.

1 I always *put my foot in it* when I'm nervous and

2 I can never *keep a straight face* so

3 I'm *getting cold feet* about the cycling race because

4 Tom and I don't *see eye to eye* about many issues so

5 My parents want me to *keep an eye* on my brother so

6 If something in a shop window *catches my eye*

A I'm useless at telling jokes.

B I say really embarrassing things.

C I won't be able to go out tonight.

D I can't resist going in to look at it.

E I don't think I've trained enough.

F I can't see our relationship lasting.

4 Complete the second sentence so that it has a similar meaning to the first sentence using the word given. Use between two and five words, including the word given.

1 I lived in London until I got married last year.
BEEN
I .... in London until I got married last year.

2 It took three days for us to walk there.
WERE
We .... three days.

3 I couldn't remember the way there, so I got a taxi.
FORGOTTEN
I .... get there, so I got a taxi.

4 It was three years since I'd visited Peru.
NOT
I .... to Peru for three years.

Eat your heart out!

5

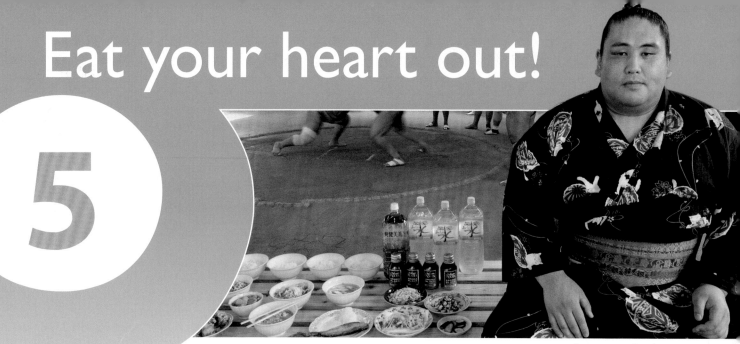

Sumo wrestler, Japan

Speaking and vocabulary

1 **Work with a partner. Look at the photos of daily diets from around the world and discuss the questions.**

1 How similar do these diets look to each other?

2 Which diet looks most similar to your own?

3 What can we tell about the countries by looking at these people's diets?

2 **Find out if your partner**

1 snacks between meals.

2 eats fast food regularly.

3 drinks a lot of tea and coffee.

4 has plenty of fresh fruit.

5 prefers organic food.

6 is allergic to any food.

3 **Complete the phrases with the words in the box.**

balanced	fat	free	low	vegetarian	vitamins

1 a high- .... diet

2 a strict .... diet

3 a diet rich in ....

4 a well- .... diet

5 a .... salt diet

6 a dairy- .... diet

4 **Use the phrases in Activities 2 and 3 to describe the diet most people have in your country. How healthy is it?**

Maasai farmer, Kenya

Student, Venezuela

LANGUAGE TIP

Rice is uncountable in English but countable in many other languages. For example, in English we say *There are **many different types of rice*** (NOT *rices*). Other English words like this include *advice, information, health, news, luggage, knowledge.*

Countable and uncountable nouns

▶ **GRAMMAR** REFERENCE p.167

5 Match the nouns in the box with the options A, B and C.

cake	cheese	chicken	chocolate	coffee	curry	egg	fat
fruit	honey	meat	rice	salt	vegetable		

A always uncountable

B always countable

C can be countable or uncountable

6 What's the difference in meaning between the countable and uncountable forms of the nouns in these examples?

1   **A**   Is there a lot of cake left?
     B   Are there a lot of cakes left?

2   **A**   I like chicken.
     B   I like chickens.

Expressions of quantity

LANGUAGE TIP

Don't get confused between *a few* and *few*
• *The party was OK; there were **a few** people I knew there.* (*a few* = some)
• *The party wasn't a success; **few** people turned up.* (*few* = hardly any). Hardly any is more natural in spoken English.

▶ **GRAMMAR** REFERENCE p.168

7 Turn to page 160 for more practice with countable and uncountable nouns.

8 What's the difference in meaning between these examples?

1   **A**   The shop sells a few cakes.
     B   The shop sells very few cakes.

2   **A**   There's a little cheese left.
     B   There's very little cheese left.

9 Work in pairs. Ask and answer questions based on the sentences in Activity 7.

Open cloze (Part 2)

▶ **EXAM** FOCUS p.201

1 Work in pairs and discuss whether you agree with the following statements.

1 I can't stand the taste of chilli. It's too hot.

2 I love food which has lots of spices and different flavours.

2 Read the text quickly and choose the correct words in these statements.

1 The writer *likes/doesn't like* chilli.

2 Chilli *can be/isn't* very addictive.

3 Look at the gaps in the text. In which four gaps should you put an expression of quantity?

EXAM TIP

In Part 2 you need to use a variety of grammatical forms, such as
• pronouns (*he, them*)
• prepositions (*at, about*)
• articles (*a, the*)
• auxiliaries (*do, are*)
• linking expressions (*despite, next*)
• comparisons (*than, as*)
• quantifiers (*any, many*).

---

4 Now think of the word which best fits each gap. Use one word in each gap. There is an example at the beginning.

5 Work in pairs and discuss the questions.

1 What do children generally dislike eating?

2 What foods did you hate at first, but enjoy now?

3 Is there any food that you refuse to eat? Why?

6 Underline all the prepositions in the text. Then find one example of

1 a phrasal verb.

2 a verb + preposition.

3 a fixed expression.

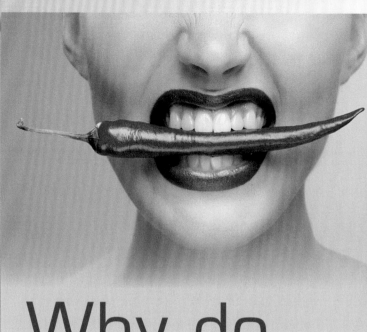

Why do people love chilli?

People don't wash their eyes in lemon juice or pour boiling hot tea over themselves, so why are we prepared to go through so **(0)** ...*much*... pain for the sake of chilli?

Chillies are one of the few foods that we simply should not enjoy and not just because of the way they taste. Not **(1)** .... people like the bitter taste of coffee to begin with but soon most of us **(2)** .... used to it. But coffee contains caffeine which has some addictive qualities, and this explains **(3)** .... it is so popular. Capsaicin, the ingredient **(4)** .... makes chillies hot, does not seem to have **(5)** .... addictive qualities whatsoever, and it also has very **(6)** .... health benefits. And yet it has **(7)** .... used in cooking in almost **(8)** .... culture for thousands of years. ■

Sentence completion (Part 2)

▶ **EXAM** FOCUS p.204

1 What have people always eaten in your culture? What have they started eating only recently?

2 You are going to listen to an extract from a radio programme in which a food writer called Sarah Willis is talking about the history of cooking. Look at the gapped sentences and say how many of the missing words are

A   nouns.

B   adjectives.

C   verbs.

3 Underline the key words and make sure you understand what each sentence means.

4 ▶ 16 For questions 1–10, listen and complete the sentences.

5 Read through your answers to check they make sense.

6 Discuss these questions.

1   How much raw food do you eat?

2   Do you think people should eat less meat?

3   What would you like to eat more or less of?

The importance of cooking

Sarah says about 60 percent of a chimpanzee's diet consists of **(1)** ....

Sarah thinks chimpanzee food tastes too **(2)** .... for humans.

Humans can't survive for long on a chimpanzee diet because they have a small **(3)** ....

Before they discovered cooking, people spent almost as much time eating food as they did **(4)** .... it.

Sarah thinks one benefit of cooking was that it helped to **(5)** .... food.

Some scientists think cooking resulted in an increase in the size of the **(6)** ....

The idea of sharing a **(7)** .... probably started when people began to cook.

Waiting until food was cooked meant there was a risk that it could be **(8)** ....

New evidence in Africa shows that early humans may have used **(9)** .... for cooking over one million years ago.

During the last ice age the extra **(10)** .... provided by cooked food helped people to survive.

Speaking

1 **Discuss the following questions.**

1 How common is it in your country to eat out in restaurants?

2 What kind of restaurants do different age groups tend to eat in?

3 What kind of food do you enjoy eating most when you go out?

Multiple choice (Part 5)

▶ **EXAM** FOCUS p.202

2 **Read the article about a restaurant food critic and say in what ways David is unusual.**

3 **Read the questions in Activity 4 (don't read the options yet) and underline the part of the text each question refers to. Then underline the key words in the options.**

4 **For questions 1–6, choose the answer (A, B, C or D) which you think fits best according to the text.**

> **EXAM TIP**
>
> Remember when you are looking for the answers in this part, the questions will follow the order of the text.

1 David wanted to go to the new restaurant because

  A he prefers Italian food to Greek food.

  B he was attracted by its appearance.

  C he wanted to write his first food review for publication.

  D he prefers eating in a restaurant to having takeout food.

2 Why was David lucky to get a table at the Salumeria Rosi?

  A The restaurant wasn't keen to serve a child on his own.

  B Most tables were reserved for celebrities.

  C The restaurant was completely booked up.

  D He couldn't afford a proper meal.

3 How did the customers react to David?

  A They were worried about him.

  B They were interested in him.

  C They wanted to hear his opinions on the food.

  D They felt they should talk to him in case he was lonely.

4 What did David appreciate about the restaurant?

  A the fuss they made of him

  B the unusual food he was given to try free

  C the fact that they explained how the food was made

  D the fact that they didn't treat him like a child

5 What does *that* refer to in line 53?

  A which part of an animal tripe was

  B why he had been given tripe

  C how the intestines were prepared

  D the kind of animal the intestines came from

6 The expression *tender years* in line 67 refers to David's

  A sweet nature.

  B extreme youth.

  C child-like behaviour.

  D lack of qualifications.

Speaking

5 **Work in pairs. Do you think people reading David's reviews would take them seriously? Why/Why not?**

Vocabulary

phrasal verbs with *turn*

6 **Match definitions 1–6 with the phrasal verbs in the box. Some of the verbs are underlined in the text.**

turn away	turn down	turn off
turn on	turn out	turn up

1 refuse an invitation

2 arrive somewhere, especially unexpectedly

3 suddenly attack someone, physically or with words

4 have a particular or unexpected result

5 make somebody decide they don't like something

6 refuse someone permission to enter a place

7 **Work in pairs. Ask and answer these questions.**

1 Are you ever turned off eating something by the smell of it cooking?

2 How would you turn down an invitation to something that you didn't want to go to? What would you say?

3 In what circumstances, if any, would you turn on a friend or family member?

4 In what situations might people be turned away from a restaurant or club?

5 In your country, is it acceptable to turn up at someone's house with no warning?

6 What have you done which turned out to be much better than you expected?

The most famous restaurant critic in America

Apparently it's never too soon to start being a restaurant food critic.

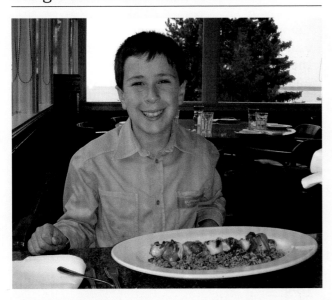

That's why David Fishman (pictured), a New York City native who had just turned twelve, decided to take himself out for dinner one night. His parents had called him at home to say they were running late, suggesting that he grab some hummus from his usual Greek takeout restaurant. David thought he could do better than that. He had recently passed by the Salumeria Rosi, a newly-opened Italian restaurant a few blocks from his home, and had been fascinated by the reflective black wall, the dried pork hanging from the ceiling, the little jars of olives and artichokes on the walls. If it was OK with his mom (and it <u>turned out</u> it was), he wanted to try that instead.

That night <u>turned out</u> to be one of the first that the restaurant was open to the public. David requested a menu, which the waitress handed to him, and decided that it was within his budget. Then he asked for a table for one and waited to see what she'd say. A year before, he had been <u>turned away</u> from a half-empty restaurant and told that it did not serve

children unaccompanied by adults. Grown-up or not, tables were hard to come by that evening – every seat was reserved, mostly by friends of the Italian chef and owner, Cesare Casella. Even TV actor Tony Danza <u>turned up</u>. But the waitress decided to squeeze in the Salumeria's first unaccompanied customer under 1.4 metres, as long as he promised to be out by 8 p.m. It was a deal.

Nobody at the restaurant seemed terribly impressed by Tony Danza, but David Fishman – now that was something. People tried not to stare, but couldn't help themselves. Where were his parents? Was he enjoying the food? Cash or credit? An Australian couple seated beside him struck up a conversation and a young couple on the other side of his table insisted on buying him a chocolate mousse. In turn, he recommended that they try the arugula salad.

David had ordered a speciality of the restaurant, as well as salad leaves with Parmesan cheese. 'Good variety,' he wrote in the leather-bound notebook he brought along, restaurant-critic-like. 'Softish jazz music. Seem to enjoy kids but not overly.' In other words, no sickly-sweet smiles or insulting offer of grilled cheese.

The kitchen workers were so fascinated by the young adventurous eater that they sent out a bowl of complimentary tripe stew, which he enjoyed, although, he admits, 'It wasn't my favorite.' He was a little surprised to learn later that tripe was prepared with intestines. His eyes went wide. 'The intestines of what?' he asked. (Somehow, that seemed to matter.) *line 53*

An only child, David grew up in a family where eating well and imaginatively at home was important. His mother encouraged him to make notes about what he liked, and it developed from there. But little did he know how dramatically his life would change after he wandered into the Salumeria Rosi. During dinner, while he was chatting with customers and taking notes, he was noticed by a woman who has a friend at the *New York Times*. The article she wrote about him led to the kind of media attention that contestants on *Pop Idol* dream will be theirs. Despite his tender years, *line 67* he is now reviewing more of the city's top restaurants, making television appearances, touring Europe, and there is even a possible film under discussion.

Passive forms

▶ **GRAMMAR** REFERENCE p.172

1 **Read the short text. What is unusual about this celebration?**

> On the last weekend in November, a feast <u>will be organised</u> in Lopburi, Thailand. A huge amount of fruit and vegetables <u>will be provided</u> by local people, and chefs <u>have been invited</u> to prepare a wonderful meal. Not so unusual, perhaps, except that the 3,000 guests are all monkeys! Monkeys <u>can be seen</u> everywhere in this jungle town, and the feast <u>is being held</u>, as it is every year, to say thank you to them. In this town at least, monkeys <u>are believed to bring</u> wealth, in the form of tourism.

2 **Look at the underlined passive forms in Activity 1 and make them active.**

Example: *People will organise a feast on the last weekend in November.*

LANGUAGE TIP

- We use the passive form when we don't know/it doesn't matter/it's obvious who does the action.
- Use a form of *to be* + past participle.

3 **Complete the sentences about other celebrations using the correct passive form of the verbs in brackets.**

1 At the wedding I went to in Italy last week, sugared almonds .... (*give away*) to all the guests.
2 Since 1368, moon cakes .... (*eat*) in China to celebrate the Harvest Festival.
3 Some people hate .... (*give*) surprise parties on their birthdays.
4 A decision must .... (*make*) about which restaurant we are going to book for Mum and Dad's wedding anniversary.
5 I hope that noodles .... (*serve*) at my Korean friend's wedding tomorrow.
6 I was really thrilled .... (*ask*) to give a speech at the wedding reception.

4 **Work in pairs. Think of popular celebrations in your country. What food is typically eaten there and how is it made?**

Passive reporting verbs

5 **Look at sentences A, B and C. Which sentence(s) avoid(s) saying *who* believes? What is the difference in form?**

A Thai people believe that monkeys bring wealth.
B Monkeys are believed to bring wealth.
C It is believed that monkeys bring wealth.

LANGUAGE TIP

We can report what people say or believe with verbs such as *think*, *believe* and two structures:
- *it* + passive reporting verb + *that* clause
- subject + passive reporting verb + present/perfect infinitive

6 **Complete the second sentence so that it has a similar meaning to the first sentence, using the word given. You must use between two and five words, including the word given.**

1 People expect tourists to carry sticks to protect themselves from curious monkeys.
ARE
Tourists .... sticks to protect themselves from curious monkeys.
2 Thai people know that the monkeys are a huge tourist attraction.
BE
Monkeys .... a huge tourist attraction.
3 Reports claim that twenty top chefs have been invited to prepare the meal.
THAT
It .... twenty top chefs have been invited to prepare the meal.
4 Locals believe that 2,000 kilos of food were consumed at the last feast.
HAVE
2,000 kilos of food .... consumed at the last feast.
5 The tourist office has estimated that over 10,000 visitors watch the feast.
BEEN
It .... that over 10,000 visitors watch the feast.
6 Some people think monkeys get very aggressive around food.
TO
Monkeys .... very aggressive around food.

7 **Work in pairs. Discuss stories which have been reported recently on TV or in the newspapers.**

Long turn (Part 2)
comparing and giving a reaction

▶ **EXAM** FOCUS p.206

> Both these photos show people eating out in restaurants. Compare the photos and say why the people might choose to eat in places like these.

1 Look at the photos and the exam task, and tick the statements you agree with. Can you think of any other points of comparison between the photos?

1 Although the food in an expensive restaurant may be wonderful, the atmosphere isn't as friendly as in fast food restaurants.

2 In expensive restaurants you often have to have full meals, whereas you can usually just get a snack in fast food places.

3 While fast food restaurants are quick and cheap, they usually serve unhealthy junk food.

4 Both formal restaurants and fast food cafés are popular with young people.

2 Underline the linking expressions in Activity 1 which are used to compare and contrast.

▶ **GRAMMAR** REFERENCE p.165

3 Work in pairs. Match the sentences 1–6 with the types of restaurants in the photos.

1 You *don't have to* dress up.
2 You *can't* hear yourself speak.
3 It's *overpriced*.
4 They're good for *special occasions*.
5 The atmosphere is more *casual*.
6 The food's a bit *basic*.

Listening

4 ▶ 17 Listen to Danuta doing the task and answer the questions.

1 What differences does she mention between the photos?
2 How does she respond to the second part of the question?

Speaking

5 Work in pairs. Turn to page 152 and complete Task 1.
Then turn to page 154 and swap roles for Task 2.

> **EXAM TIP**
>
> Make sure you allow enough time to answer the second part of the question or you will miss the focus of the task. You have only one minute to do both.

Reading

Describing a personal experience

1 **Read the restaurant review and tick the things that are mentioned.**

staff	writer's expectations	location
décor	other diners	atmosphere
prices	food	service

2 **Work in pairs and discuss the questions.**

1 Would you go to the Hard Rock Café in London after reading this review?

2 Have you ever been disappointed or pleasantly surprised by a meal in a restaurant?

3 **Copy and complete the table with words/ phrases from the review.**

food	staff	atmosphere
poor quality		full of tourists

4 **Underline examples of where the writer uses structures 1–4. Say why they are used.**

1 phrases containing negatives which have positive meanings

2 adverbs

3 the passive

4 the past perfect

5 **In which paragraph does the writer**

A give details about the food?

B say who she recommends the restaurant for?

C give some basic information about the restaurant?

| 🏠 Home | Restaurants | Diners | Cafés | Bars | ★ Star reviews |

The Hard Rock Café

EXCELLENT ★★★★★

I'd always avoided visiting the legendary Hard Rock Café in London's Piccadilly, as I thought it would be full of tourists and the food would be poor quality and overpriced. But I have to say I was pleasantly surprised. The food was outstanding, the staff extremely welcoming and the atmosphere certainly didn't disappoint.

As a vegetarian, I thought there wouldn't be much to tempt me on the menu. I decided to try the veggie burger, even though these are quite often stodgy and bland. But this one wasn't. It was perfectly cooked and far from bland. I'd heard that you sometimes have to wait a long time for your food but mine was served in just twelve minutes.

The only downside was the fact it got so busy; literally the place was already packed by 7p.m. And when I needed to pay the bill, I had to wait a while. But the staff are so friendly and helpful it almost seems mean to mention it. On the whole, I'd really recommend going there. It's a great place for a fun night out with friends.

Review (Part 2)

▶ **WRITING** REFERENCE p.186

6 **Read the exam task and write a review, using some of the ideas and language from the review of the Hard Rock Café. You should write 140–190 words.**

You see this advertisement in the local paper.

Wanted: Restaurant Critics!

Have you tried a new restaurant in your area recently? We'd like to know your opinion, not only of the food but also the staff, the atmosphere and the prices. Tell us whether you would recommend the restaurant to other people. The best review will be published in next week's paper.

Write your **review**.

1 Complete the sentences with the prepositions in the box. You may need to use them more than once.

after away down off on out over up

1 I wasn't expecting him to arrive. He just turned .... with no warning.

2 I had to turn .... the invitation to dinner because I was working late.

3 The restaurant is so popular that people are often turned .... at the door.

4 Getting food poisoning from shellfish really turned me .... eating it again.

5 The play turned .... to be a disappointment after a great start.

6 The chef turned .... me and blamed me for burning the meal.

7 When I have more time, I'm going to take .... tennis.

8 I had to leave work at five but a friend took .... for the last hour.

9 The band have completely taken .... in America: everyone loves them.

10 I think he must take .... his mother. She's really clever, too.

2 Choose the best answer, A, B, C or D.

1 He snacks a lot .... meals.
A besides   B on   C between   D from

2 It's important to eat a diet .... in vitamins.
A rich   B high   C full   D plenty

3 People would be healthier if they ate less .... food.
A fast   B quick   C hurried   D speedy

4 Never add salt to any dish without .... it first to see if it's needed.
A tasting   B cooking   C flavouring   D pouring

5 Some cultures are known .... their spicy food.
A by   B for   C about   D with

6 What .... are needed to make that dish?
A parts   B items   C ingredients   D pieces

3 Complete these sentences with one word.

1 We've got very .... cheese left. Can you go to the shops for me?

2 I don't eat .... eggs these days; just two a week.

3 There's .... milk left in the fridge. Who's drunk it all?

4 She eats .... any chocolate these days.

5 I think I am .... followed by someone.

6 A lot of excellent work .... been done today.

7 The onions must .... fried until they are soft.

8 Those chefs .... said to be extremely talented.

4 There is a mistake in each of the following sentences. Underline the mistakes and correct them. There may be more than one possibility.

1 They live there for more than twenty years.

2 I run more fastly than he does.

3 My friend isn't having much money at the moment.

4 The team tried very hardly to win the match.

5 I'm afraid there are a very few tickets left for that performance.

6 That was by far the more expensive holiday we've ever had.

7 He has run, which is why he's tired.

8 That band gets really popular these days.

9 He works like a waiter during his holidays.

10 During the storm, lot of roofs were blown off.

11 We were all absolutely frightened by that film.

12 She is used to travel long distances for her job now.

13 I tried to get in touch with him but he already left.

14 He was playing the golf when it started raining.

15 Did you promise taking her to the shops?

5 Choose the correct alternative in each of these sentences.

1 While I was tidying my room, I came *over/across* a story I had written.

2 My *taste/feeling* in music has changed a lot over the years.

3 My sister's favourite band have just *brought/released* a new album.

4 My maths teacher's mood is rather *unpredicted/unpredictable*.

5 What is the *different/difference* between these two words?

6 Some actors are out of work for years before they finally *do/make* it.

7 I get really annoyed *of/by* my brother's behaviour.

8 I am a bit *short/low* of money at the moment.

9 Suddenly, a movement *caught/attracted* my eye.

10 We decided not to go because of the *hard/strong* wind.

11 The boss was very *freezing/icy* towards us when we returned late.

12 It's a pity that you had to be so *impatient/unpatient* with him.

13 Tom is not very good at *taking/doing* responsibility.

14 It looks *though/like* it's going to rain later on.

15 The situation is extremely *embarrassed/embarrassing*.

Gold First by Bell & Thomas
© Pearson

Multiple-choice cloze (Part 1)

6 For questions 1–8, read the text below and decide which answer (A, B, C or D) best fits each gap. There is an example at the beginning.

Happy families

It came as no surprise to me when a newspaper article I read **(0)** *B recently* claimed to prove that the happiest children tend to be **(1)** .... children.

When I was younger, I used to **(2)** .... having a brother because I thought that parents with just one child were bound to **(3)** .... them more attention and love them more.

My most unhappy childhood memories involve my older brother Thomas. I didn't get **(4)** .... with him at all and, because he was much bigger than me, he would always **(5)** .... any fights we had. My parents took the view that they should not interfere in our arguments, and made us sort them **(6)** .... ourselves, which meant that Thomas could do whatever he wanted.

However, the good news about siblings is that as they get older, they seem to start valuing each other more. In fact, nowadays Thomas and I are quite **(7)** ....
I suppose this is not surprising, since we share a **(8)** .... that goes back a long way, and no one else knows much about it or is very interested in it.

0	**A** lately	**B** recently	**C** currently	**D** presently
1	**A** only	**B** single	**C** unique	**D** individual
2	**A** miss	**B** hope	**C** wish	**D** regret
3	**A** pay	**B** make	**C** allow	**D** provide
4	**A** on	**B** by	**C** round	**D** away
5	**A** win	**B** beat	**C** succeed	**D** overcome
6	**A** of	**B** over	**C** out	**D** through
7	**A** near	**B** close	**C** familiar	**D** attached
8	**A** story	**B** record	**C** history	**D** narrative

Open cloze (Part 2)

7 For questions 9–16, read the text below and think of the word that best fits each gap. Use only one word in each gap. There is an example at the beginning.

The coldest city on earth

Although the remote region of Yakutsk in Siberia covers more than a million square miles, it is home to **(0)** *fewer* than one million people and has hardly any large towns. In January the temperatures are -45°C, causing the metal on people's spectacles to stick to **(9)** .... cheeks.

Locals claim there are **(10)** .... lakes and rivers in the region for each inhabitant to have one. According **(11)** .... legend, when the god of creation arrived in Yakutsk, he got **(12)** .... cold that his hands were frozen and he dropped all the natural resources there. The capital of the region, also called Yakutsk, is six time zones away from Moscow.

There's no railway, so travellers have the option of a 1,000-mile boat ride up the Lena river during **(13)** .... few months of the year when it isn't frozen, or they have to use the 'Road of Bones', **(14)** .... was built by prisoners and can only be used in winter, when the rivers freeze over. Truck drivers bringing supplies to remote villages go in pairs and never turn their engines **(15)** .... during the two-week drive. **(16)** .... they break down on the little-used road, it means almost certain death.

Word formation (Part 3)

8 For questions 17–24, read the text below. Use the word given in capitals at the end of some of the lines to form a word that fits the gap in the same line. There is an example at the beginning.

Anyone for bugs?

In the kitchen of the Archipelago restaurant in London, the head chef is making final **(0)** _preparations_ to one of the salads that has helped to make his restaurant so famous. Taking a wok off the stove, he spoons a **(17)** .... red sauce onto a bed of salad leaves. At first **(18)** ...., this could be any other Thai salad, with its chilli, garlic and many other **(19)** .... ingredients.

But it's not long before you can recognise the shape of an insect – the thin legs, huge eyes and a long tail of a locust. The less **(20)** .... among us would not be too keen on eating insects such as locusts and crickets but they are, in fact, **(21)** .... tasty. Many people find the idea of eating insects **(22)** .... However, for around 2.5 billion of the world's population, insects like these form part of their **(23)** .... diet. This is very **(24)** .... as they are low in fat, high in protein and full of vitamins as well as being energy efficient.

PREPARE

SPICE
SEE

COLOUR

ADVENTURE

SURPRISE

FASCINATE

DAY
FORTUNE

Key word transformations (Part 4)

9 For questions 25–30, complete the second sentence so that it has a similar meaning to the first sentence, using the word given. Do not change the word given. You must use between two and five words, including the word given.

Example:

I don't think John has got his father's musical talent.

AFTER

John doesn't appear _to take after_ his father as far as musical talent is concerned.

25 Julia can sing better than me.

WELL

I .... as Julia.

26 A fast food chain has taken over two of our local restaurants.

BY

Two of our local restaurants .... a fast food chain.

27 Nearly all the shops in this town are expensive.

HARDLY

There .... shops in this town.

28 It's ages since I've seen him.

NOT

I .... ages.

29 I think I forgot to lock the door.

REMEMBER

I .... the door.

30 My brother often arrives unexpectedly.

TURNING

My brother is .... unexpectedly.

(Pearson 2014, Gold First)

On camera

6

Speaking

1 **Work in pairs and discuss the questions.**

1 What kind of live performances do you enjoy?

2 Do you ever give money to street performers? Why/Why not?

2 **Choose the word which does NOT fit in phrases 1–3.**

1 The *main/most obvious/highest/key* (dis)advantage of (being a street performer) is…

2 *Another/One further/One different/An additional* (dis)advantage of (working in X) is…

3 …is a *huge/considerable/major/large* (dis)advantage.

3 **Work in pairs. What might the advantages and disadvantages of being a circus performer and a street performer be? Use the phrases in Activity 2 and the ideas in the box to help you.**

fun	pay	practice	the risk of injury
the stress of performing		travel	working hours

Discussion (Part 4)

▶ **EXAM** FOCUS p.207

4 ▶ 18 **Read the questions and listen to two students, Roberto and Beata, answering question 1. Do you agree with their opinions?**

1 Which do you think you need more of, luck or talent, to succeed in the arts?

2 How important do you think it is for schools to offer art, dance and drama classes to all students?

3 What do you think of people who take part in TV talent shows like *The X Factor*?

5 **What language did Roberto/Beata use to**

1 ask his/her partner a question?

2 summarise his/her partner's opinion?

3 accept his/her partner's argument?

EXAM TIP

Try to include your partner in the discussion and listen to what he/she says.

6 Do you think Roberto and Beata answered the question well?

7 Work in pairs. Discuss the questions in Activity 4.

Vocabulary
the arts

8 Complete the sentences with the words in the box.

critics   production   set   script

1 The .... took months to make.
2 The play received good reviews from the ....
3 This .... was first performed in 1922.
4 The .... was difficult for the actors to learn.

9 Look at the paintings. Do you recognise them? Which one do you like the most? Match the words with the pictures.

abstract   graffiti   landscape   portrait   still life

1

2

4

3

10 Work in pairs. Take turns to describe a favourite painting or photograph. Find out as much information as you can about your partner's favourite artist or photographer.

It was painted by…

It's on display in…

It makes me feel…

It shows…

5

Multiple choice: short extracts (Part 1)

▶ **EXAM** FOCUS p.204

1 ▶ **19 You will hear people talking in eight different situations. First, underline the key words in question 1. Then listen and choose the best answer, A, B or C.**

1   On the radio, you hear a woman talking about a play. What did she dislike about the play?

   A the lighting   **B** the music   **C** the costumes

2 **Check with a partner and answer these questions. Then listen to question 1 again.**

1   Was the information in the recording in the same order as options A, B and C?

2   Did you hear any of the key words in options A, B or C?

3   Does the woman make negative comments about all the options, A, B or C?

4   Which words did you hear that refer to lighting, music and costumes?

5   Which words signal what the woman disliked about the play?

3 ▶ **20 Listen to questions 2–8 and choose the best answer, A, B or C.**

EXAM TIP

Don't worry if you don't understand every word. Just focus on choosing the best option to answer the question.

2   You overhear a man and a woman talking about a visit to the theatre. Why do they decide to meet at 6p.m.?

   A The show starts earlier than they had thought.

   B They want to eat before the performance.

   C They need to get tickets.

3   You hear someone talking about a famous actor. Where will fans be able to see the actor next week?

   A on the set of his new film

   B performing on stage

   C on a TV chat show

4   You hear a woman giving some information on the radio about a comedy festival. Why is the festival going to be different this year?

   A The tickets will be more expensive.

   B It will be held in a smaller venue.

   C It will be on different dates.

5   You hear a man interviewing a ballet dancer on the radio. Why is she going to retire later this year?

   A She is worried about getting injured.

   B She no longer enjoys performing.

   C She wants to see more of her family.

6   You hear a man and a woman talking on the radio about a new art exhibition. What is special about it?

   A its content

   B its location

   C its size

7   You hear an actress being interviewed on the radio. What is the actress doing?

   A giving her opinion

   B describing future events

   C stating an intention

8   You hear two friends talking in a café. What are they talking about?

   A a play they're going to see

   B their favourite actress

   C a college production

4 **Work in pairs and discuss the questions.**

1   How often do you go to the theatre/the cinema/ art galleries?

2   Would you be prepared to queue for three hours to see a famous painting? Why? Why not?

Future forms

▶ **GRAMMAR** REFERENCE p.177

1 **Look at the underlined verbs. Which ones are examples of the present continuous, present simple, *will, going to* and modal verbs?**

A: Who do you think will get the main part?

B: I expect **(1)** it'll be Zoe. She's a good singer and dancer. But it **(2)** could be Molly. I thought she did a good audition too. Mr Paton says **(3)** he's going to tell us in class this week.

A: When **(4)** are you starting rehearsals?

B: On Friday. **(5)** It's going to be really hard work because performances **(6)** start in three weeks.

A: **(7)** I'll help you learn your lines, if you like.

B: Thanks. That would be very helpful.

2 **Match the numbered future forms in the dialogue with their uses A–G.**

A an offer

B a fixed arrangement

C a timetabled event in the future

D an intention – something that someone has decided to do in the future

E a prediction based on a belief or opinion

F a prediction – based on fact

G a future possibility

3 **What words can you use instead of *could* for example 2 in Activity 1?**

4 **21 Complete the dialogues with the correct future form of the verbs in brackets. Then listen and check.**

1 *will / present simple / present continuous*

A: What **(1)** .... (*do*) this weekend?

B: I **(2)** .... (*go*) to the dance festival in the park. It's on all weekend.

A: Oh I'd really like to go but my brother **(3)** .... (*move*) house and I have to help him.

B: That's a shame!

A: Never mind. I'm sure you **(4)** .... (*enjoy*) it.

B: Yes. It should be fun, especially as I think the weather'll be good.

2 *going to / will / present simple*

A: Hi Ben! Are you going to the film festival at the weekend?

B: Yes, on Saturday. I **(5)** .... (*buy*) the tickets online today.

A: How much are they?

B: Only £15. I **(6)** .... (*get*) you one if you like.

A: That would be great. What time **(7)** .... (*start*)?

B: At 7.30. But I **(8)** .... (*leave*) home early, at six o'clock because of the traffic. I'll pick you up on my way if you want.

5 **Listen again and underline the stressed words in each sentence.**

Example: *What are you doing this weekend?*

6 **Practise the dialogues in pairs, paying attention to contractions, weak forms and the main stress in each sentence.**

LANGUAGE TIP

Future time expressions: *as soon as, when, before, after* are used with the present simple.

As soon as the film ends we'll call a taxi.

We'll have dinner when she arrives.

Before you see the film, you must read the book.

She's hoping to become an actress after she leaves school.

Speaking

7 **Tell your partner one hope, arrangement, intention or prediction for**

1 later today.

2 next weekend.

3 your next holiday.

4 next year.

Speaking

1 **Work in pairs and discuss the questions.**

1   Why do you think people still go to the cinema rather than watching films at home?

2   Which are more popular in your country: international blockbusters or independent films made in your own country?

Gapped text (Part 6)

▶ **EXAM** FOCUS p.202

2 **Read the title and introduction carefully. Then read the article quickly. Why are blockbusters and 'niche' products doing so well these days?**

3 **Six sentences have been removed from the text. Look at the text around the first gap and answer the questions.**

1   What does *That* refer back to?

2   How does the information after the gap relate to the information before the gap?

3   What kind of information do you think is missing?

4   What kind of linking word or expression would you expect to find in the missing sentence?

4 **Look at the options A–G and choose the one that fits the first gap. Then do the same for the rest of the gaps (2–6). There is one extra sentence which you do not need to use.**

EXAM TIP

Try to predict what kind of information will be in the gap before looking at the options.

Speaking

5 **Discuss the questions in pairs.**

1   Which 'niche' or small independent films have been successful in your country?

2   How do you choose what films to see or books to read?

3   What effect has digital technology had on the film industry so far? What do you think the future of the cinema and entertainment in general will be?

Vocabulary

word formation: adjectives from nouns; nouns from verbs

6 **Work in pairs to form the words in questions 1 and 2. Then check with the underlined words in the article.**

1   What are the adjectives from these nouns?

| access | anxiety | romance | succeed |

2   What are the nouns from these verbs?

| choose | entertain | grow | live |
| produce | separate | supply | |

7 **Tick the statements you agree with. Then discuss your opinions in groups, giving reasons and examples.**

The films I enjoy the most

A   tend to have a happy ending.

B   are usually romantic comedies.

C   generally have amazing special effects.

D   always have a great soundtrack.

E   are often blockbusters.

The future of entertainment

More than ever, media is separating into mass market blockbusters on the one hand and 'niche' products – attracting small groups of people with similar interests – on the other. Everything else is struggling to compete.

Joe Swanberg makes films about the romantic lives of young people in the city. He shoots quickly with a digital camera and asks actors to wear their own clothes. His low-budget films are hardly ever shown in cinemas. By keeping his costs down and distributing digitally, Mr Swanberg is making a living.

Technology was expected to help young people like him. A few years ago it was predicted that the internet would vastly increase the supply of small independent films and other niche media products and increase their audiences. That has certainly happened. [1] Blockbusters are also tightening their grip on audiences, whether it's in the area of film, music, television or books. The growth of both niche products and huge sell-out successes has been at the expense of the things in the middle which are just quite popular – the near misses.

[2] As in the past, people still want to have something to talk about with their friends. Which is why talent shows such as *American Idol* do pretty much as well as they did ten years ago, and why the latest blockbuster still breaks new records at the box office. Research shows that people still choose blockbusters more often than less well-known books and films. This is probably because people tend to try only things they have heard of – which for many people means only media-hyped blockbusters.

Furthermore, all the technology that has made niche content so much more accessible has also proved handy for pushing blockbusters. Missed the last popular film? [3]

Blockbusters are doing well not in spite of the fact that people have more choice in entertainment, but because of it. Imagine walking into a music shop which has more than 10 million songs, as iTunes does, all of them arranged alphabetically. Making up your mind would be impossible! [4]

Is this increasingly more common separation into blockbusters and niches good or bad? It certainly makes life harder for media companies. In a world where entertainment choices are growing, it is more important than ever to make a big impact with your product. [5] The possibility of failing can make people anxious and more conservative. Television programmes must be successful quickly or they will be cancelled. It is becoming even harder to talk the decision-makers in the movie industry into approving films if they are not confident there is a demand for them.

These days, with so many options, there is rarely nothing good on television. So the media industry must raise its game. Intelligent people naturally wish that more money were available to produce the kind of music, films and television programmes they like. [6] Some may love watching a programme about the history of dance; others may want to spend an hour being told how to look after pet snakes. But not many want to do either of these things, which explains why such programmes are niche products. There are only a few things that can be guaranteed to delight large numbers of people. They are known as blockbusters.

A Don't worry, because there will be other chances to see it, in a wide variety of formats.

B The problem is that everybody has different ideas about exactly what they want to watch.

C If it isn't a hit, it will have to fight for attention together with thousands – perhaps millions – of other offerings.

D State broadcasters like the BBC have some protection from the poor economic climate.

E However, so has the opposite.

F So, rather than having to decide, it's much easier to just grab what everybody is talking about.

G There are several reasons why big hits still do so well.

Future perfect and continuous

▶ **GRAMMAR** REFERENCE p.177

1 **Do you agree with these predictions?**

> By 2020, we'll all be watching TV programmes in 3D. They might even have found a way to project our faces onto the characters on the screen by then.

> In twenty-five years, people will have learnt how to monitor the electronic activity of your brain and when you play video games, your thoughts will be controlling your avatar.

2 **Look at the predictions again.**

1 Write down the time linkers connected to the future.
2 Underline two actions which began before a specific time in the future and will continue after it.
3 Circle two actions which are already over before a specific time in the future.

3 **Complete the notes.**

- future continuous: *will/may/might* + ... + *-ing*
- future perfect: *will/may/might* + ... + ... participle

4 **Choose the correct alternative to complete the sentences.**

By 2050 …

1 most cinemas will *be closing down/have closed* down.
2 everybody will *be using/have used* surround sound systems with their TVs.
3 we'll *be choosing/have chosen* from a huge cyber library whatever television programme we want to watch.
4 we will not *be interacting/have interacted* with the screen when we move and speak.
5 they will *be inventing/have invented* contact lenses with a chip inside so that we can watch the screen in 3D.
6 holographic TV screens will *be projecting/have projected* images around our rooms at home.

5 **Tick the sentences you agree with in Activity 4. Then discuss your opinions in pairs.**

6 **Work in pairs. What do you think the world will be like in fifty years' time? What will have changed and what will be happening? Use the ideas in the box to help you.**

the environment   the family   food
leisure time   medicine and technology
travel   work

Vocabulary
expressions with *get*

1 *Get* has lots of different meanings. Replace *get* in questions 1–6 with one of the verbs in the box. Then ask each other the questions in pairs.

become	have	move/travel	persuade
receive	understand		

1 Was there a subject at school that you really didn't get?
2 What techniques do you use to get people to do what you want?
3 When do you normally get the time to relax?
4 In which situations do you get angry?
5 How do you get from one place to another?
6 How many texts do you get in an average day?

Multiple-choice cloze (Part 1)

▶ **EXAM** FOCUS p.200

2 Read the text quickly. What did science fiction get right and wrong when it predicted the future? What did it not predict?

EXAM TIP

Part 1 tests language (focusing on vocabulary) such as
- phrasal verbs (*get away*)
- collocations (*do your homework*)
- words with similar meanings (*travel, trip, journey*)
- linking words (*although*)
- set phrases (*on purpose*).

	A		B		C		D	
0	**A** say	**B** call	**C** tell	**D** name
1	**A** true	**B** right	**C** exact	**D** correct
2	**A** get	**B** arrive	**C** reach	**D** appear
3	**A** on	**B** by	**C** with	**D** at
4	**A** drive	**B** travel	**C** voyage	**D** journey
5	**A** for	**B** to	**C** in	**D** against
6	**A** up	**B** off	**C** over	**D** down
7	**A** make	**B** do	**C** get	**D** take
8	**A** end	**B** effect	**C** result	**D** solution

3 Read the text again and decide which answer (A, B, C or D) best fits each gap.

4 Do you agree with the writer about the importance of the computer? What other inventions do you think have had a huge impact on our lives?

From fiction to reality

Science fiction films have promised us many exciting gadgets. We have seen hoverboards, domestic robots and flying cars, to (0) __*D name*__ just a few, but most of these predictions have not come (1) .... yet. For example, this morning I didn't (2) .... to the office on a hoverboard. I came (3) .... bike instead. The bicycle was invented in the nineteenth century. Almost the whole (4) .... was on a form of Tarmac, also invented that same century. Instead of a pill for breakfast, I had a bacon roll. Also, (5) .... some people's surprise, robots haven't taken (6) .... either the home or the workplace yet.

On the other hand, in 1987, *Star Trek* predicted we would be using touch screen technology. So perhaps fiction doesn't always (7) .... it wrong after all. Maybe the most astonishing development has been the microchip and its place in computers. The (8) .... on our lives has been amazing, and this was never really predicted.

Report (Part 2)
text organisation

▶ **WRITING** REFERENCE p.184

1 Read the report which a teacher was asked to write for the director of her language college. Answer the questions in pairs.

1 What was the purpose of her report?

2 What is her recommendation?

3 Is it written in an informal or a semi-formal style? Give examples.

Report on suggestion for a college cinema

(1) ....

The aim of this report is to outline the advantages and potential problems of investing money in a small cinema, and make recommendations. In order to do this, both students and staff were consulted.

(2) ....

It was generally believed that a college cinema could have wide-reaching benefits for both students and teachers. It was suggested that films in other languages as well as English could be shown, which would widen the appeal, and that the cinema might also be used for conversation classes.

(3) ....

The main concerns that were raised are as follows:

1 It would be expensive to set up and run.

2 Since many students watch DVDs on their laptops, they might not be prepared to pay to watch films.

3 Only big cinemas have access to blockbusters when they first come out.

(4) ....

I am concerned that the cinema may not pay its way at first. However, all things considered, the benefits outweigh the disadvantages. I would therefore recommend going ahead with the project.

2 Give each of the four sections of the report a heading, so that it is easier to read.

Advantages   Potential problems
Introduction   Recommendations

3 Look at the underlined phrases in the text. Find examples of the following and discuss why they are commonly used in reports.

1 passive forms/reporting verbs

2 linking words

3 clauses of purpose

4 Read the exam task and underline the key words.

> The director of your college has asked you to write a report on a visit you made to a self-study centre at a local university. You should explain how successful it has been and recommend whether or not your college should have one.
>
> Write your **report** to the director. Write your answer in **140–190** words in an appropriate style.

5 Divide these points into the advantages and disadvantages of the study centre you saw.

1 It is under-used at weekends.

2 People from the community use the facilities, which helps to fund it.

3 Many students still prefer to study in their own rooms.

4 The worksheets provided give extra practice of classroom work.

5 A full-time assistant has to be on duty even if the centre is empty.

6 The facility helps to attract potential students to the college.

7 It cost a lot to set up because of all the computers, etc.

8 Writing materials for the centre is time-consuming for the teachers.

6 Write your report. You can use some of the points in Activity 5 as well as your own ideas.

EXAM TIP

Organise your report under clear headings and include numbers or bullet points to make your points clearly.

1 **Complete the following sentences, using the correct form of the word in capitals.**

1 Comedy stand-up has been my favourite form of .... since I was a teenager. **ENTERTAIN**

2 The rapid .... of our national film industry has been very welcome. **GROW**

3 Although I wasn't .... in the audition, I was glad I'd taken part. **SUCCEED**

4 The theatre has invested money so that the building is .... to people in wheelchairs. **ACCESS**

5 He wants to be an actor but he is .... about getting a job. **ANXIETY**

6 We wanted to see a film, but there wasn't much .... **CHOOSE**

2 **Choose the correct word to complete the sentences.**

1 Sorry, I can't come on Saturday. I .... an old school friend for lunch.

  A meet   **B** am meeting   **C** will meet

2 As soon as she ...., will you text me?

  A phones   **B** will phone   **C** will be phoning

3 I .... my drama course by the end of next year.

  A will be completing   **B** will have completed

  C am completing

4 This time tomorrow, I .... in front of hundreds of people.

  A will dance   **B** will be dancing   **C** dance

5 Don't worry, I haven't forgotten. I .... to him later.

  A speak   **B** will have spoken

  C am going to speak

6 I'll meet you after I .... work.

  A finish   **B** am finishing   **C** will finish

7 Don't be nervous. I'm sure you .... really well tomorrow.

  A do   **B** are doing   **C** will do

8 Let's hurry! They .... the theatre doors at 7.30 and then you have to wait until the interval to go in.

  A close   **B** are going to close   **C** are closing

3 **Complete the sentences with the words in the box.**

away	down	into
over	round	through

1 The only way I can get .... to my cousin is by talking about dance.

2 *City Lights* is on TV tonight. I never got .... to seeing that in the cinema.

3 It took him ages to get .... the disappointment of not being in the play.

4 If I stay in every night watching TV, it gets me ....

5 Comedians can't get .... with simply repeating the same jokes at every performance.

6 Everyone says it's a really good series. I just can't get .... it.

4 **Complete the sentences with the future continuous form or the future perfect form of the verbs in brackets.**

1 I think I'll still .... (*learn*) my lines until just before the play starts.

2 The film may already .... (*start*) by the time we get there.

3 I hope they'll .... (*show*) his still lifes at the exhibition.

4 We might .... (*use*) the same costumes in our next production.

5 People will probably still .... (*watch*) live theatre in fifty years' time.

6 I think people will .... (*lose*) interest in computer games a long time before 2020.

A home from home

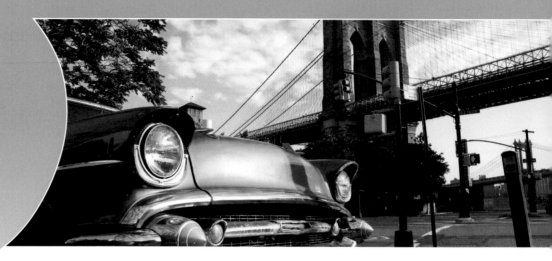

Speaking

1 You are going to read an extract from a novel about Eilis, a young girl in the 1950s, who is about to leave her home in Ireland to go and live in America. Work in pairs and discuss how you would feel about leaving your family, town and country to emigrate.

Library ≣   AA Q

line 1 Until now, Eilis had always presumed that she would live in the town all her life, as her mother had done, knowing everyone, having the same friends and neighbours, the same routines in the same streets. She had expected that she would find a job in the town and then
line 3 marry someone and give up the job and have children. Now, she felt that she was being singled out for something for which she was not in any way prepared, and this, despite the fear it carried with it, gave her a feeling, or more a set of feelings, she thought she might experience in the days before her wedding, days in which everyone looked at her in the rush of arrangements with light in their eyes, days in which she herself was fizzy with excitement but careful not to think too precisely about what the next few weeks would be like in
line 7 case she lost her nerve.

There was no day that passed without an event. … Father Flood wrote with more details, of where she would stay when she arrived and how close it would be to her place of work; her ticket arrived for the ship to New York, which would leave from Liverpool. … The house was, she thought, unusually, almost unnaturally happy, and the meals they shared were full of too much talk and laughter. It reminded her of the weeks before Jack had left for Birmingham when they would do anything to distract themselves from the thought that they were losing him.

One day, when a neighbour called and sat in the kitchen with them having tea, Eilis realised that her mother and Rose were doing everything to hide their feelings. The neighbour, almost casually, as a way of making conversation, said: 'You'll miss her when she's gone, I'd say.'

'Oh, it'll kill me when she goes,' her mother said. Her face wore a dark strained look that Eilis had not seen since the months after
line 17 their father died. Then, in the moments that followed, the neighbour appearing to have been taken aback by her mother's tone, her mother's expression became almost darker and she had to stand up and walk quietly out of the room. It was clear to Eilis that she was
line 19 going to cry. Eilis was so surprised that, instead of following her mother into the hallway or the dining room, she made small talk with
line 20 their neighbour, hoping her mother would soon return and they could resume what had seemed like an ordinary conversation.

Even when she woke in the night and thought about it, she did not allow herself to conclude that she did not want to go. … It struck her on one of those nights, as she lay awake, that the next time she would open the suitcase it would be in a different room in
line 23 a different country, and then the thought came unbidden into her mind that she would be happier if it were opened by another person who could keep the clothes and shoes and wear them every day. She would prefer to stay at home, sleep in this room, live in this house, do without the clothes and shoes. The arrangements being made, all the bustle and talk, would be better if they were for someone else, she thought, someone like her, someone the same age and size, who maybe even looked the same as she did, as long as she, the person who was thinking now, could wake in this bed every morning and move as the day went on in these familiar streets and come home to the kitchen, to her mother and Rose.

line 29 Even though she let these thoughts run as fast as they would, she still stopped when her mind moved towards real fear or dread, or worse, towards the thought that she was going to lose this world for ever, that she would never have an ordinary day again in this ordinary place, that the rest of her life would be a struggle with the unfamiliar. Downstairs, once Rose and her mother were there, she talked about practical things and remained bright.

· · · · · · · ▫ · · · · · ·

Multiple choice (Part 5)

reading for detail

▶ **EXAM** FOCUS p.202

2 Read the extract quickly. Does Eilis feel positive about the move?

3 Read the extract again and answer questions 1–3. Choose the answer which you think fits best according to the text.

1 From the first paragraph we understand that Eilis is

   A worried about adjusting to the new plans for her future.

   B anxious that she won't be ready in time for her departure.

   C disappointed about not being able to get married in Ireland.

   D upset that she might lose touch with everyone she cares about.

2 What impression do you get of Eilis's family?

   A They don't pay much attention to each other's lives.

   B They have not yet got over the death of Eilis's father.

   C They are used to family members leaving to go abroad.

   D They tend to avoid talking to each other about their emotions.

3 What did Eilis worry about in bed at night?

   A whether the clothes she had packed were appropriate

   B whether she would ever feel at home anywhere again

   C whether she would like the place where she was going

   D whether her mother would be lonely when she had gone

> **EXAM TIP**
>
> The other options may seem tempting but there is only evidence for one answer in the text.

4 Work in pairs and discuss why you chose the answers you did, and why the other ones weren't possible.

5 In what ways do you think emigrating in the 1950s would have been a more life-changing experience than it is these days?

Vocabulary deducing meaning

6 Work in pairs. For each question, which option is correct? How did you guess?

1 In line 19 *small talk* means

   A talked very little.   **C** talked about unimportant things.

   B talked very quietly.   **D** talked about childish things.

2 In line 20 *resume* means

   A start doing something again.   **C** discuss the meaning of something.

   B make a summary of something.   **D** try to understand why something happened.

7 In pairs, try to work out the meanings of these words and expressions from the context.

1 *presumed* (line 1)   **3** *lost her nerve* (line 7)   **5** *unbidden* (line 23)

2 *singled out* (line 3)   **4** *taken aback* (line 17)   **6** *dread* (line 29)

8 Work in groups and discuss the questions.

1 What would you miss most about your home town if you had to emigrate?

2 Are you happiest in familiar places and with people you know or are you always looking for new experiences?

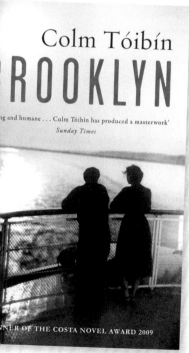

Colm Tóibín

BROOKLYN

...g and humane . . . Colm Tóibín has produced a masterwork'
Sunday Times

...NER OF THE COSTA NOVEL AWARD 2009

Modal verbs

possibility and certainty

▶ **GRAMMAR** REFERENCE p.170

1 **Agree or disagree with opinions 1–5 about the novel extract on page 68. Give reasons.**

Example: *Father Flood must be a relation of Eilis.*
No, he could be a family friend.

1 Jack could be Eilis's father.
2 Rose might be Eilis's sister.
3 Father Flood can't be living in New York.
4 Eilis couldn't have realised how her mother was feeling about her leaving.
5 Father Flood may have found Eilis the job in America.

2 **Look at sentences 1–5 again and underline a modal verb in each one. Then complete the gaps in rules A–C with the modal verbs.**

A When we are sure something is true, we use
....

B When we are sure something is not true, we use
.... or ....

C When we think something is possibly true we use
....................., ... or ....

3 **Answer the questions.**

1 Which sentences in Activity 1 refer to the present? Which refer to the past?

2 What verb form do we use after the modal in a) the present? b) the past?

LANGUAGE TIP

Use the weak form of *have* /əv/ in past modals.
She must have /mʌstəv/ *missed the bus.*

---

4 **Choose the best alternative in the following sentences.**

1 He *might/must* be here somewhere because he promised to meet me.

2 The boat for New York *can't/could* be leaving already. It's too early.

3 She *must have decided/ must be deciding* to stay in the USA. I haven't seen her for ages.

4 Surely they *can't be playing/must be playing* football. It's snowing!

5 Sam *couldn't be/can't have been* driving the car. He was at home with me.

6 He *may have seen/might be seeing* a ghost. But I never really believed him.

5 **Work in pairs. Take turns to use the cues in brackets to make responses to the statements. Remember to use the weak form of *have* for past forms.**

1 A: James looks very relaxed these days.
   B: .... (*must/give up/work*)

2 A: I think that's Alfie who's running towards us.
   B: .... (*can't/never take/any exercise*)

3 A: Florence keeps checking her phone.
   B: .... (*may/expect/a message*)

4 A: It's unusual for Amy not to come out clubbing.
   B: .... (*might/run out/of money*)

5 A: It's strange that we haven't seen Jo and Rebecca for ages.
   B: .... (*may/go/on holiday*)

6 A: Jess isn't wearing her glasses, but she's as blind as a bat without them.
   B: .... (*may/wear/contact lenses*)

7 A: Do you like their new car?
   B: .... (*must/spend/a fortune on it*)

8 A: I can't understand where the cat is in all this rain.
   B: .... (*may/hide/in the shed*)

6 **Look at the picture below. What do you think might be happening?**

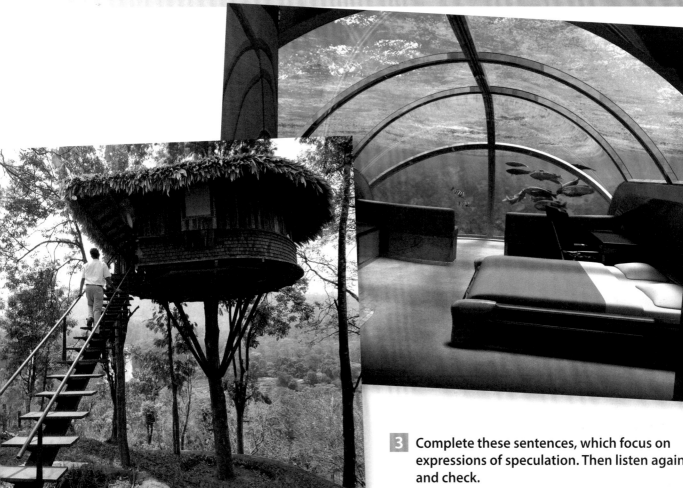

Long turn (Part 2)

stating preferences and speculating

▶ **EXAM** FOCUS p.206

1 Work in pairs and compare the photographs. Use some of these expressions of certainty, probability and doubt.

They seem/appear (to be)…
It looks like/as if (they are)…
It must/could/may/can't (be/have done)…
I'd imagine (that they are)…
I'm fairly/absolutely certain (they are)…
As far as I can see, (they are)…
I suppose (they are)…
They are definitely…

Listening

2 ▶ 22 **Read the exam task. Then listen to a student doing it. Which place did he choose?**

Look at the photos, which show unusual places to stay. Compare the photographs and say which of the places you think would be more enjoyable to stay at.

3 Complete these sentences, which focus on expressions of speculation. Then listen again and check.

1 I'm not absolutely .... what the place on the right is.
2 It .... be an underwater hotel.
3 The other one .... to have been built in the trees.
4 The underwater hotel .... quite luxurious.
5 The treehouse .... to be more basic.
6 It would .... be less expensive to stay at.
7 It .... be an interesting experience to stay at both of them.
8 I'd .... the treehouse might not be such fun in bad weather.

4 ▶ 23 **Listen again to the sentences from Activity 3 and underline the words which are stressed. Practise saying them with the same 'certain' or 'uncertain' intonation.**

EXAM TIP

In the first part, summarise the main similarity and difference. Mention any other similarities and differences if you have time. Don't describe one picture in detail.

5 Work in pairs.
Turn to page 153 and complete Task 1.
Then turn to page 155 and swap roles for Task 2.

Vocabulary
describing places

1 Look at the photo of a monastery in Tibet. Which of these adjectives do you think you could use to describe it?

breathtaking	inspirational	luxurious
magnificent	mysterious	peaceful
remote	spiritual	

2 ▶ 24 Underline the stressed syllable in each adjective in Activity 1 and then listen and check. Practise saying the words.

3 Look at the dictionary entry and answer the questions.

Shangri-La /ˌʃæŋgri ˈlɑː/ *n*
1 an imaginary remote paradise on earth; utopia
2 a distant beautiful imaginary place where everyone is happy

from the Longman Dictionary of Contemporary English

1 What do you know about Shangri-La?
2 What's your idea of paradise on earth? How do you imagine the landscape, the people, the way of life?

The classic tale of Shangri-La
LOST HORIZON
JAMES HILTON

Multiple choice (Part 4)

▶ **EXAM** FOCUS p.205

4 ▶ **25** **You will hear a journalist interviewing a travel writer called Olivia Rees about a place called Shangri-La. First read the questions and options and underline the key words. Then listen and choose the best answer, A, B or C.**

EXAM TIP

If you can't answer a question during the first listening, continue answering the other questions and wait until the second listening before deciding on an answer. Guess if you are not sure.

---

1 Why does Olivia say the novel *Lost Horizon* was so popular in the 1930s?

A People needed to escape from reality.

B People believed Shangri-La was a real place.

C People were interested in finding out about Tibet.

2 How did the travellers in *Lost Horizon* get to Shangri-La?

A Guides took them there.

B Their plane crashed there.

C They found it using an old map.

3 What was special about the people of Shangri-La?

A They were very wise.

B They lived a very long time.

C They could speak every language.

4 What does Olivia say about the author, James Hilton?

A He became a Buddhist.

B He only made one trip to Tibet.

C He got his ideas from books and magazines.

5 Olivia says the similarities between the stories of Shambhala and Shangri-La show that Hilton

A was interested in Tibetan culture.

B believed such a society could really exist.

C was unable to think of original ideas.

6 What information is given about the county of Zhongdian?

A It was originally called Shangri-La.

B It has a large number of monasteries.

C It has found a new source of income.

7 Olivia says people who visit modern-day Shangri-La may be

A shocked.

B confused.

C disappointed.

5 **Listen again and check your answers to question 1 in Activity 4.**

1 Which words from options A, B and C are mentioned in the recording?

2 Which words are a paraphrase of the correct answer?

3 Which words show why the wrong options are wrong?

6 **What places in the world**

1 have a relaxed pace of life?

2 have/haven't lived up to your expectations?

3 are cut off from the outside world?

Vocabulary

travel and expressions with *world*

7 **Choose the word which does NOT collocate with the noun.**

1 a *domestic/direct/long distance/seasonal* flight

2 a *season/direct/one-way/open/return* ticket

3 a *sightseeing/package/round/guided* tour

4 a *package/camping/shopping/tourist* expedition

5 a *tourist/weekend/long-distance/sightseeing* excursion

6 a *business/coach/day/round/direct* trip

8 **Complete the expressions with the correct preposition.**

1 It's very remote, completely *cut* .... *from* the outside world.

2 He travels *all* .... *the world* with his job.

3 It's the most magical place, quite .... *of this world*.

4 *There's a world* .... *difference between* the north and south of the country.

5 He has no idea what's going on. He's .... *a world of his own*.

6 They've got *the world* .... *their feet*. There's nothing they can't achieve.

7 I wouldn't live anywhere else. This house *means the world* .... *me*.

8 I'm so lucky. I've got the best job .... *the world*.

9 **Which of the expressions in Activity 8 are similar to expressions in your language?**

10 **Think of somewhere that's special to you and use some of the expressions to describe it and how it makes you feel.**

Relative clauses

▶ **GRAMMAR** REFERENCE p.172

1 **Read the text and guess which place is being described.**

2 **Decide which lines contain**

A a defining relative clause (provides essential information).

B a non-defining relative clause (adds extra information).

3 **In which line(s) could the relative pronoun**

A be replaced by *that*?

B be left out?

C be replaced by *where*?

LANGUAGE TIP

that • can't be used in non-defining relative clauses.
• can be used instead of *which* or *who* in defining relative clauses.
• can be used for both people and things.

---

4 **Join these pairs of sentences using relative clauses. Add commas where necessary.**

1 The nearest town doesn't have a train station. It's 5km from here.

2 The local people now work in tourism. They used to work in the fishing industry.

3 Where's the bus? It goes to the beach.

4 This hotel belongs to a woman. She's not here at the moment.

5 In summer the water is warm. You can go swimming.

6 That man is a tour guide. I met him yesterday.

7 The road takes you to the top of the mountain. It's very steep.

8 It's a very beautiful place. We stayed there last summer.

5 **Describe one of the most popular places in your country and why people go there. Use these phrases.**

It's a place which …

It's somewhere that …

The people who live there …

One reason why people like it is …

The land of ice and fire

1 The island, which is bigger than Ireland, has a population of only 370,000. Around two thirds of people live in the southwest of the country, where the capital Reykjavík 5 is situated. In recent years the island, whose main attraction is its abundance of volcanoes and geysers, has become increasingly dependent on tourism. It's easy to understand why most tourists who 10 come to the island choose to come in summer, when there are over twenty hours of daylight. But although it's known as 'the land of ice and fire', winter temperatures, which average about $-1\,^{\circ}\text{C}$, are not as 15 cold as you might expect. One of the places which tourists most want to visit is the Blue Lagoon, a naturally heated pool of seawater in the middle of a lava field, in which you can bathe all year round.

so, such, too, enough, very

▶ **GRAMMAR** REFERENCE p.175

1 **Choose the correct words to complete the sentences.**

1 It rains *so/such* a lot that no one bothers to carry an umbrella because they're *so/enough* used to getting wet.
2 Going by taxi is *very/too* expensive but it takes *too/very* long to walk.
3 The hotel is a *very/such* relaxing place because it's *so/too* near the beach.
4 There are *too/very* many cars on the road and not *enough/such* bicycles.
5 He's done *so/too* much travelling recently that he's tired *too/enough* to sleep for a week!
6 *Very/Such* few people have visited it because the location is *so/such* remote.

2 **Look at the examples in Activity 1 and complete the rules with *so, such, too, enough* or *very*.**

1 ...., ... and .... are used before an adjective.
2 .... is used after an adjective.
3 .... is used before countable and uncountable nouns.
4 ...., ... and .... are used before the determiner *much*.
5 .... is used to show that there is an excessive amount of something.
6 ...., ... and .... are used before the determiner *few*.

Speaking

3 **Complete the sentences so they are true about you. Then compare with a partner.**

1 I haven't got enough time to …
2 It's such a long time since I've …
3 I'm feeling so excited about …
4 I don't think I'm old enough to …
5 I don't think I have enough …
6 I find it too expensive …

Key word transformations (Part 4)

▶ **EXAM** FOCUS p.201

4 **Complete the second sentence so that it has a similar meaning to the first sentence, using the word given. Do not change the word given. You must use between two and five words, including the word given.**

EXAM TIP

Don't write more than five words – remember contractions, e.g. *isn't*, count as two words.

Example: *It was the most depressing story I have ever heard.*
NEVER
I have _never heard such a_ *depressing story.*

1 It was too foggy for us to ski.
  SO
  It was .... not ski.
2 He couldn't afford a taxi, so he went by bus.
  ENOUGH
  He .... for a taxi, so he went by bus.
3 There was so much traffic that we missed the show.
  SUCH
  There was .... that we missed the show.
4 It's possible that you saw a ghost, but I'm not convinced.
  COULD
  You .... a ghost, but I'm not convinced.
5 She is definitely lying.
  BE
  She .... the truth.
6 This is possibly where the photograph was taken.
  MAY
  The photograph .... here.

Essay (Part 1)
including a range of structures

▶ **WRITING** REFERENCE p.180

1 **Discuss whether you agree or disagree with the statements about travel and say why.**

1 It broadens the mind.

2 It is better to spend money on possessions.

3 You don't need to travel because you can experience what countries are like online.

4 Travel develops skills such as self-reliance.

5 Travel is good for the CV.

2 **Look at the essay title and think of points for and against. How would you organise the essay?**

Some people argue that travelling abroad is a valuable part of every young person's education. To what extent would you agree with this opinion?

Notes
Write about:

1 the cost
2 being independent
3 _job advantages_ (your own idea)

3 **Read the model essay. What are the main points and the supporting information in each paragraph?**

4 **Complete the sentences with the linking words/phrases in the box.**

This	If	Even if	unless	which	
so that					

1 .... you apply for a programme .... provides accommodation, you still have to pay for the flight.

2 Many young people work in a restaurant .... they can save enough for the fare.

3 You don't gain independence from going abroad .... you learn the language. .... allows you to mix with the people.

4 .... you spend your time with people of your own nationality, it can turn out to be just like an extended holiday.

Some people argue that travelling abroad is a valuable part of every young person's education. To what extent would you agree with this opinion?

In some parts of the world, travelling abroad before starting university or finding a job is seen as a very useful experience to have.

However, obviously not everyone can afford it. Even if you apply for a volunteer programme which provides food and accommodation, you still have to find the money to travel there. Many young people work in a shop or restaurant so that they can save up enough for the air fare.

In addition, it could be argued that you don't necessarily gain independence from going abroad unless you learn the language. This allows you to mix with the people living there. If you spend most of your time with people of your own nationality, it can turn out to be just like an extended holiday. You may not learn a lot from it.

On the positive side, having lived in another country is often an advantage when applying for jobs because it shows you have experienced other cultures and developed some life skills.

Personally, I think the ideal time to travel is when you are young and have no commitments. Having said that, it is not practical for everyone.

5 **Work in pairs. Turn to page 159 and follow the instructions.**

EXAM TIP

Include a range of simple and complex sentences to make your essay more effective.

LANGUAGE TIP

Try to include adverbs which show your attitude, such as *Personally, Obviously, Unfortunately*.

6 **Exchange essays with another student and think about the questions.**

1 Have you included all the information required?

2 Have you organised the essay into paragraphs? Have you included linking words?

3 Are your main points backed up with supporting detail?

4 Have you included a mix of simple and complex sentences?

1 Complete this story about Mothman, using the correct form of the modals in brackets.

Mothman

Many years ago a strange creature was spotted in West Virginia in the USA. It looked like a man with wings and most witnesses claim it **(1)** .... (*must/be*) nearly two metres tall; others say it **(2)** .... (*may/have*) eyes in its chest. Nobody is very sure what this creature **(3)** .... (*could/be*). Some people today think these witnesses **(4)** .... (*might/mistake*) big owls flying around for the creature. Others feel it **(5)** .... (*must/be*) a UFO because there were also strange lights around it. And even people who think there **(6)** .... (*can/be*) such things as a Mothman enjoy watching the films about it or visiting the four-metre sculpture in West Virginia.

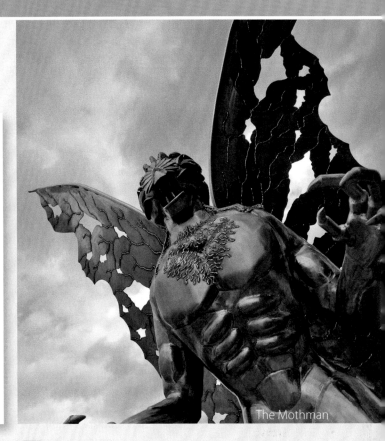

The Mothman

2 Complete the text by putting the correct relative pronoun in each gap.

Cape Cod

Cape Cod, **(1)** .... is referred to locally as 'the Cape', is famous around the world as a summer playground for the rich and powerful, **(2)** .... own charming seafront summer houses there. But it is also the destination of choice for many East-Coast middle-class families **(3)** .... come to enjoy the relaxing pace of life. It's a place **(4)** .... people come to fish, sail and generally get in tune with nature. It is hard to overestimate the Cape's stunning beauty. The coast, **(5)** .... faces the Atlantic, amounts to one long, awesome beach, **(6)** .... is backed by giant sand dunes and protected from development. The towns and villages are very attractive, with pretty cottages and clapboard houses, **(7)** .... were built by sea captains 200 years ago.

However, unlike other US beach destinations such as Florida or California, **(8)** .... it is consistently hot, Cape Cod can be misty and even chilly occasionally during the summer season.

3 Choose the correct word to complete the sentences.

1 We went on an interesting guided .... of a fishing village.

A journey   C tour

B expedition   D visit

2 I need to get a .... ticket because I am coming back this evening.

A round   C package

B return   D direct

3 We had to .... the car and walk home when it broke down.

A cut   C abandon

B miss   D lose

4 She was sure she must have been there before as the place seemed so ....

A routine   C usual

B ordinary   D familiar

5 It's a very remote location, completely cut .... from the outside world.

A by   C off

B out   D down

6 The first time people try sky-diving they sometimes lose their .... and can't jump out of the plane.

A fear   C dread

B nerve   D worry

Moving on

8

Multiple matching (Part 3)

▶ **EXAM** FOCUS p.205

1 You will hear five different people talking about the future of their profession. What do you think these jobs involve?

robotics engineer   social-networking counsellor   spaceship pilot
vertical farmer   virtual lawyer

EXAM TIP

Hearing exactly the same word on the recording as in one of the options doesn't necessarily mean that option is the correct answer.

2 ▶ 26 Listen and choose from the list A–H what each speaker's job will involve in the future. Use the letters only once. There are three extra letters which you do not need to use.

A	working with new employees	Speaker 1 ☐
B	getting new qualifications	Speaker 2 ☐
C	helping a wide range of people	Speaker 3 ☐
D	providing a service that costs less than today	Speaker 4 ☐
E	being available on demand	Speaker 5 ☐
F	designing new products	
G	working longer hours	
H	providing a fast and efficient service	

3 Check your answer for Speaker 1 by looking at the audio script on page 160. Underline the part of the text that gives the correct answer.

4 Now listen to Speakers 2–5 again. Identify the key phrases that give the answers.

Speaking

5 Discuss the questions in pairs.

1 Which job would you most like to have? Why?

2 Which of the jobs wouldn't you consider doing? Why?

3 Which of the jobs do you think is the most: worthwhile? highly-skilled? stressful? physically demanding?

Vocabulary

collocations and phrasal verbs with *work*

6 **Choose the correct word.**

1 Helping people gives me a lot of *work/job/employment* satisfaction.
2 I expect there isn't much *job/work/career* security in counselling.
3 Until quite recently, engineering used to be seen as a male *employment/career/occupation*.
4 When I leave university, I hope to join the medical *profession/career/occupation*.
5 The *work/profession/employment* agency found me my first job in sales.
6 It's important to look for a job that offers good *work/career/profession* opportunities.

7 **Match the phrasal verbs with the definitions A–F.**

1 We finally *worked out* how much tax we would have to pay.
2 Things *worked out* really *well* for him after he moved abroad for his job.
3 I *get worked up* about things too easily at work, especially if a customer is rude or difficult.
4 I *work out* at the gym three or four times a week during my lunch hour.
5 We need to *work out* who would be the best person to talk to the boss.
6 If the meeting is cancelled, we'll just have to *work around* it and sort the problem out ourselves.

A do exercise
B become angry or upset
C have a (good/bad) result
D calculate
E deal with
F plan/decide

8 **Discuss the questions with a partner.**

1 What do you get worked up about?
2 Do you think working out at the gym is the best way to keep fit?
3 Have you had to work around any obstacles recently?
4 How easy is it for you to work out solutions to problems?

LANGUAGE TIP

Some phrasal verbs have more than one meaning. But they are not all used in the same way. For example *work out* (solve) takes a direct object.
I **worked out** the *problem*.
I **worked** the *problem* **out**.
But *work out* (take exercise at the gym) does not.
I **work out** every day.

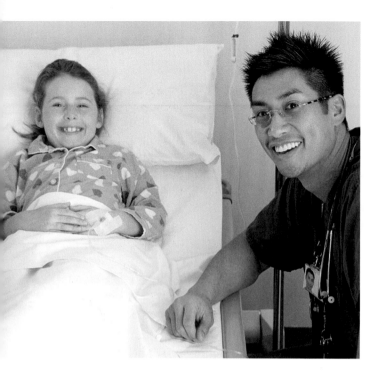

Collaborative task and discussion (Parts 3 and 4)

agreeing and disagreeing

▶ **EXAM** FOCUS p.207

1 Look at the examiner's instructions and the speaking task and underline the key words.

> I'd like you to imagine that a college is offering career advice for students on different kinds of jobs. Here are some of the jobs that students could choose in the future and a question for you to discuss. First you have some time to look at the task.

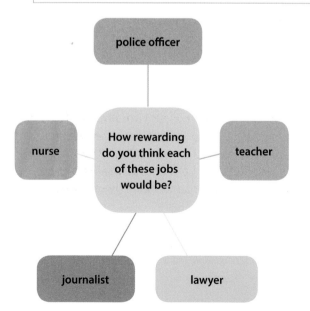

police officer

nurse

How rewarding do you think each of these jobs would be?

teacher

journalist

lawyer

2 Look at the statements made by some students. For each one, mark whether you agree (✓), disagree (✗) or are not sure (?).

> **1** Teaching should be rewarding but a lot of the time teachers have to teach children who aren't interested in their subject and that must be very unrewarding.

> **2** I think the only kind of journalism that's rewarding is for journalists who are bringing attention to important events around the world that can make a difference to people's lives.

> **3** Nurses have to work long hours and they don't get paid well, so for me that wouldn't be rewarding at all.

3 ▶ 27 Listen and copy the intonation patterns in these phrases for agreeing and disagreeing.

1 Actually, I'm not sure about that.
2 I agree up to a point but…
3 I suppose so.
4 That's just what I was going to say!

4 Work in pairs. Take turns reading out the statements in Activity 2 and using the phrases in Activity 3 to agree and disagree with them.

5 Do the speaking task in Activity 1.

EXAM TIP

Try to discuss each prompt in the exam task without spending too long on any one of them.

6 Work in pairs. Decide which of the jobs would be the most rewarding. You have a minute to do this.

7 Discuss the questions.

1 Do you think people should be paid more for doing a dangerous job?
2 Would you want to have the same job/career for your whole life?
3 Do you think it's possible for anyone to become a police officer?

Listening

1 ▶ 28 **You will hear people talking in three different situations. For each question, choose the best answer, A, B or C.**

1 You hear a manager talking to an employee. What is he doing?

A requesting some information

B advising her about a problem

C explaining how to do something

2 You hear part of a radio programme on the subject of job interviews. What does the presenter recommend?

A doing research about the company

B asking lots of questions

C appearing very confident

3 You hear a discussion between two colleagues. What is the woman doing?

A reminding the man to do something

B accusing the man of not telling her something

C apologising for forgetting something

Reporting verbs

▶ **GRAMMAR** REFERENCE p.173

2 **Use the verbs in the box to report the information in Activity 1. More than one verb may be possible.**

accused	advised	asked	denied
explained	offered	recommended	
reminded	suggested	told	warned

1 The manager .... Amy to keep the report brief.

2 The manager .... that she should keep the report brief.

3 The presenter .... finding out as much as you can about your prospective employer.

4 The woman .... Mike of forgetting to give her a message.

5 Mike .... taking any calls from the customer.

6 Mike .... to find out what had gone wrong.

LANGUAGE TIP

recommend and *suggest* do not take a direct object:
He **recommended** *something* **to me**.
NOT
~~He recommended me something~~.

---

3 **Look at the examples in Activity 2 and match the reporting verbs in the box with the patterns. For some verbs more than one pattern is possible.**

A verb + object + infinitive, e.g. *advise, ask, remind*

B verb + infinitive

C verb + *-ing*

D verb + object + *of* + *-ing*

E verb + *that* + clause

Speaking

4 **Work in groups. Prepare four pieces of advice about what to do at a job/college interview. Exchange advice with another group. Then use the verbs in Activity 2 to report the recommendations you have been given.**

Speaking

1 **You are going to read an article about five people whose work involves them living abroad. Work in pairs and answer the questions.**

1 Why do some people choose to go and work in another country?

2 What do you think the disadvantages of living abroad would be?

Multiple matching (Part 7)

▶ **EXAM** FOCUS p.203

2 **Read questions 1–10 and underline the key words and phrases. This will make it easier to locate the information that you're looking for. The first one is done for you.**

EXAM TIP

The information in the text may not come in the same order as the questions.

3 **For questions 2–10, choose the best answer from the people A–E.**

Which person

has always had a <u>passion to see the world</u>?	1	B
wanted work to be more of a challenge?	2	
decided to live abroad because it was less expensive?	3	
took a while to adapt to a new way of living?	4	
found the ideal job by accident?	5	
discovered unexpected things about the place?	6	
regularly travels long distances to do a specific job?	7	
sacrificed career opportunities in order to live abroad?	8	
appreciates the long holidays which the job makes possible?	9	
lives in a very primitive environment?	10	

Speaking

4 **Discuss the questions in pairs.**

1 Which of these jobs would you find most interesting? Why?

2 Which do you think is more important: the job you do or the place that you live in?

Vocabulary

linking words and expressions

5 **Look at the linking expressions underlined in the text. Which are used to**

1 give extra information?

2 express reason/result?

3 express a purpose for doing something?

4 contrast information?

6 **Look carefully at how the linking expressions are used in context, including the punctuation. Complete the sentences with the linking words or phrases in the box.**

although	as well as	despite	however
in order to	so	that's why	too

1 I applied for the job. .... , I didn't get it, unfortunately.

2 I didn't even get an interview, ... I am more than qualified for the job.

3 I love travelling. .... the work was perfect for me.

4 I think the reason I didn't get the job was my poor Spanish, ... I have enrolled on a beginners' course.

5 .... learning Spanish, I am trying to improve my French.

6 I am watching French films .... improve my vocabulary.

7 .... the high salary I was offered, I decided to turn down the job.

8 I enjoyed my time at the law firm. I made a lot of friends there ....

To the ends of the earth

Five people tell us how they've found success living and working in exotic locations.

A **Emma** <u>While</u> I enjoyed my job at a busy surgery in Oxford, checking people's blood pressure wasn't really stretching me enough, <u>so</u> I applied for and got a job with the Flying Doctor service in Australia. We doctors are dropped off by plane at remote houses in the bush, which we use as clinics. Common problems we have to treat are injuries after falls from horses, farm accidents, snake bites, <u>as well as</u> road accidents in the middle of nowhere. I wanted a job which would enable me to experience extraordinary places and people, and this job certainly does that.

B **Heather** I've had the travel bug ever since I was very young. As soon as I left university, where I studied journalism, I got myself an administrative job and saved up enough money to go backpacking to New Zealand. When I got back, I started job-hunting <u>so that</u> I could save money for another big trip, which is when I stumbled across an advert for a job with a publisher of travel guides. When I was offered the job and sent to South Africa <u>to</u> write a blog, I could have burst with excitement. The best part of my job is being able to take time off to go travelling for a couple of months. <u>Although</u> I travel for work, it's not the same as a holiday, when I can switch off and don't have deadlines. <u>Still</u>, I can't think of any job I'd rather be doing.

C **Jonathan** I'm a graphic designer, and when I was made redundant I decided to set up my own business with my wife. The only problem was meeting the same standard of living – apartment, car, meals out. <u>That's why</u> I hit on the idea of moving somewhere in the world where you can enjoy the same lifestyle for far less. <u>In order to</u> help us make the decision, we made contact through Facebook and Twitter with other people who have done the same thing.

D **Annie** I was on a business trip to Buenos Aires for a couple of weeks when I met an Italian who became the love of my life. <u>Since</u> I was freelance and he was a TV producer in Argentina it made sense that I would be the one to move. <u>Despite</u> this, the decision was agonising <u>as</u> I was building a career as a newspaper correspondent and all my contacts were in London. There was <u>also</u> the issue of leaving my family, friends and home but I knew if I didn't give it a try I'd regret it forever. Fede took time off to help me settle in, but then I began to realise the enormity of what I'd done. <u>Because</u> I didn't speak Spanish very well, I felt frustrated and stupid but four months on I don't regret a thing.

E **Phil** As an engineer, I happily accepted an invitation to build a scientific research centre in Antarctica. Everything is different here, and we have only the basic requirements for human survival. From the moment you arrive you are faced with danger, whether it is landing in a plane on an ice runway or travelling across sea ice. <u>However</u>, seeing giant icebergs for the first time blew my mind. There are lots of surprises <u>too</u>, such as suffering from sunburn and the twenty-four hours of sunlight a day which makes it difficult to sleep <u>even though</u> you are exhausted.

Listening

1 ▶ 29 **You'll hear part of a job interview with Lauren. Listen and underline eight mistakes in Lauren's email to her mum.**

2 **Work in pairs. Correct the incorrect details. Then listen again and check your answers.**

Example: *She told her she'd spotted the advert on the internet.*

Hi Mum,

The interview for the job in Greece went well, I think. First the interviewer asked me how I'd heard about it. I told her I'd spotted the advert in a local newspaper and thought it was something I'd enjoy doing.

Then she said the job would involve looking after young teenagers and asked me whether I'd had any experience of doing this. So I told her that I look after Sandra and Davy now and again and that I was taking them camping the next day. She said I might be unlucky, as she'd heard it was going to snow. Then she told me to enjoy the weekend and said she'd phone soon. She told me not to worry if I didn't hear anything for a few weeks.

Fingers crossed,

Lx

Reported statements

▶ **GRAMMAR** REFERENCE p.174

3 **Turn to page 159 and follow the instructions.**

4 **Complete the table to show how direct speech changes to reported statements. Use the audio script on page 159 to help you.**

Direct speech	Reported statements
past simple	*past perfect*
present perfect	
present simple	
will	
present continuous	
be going to	
would, might	

Reported questions and imperatives

▶ **GRAMMAR** REFERENCE p.174

5 **How did the interviewer say sentences A–D in direct speech?**

A She asked me how I'd heard about the job.
B She asked me whether I'd had any experience of this.
C She told me to enjoy my weekend.
D She told me not to worry.

6 **Look at the things that Lauren's friend Jack asked or said after she started the job. Change them to reported speech, using *tell, ask,* etc. or a reporting verb.**

1 'Do you get paid well?'
2 'Let me know if there are any more job vacancies!'
3 'Who are you going to be working with next week?'
4 'What did you do yesterday?'
5 'Don't forget to take some photos.'
6 'We'll email you if we come over to Greece.'

7 **Work in pairs and follow the instructions.**

1 Tell your partner four things about yourself. One of them should be false.
2 Join up with another pair. Tell the others what your partner told you.
3 Guess which of the four things they tell you is untrue.

Vocabulary

concrete and abstract nouns

1 Which word in each pair is a concrete noun such as a person and which is an abstract noun?

engineering/engineer   journalist/journalism
music/musician   visitor/visit

2 What suffixes do you often add to a word to make a concrete noun? Complete the table.

	Abstract noun	Concrete noun
1	creation	*creator*
2	advice	
3		employer/ee
4	tourism	
5		applicant
6		representative
7	childhood	
8		politician

3 Divide these words into verbs and adjectives. What is the abstract noun for each?

angry   arrive   behave   confide
difficult   friendly   know   permit
progress   sad   short   strong

4 Change the word in brackets to a noun. Add *a/an* if necessary.

1 The school won't give us .... (*permit*) to take a week off during term time.

2 I'm finally beginning to make .... (*progress*) with my maths and science.

3 She had .... (*difficult*) understanding what I wanted her to do.

4 We're going on .... (*visit*) to Rome next week.

5 I can't carry this any further, I haven't got the .... (*strong*)!

6 Cara and I have .... (*friend*) built on respect and trust.

Word formation (Part 3)

▶ **EXAM** FOCUS p.201

5 Use the word given in capitals at the end of each line to form a word that fits the gap in the same line.

The video game designer

At the office where video games are designed, everyone is working hard on the **(0)** .production. of their latest game. The licence for the game cost millions of dollars – so there's no room for any **(1)** .... However, everyone seems calm so far. A man called Tim, who has **(2)** .... for the design, explains why it takes over 100 people to make just one video game. Apparently it's because of the complex **(3)** .... which is involved. He himself is not actually **(4)** .... involved in doing the diagrams. That job is done by the team of **(5)** .... which he employs to work for him. Neither is he involved in the computer side of the games. What he has to do is to make all the plans and **(6)** .... One would imagine this is not always totally straightforward!
Despite the time pressures, Tim claims to find his work **(7)** .... and appears to welcome the **(8)** .... challenges he must have to face every day.

PRODUCE

FLEXIBLE

RESPONSIBLE

TECHNICIAN
PERSON

ART

DECIDE

ENJOY
VARY

6 Would you like to do this job? Why/Why not?

Reading

1 Read the letter of application. What job is Magda applying for?

Dear Sir/Madam,

Following your recent advertisement in *The Traveller*, I would like to apply for the **(1)** *job/position* of hotel receptionist.

(2) *Right now/At present* I am completing my second year at Poznan University, where I have been studying Spanish. I would now like to spend some time developing my confidence in spoken Spanish.

As well as Polish and Spanish, I also speak fluent English. I **(3)** *got/obtained* the diploma you **(4)** *require/want* three years ago and I have worked in hotels **(5)** *on a number of occasions/lots of times.* **(6)** *In addition/Also,* **(7)** *I possess/I've got* the energy and good communication skills which you are looking for.

I would be grateful if you could send me further details of the job, including the salary. I enclose my CV and I **(8)** *look forward/am looking forward* to hearing from you **(9)** *soon/in the near future.* I have only three weeks **(10)** *left/remaining* of my university year. After that time, I will be **(11)** *free/available* if **(12)** *I am required/you need me* to come for an interview.

Yours faithfully,

Magda Koblewska

2 Look at the options in italics in the letter and underline the most appropriate one.

3 In which paragraph is Magda

A giving her qualifications and experience?

B giving a reason for writing?

C saying when she can meet her possible employers?

D saying why she wants the job?

E asking for information?

4 Look at the letter again and find fixed phrases for 1–5.

1 to say where you heard about the job

2 to say which job you're interested in

3 to give details of your qualifications

4 to ask for further information

5 to explain what you are sending with the letter

Letter of application (Part 2)

using semi-formal language

▶ **WRITING** REFERENCE p.183

5 Read the exam task and the advertisement. Underline the important information in the advertisement.

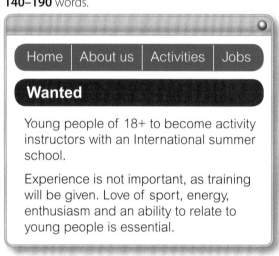

You have seen a job advertisement on the internet and have decided to apply for it. Read the advertisement and write your **letter** in **140–190** words.

| Home | About us | Activities | Jobs |

Wanted

Young people of 18+ to become activity instructors with an International summer school.

Experience is not important, as training will be given. Love of sport, energy, enthusiasm and an ability to relate to young people is essential.

6 Read the exam task again. Make a detailed plan about what will be in each paragraph of your letter. Follow the structure of Magda's letter.

EXAM TIP

If you begin the letter with the name of the person you are writing to, end the letter *Yours sincerely*. If you start with *Dear Sir/Madam*, end with *Yours faithfully*.

7 Write your letter. When you have finished check your work, using the checklist on page 179 to help you.

1 **Choose the correct word to complete the sentences.**

1 I'm happy at my place of work but there aren't many .... opportunities.

   A profession   **B** work   **C** career

2 Have you managed to work .... how much overtime we've earned this week?

   A out   **B** in   **C** up

3 I enjoy working there, ... there's a lot of pressure at times.

   A although   **B** despite   **C** however

4 I have an interview next week .... I'm going to get something smart to wear.

   A that's why   **B** so   **C** in order to

5 Can I borrow your computer .... I can do my CV?

   A so that   **B** to   **C** in order

6 There is a problem with staffing at the moment but we'll have to work .... it.

   A for   **B** around   **C** over

2 **Use the word in capitals to form a word that fits the gap.**

1 .... from ten different companies will give talks at the Careers Fair.   **REPRESENT**

2 Because of the economic crisis, there is a lot of .... in the area.   **EMPLOY**

3 I need to send in an .... for a summer job.   **APPLY**

4 Unfortunately, there is a job .... at the moment.   **SHORT**

5 When she resigned, there was a lot of ....   **SAD**

6 .... usually appreciate being met at the airport.   **TOUR**

7 On .... , most holidaymakers are taken to their hotel by coach.   **ARRIVE**

8 It's useful to employ people who have some .... of the local area.   **KNOW**

3 **Complete the second sentence so that it has a similar meaning to the first sentence using the word given. You must use between two and five words, including the word given.**

1 'Make sure you lock up when you leave the office tonight,' Jake told his colleagues.
   REMINDED
   Jake .... lock up when they left the office that night.

2 'Carol, why not take a break while things are quiet?' the manager said.
   SUGGESTED
   The manager .... take a break while things were quiet.

3 'It was Anna who lost the contract,' said Jon.
   ACCUSED
   Jon .... losing the contract.

4 'You mustn't talk to the press about the incident,' the boss said to us.
   WARNED
   The boss .... talk to the press about the incident.

5 'I'm really sorry that I didn't meet the deadline,' said Joanna.
   APOLOGISED
   Joanna .... meeting the deadline.

6 'I'm going to hand in my notice tomorrow,' said Alfie.
   THE
   Alfie decided to hand in .... day.

7 'If I were you, I would look for another job,' said Max.
   RECOMMENDED
   Max .... for another job.

8 'I didn't break the photocopier,' said Maria.
   DENIED
   Maria .... the photocopier.

Lucky break?

9

Speaking

1 **Discuss the questions.**

1 Who is your role model or hero from the sports world?
2 What qualities do you think a great sprinter must have?

Gapped text (Part 6)

▶ **EXAM** FOCUS p.202

2 **Quickly read the article about Usain Bolt and compare it with your ideas in Activity 1.**

EXAM TIP

Make sure you read the text for gist before focusing on the missing sentences.

3 **Six sentences have been removed from the article. Choose from the sentences A–G the one which fits each gap 1–6. There is one extra sentence which you do not need to use.**

A It took a lot of persuasion because Bolt had been running the distance for less than a year and was surviving on a diet of junk food.
B But before that he has more to achieve on the track.
C This condition should have made it impossible for him to have a career in sport.
D I ask him what's it like to run so fast, to race the wind.
E 'I try not to let them, but they do.'
F His manager says he runs like a cheetah.
G Winning that race changed his whole life, but for much of the next three years he was injured.

Speaking

4 **Discuss these questions.**

1 How is Bolt different from most sportspeople?
2 How easy is it for a very successful person to stay grounded?
3 When does a successful person become a legend, and why? Give some examples.

Usain Bolt:
fast and loose

When Usain Bolt was a young boy growing up in Jamaica, his parents took him to the doctor because he couldn't keep still. He was gifted at cricket, his first love. 'But I just happened to run fast. They said, 'Try track and field,' and I continued because it was easy and I was winning. And my dad said I should concentrate on running because it's an individual sport and, if you do good, you do good for yourself.'

Nobody can hold a light to Usain Bolt – he is a one-off. There's the size, for a start: 1.96 metres (ideal sprinters are thought to be no more than 1.85 metres). Then there's the scoliosis, a curved spine which means one leg is shorter than the other. ⬚ 1 ⬚ And the attitude – at warm-up his rivals look as if they will explode with tension, but Bolt smiles, even dances. And, of course, Bolt is said to be the fastest man ever, although he wasn't even giving his all when he broke the 100 and 200 metre records.

Bolt maintains that he isn't quite as cool and laid-back as he appears to be. There are things that bother him. ⬚ 2 ⬚ For example, he says he was so uptight before the Junior World Championships final – where he became the youngest gold medallist at the age of fifteen – that he put his shoes on the wrong feet. 'I've never been so nervous in my whole life. I was shaking because everyone was expecting me to get a medal.' ⬚ 3 ⬚ That's when Jamaica turned on him. His own people said he was undisciplined, he partied too much. And yes, he did; but the truth was he was suffering with his spine.

People, he says, are quick to criticise. Even now. 'People say I'm always partying. Well, I do party. I work hard and I'm going to enjoy myself. I'm not going to let people hold me back. That's when the stress comes in and when you get stressed you start to lose it.'

Bolt arrived in athletics at a time when the profession had lost a lot of respect over drug-taking. Here was a man who looked and acted differently. In 2008, though, he had to beg his coach to let him run the 100 metres at the Beijing Olympics. ⬚ 4 ⬚ Despite that, not only did he win gold but he broke the 100 metre world record. He broke his own record at the 2009 World Championships and went on to win gold in the 2012 London Olympics in the 100 metre and 200 metre races and the relay.

'He's lazy,' says his manager. 'But when he trains, he trains very hard. The image on the track is that he just turns up and runs but it isn't true. He's very competitive.' And the thing is, says Bolt, if he weren't easy-going, he wouldn't run so fast. He looks a little blank when I ask him what makes him such a good runner. Perhaps his height helps, and those huge strides, he suggests. ⬚ 5 ⬚ 'The way his feet move, the way the mechanics are so perfect. And the strength he can generate from his hips and his hamstrings, everything is perfect for running.'

I've never met a sportsman quite like Bolt. While so many are uncommunicative, conventional and self-important, he is opinionated, funny and grounded. I ask him about his ambitions. Eventually, he says, he'd like to make a go of playing football professionally. ⬚ 6 ⬚ 'People say I'm a legend but I'm not until I've fulfilled my potential.'

Vocabulary
collocations: success and failure

5 Complete the sentences with the verbs in the box. They may be used more than once.

be   fulfil   have   make   overcome   set

1 To be successful, sportspeople need to .... a strong competitive streak.
2 They often have to .... setbacks, so it's important for them to .... motivated and determined.
3 Sportspeople often .... themselves goals or deadlines.
4 A lot of young athletes don't .... their potential.
5 If you want to .... a go of a career in sport, you need to .... a lot of stamina.
6 Winners are usually single-minded and .... a lot of commitment.

6 Complete the phrases with the words in the box.

down   in   for   on   with   up

1 cope .... pressure
2 focus .... achieving their goal
3 aim .... the top
4 take .... new rivals
5 give .... to pressure
6 face .... to problems
7 let your team ....
8 succeed .... your career

7 Work in pairs. Use some of the language from Activities 5 and 6. Compare your attitudes to success and failure.

1 How well do you think you cope with success and failure?
2 Do you have a drive to succeed or are you more laid-back?

Listening

1 Work in pairs. What do you think makes some people more successful than other people?

2 ▶ 30 Listen to two students answering a similar question. Which of these factors do they mention?

ambition	dedication	family support	
good health	money	personality	talent

Compensation strategies

3 Match strategies A–C to examples 1–3. Then listen again and tick the language the students use.

A correcting yourself/explaining something in other words
B giving yourself time to think
C checking you understand

1 Do you mean …?
I'm sorry, did you say …?
So, what you're saying is …?

2 OK, let me see
Well, it's difficult to say, of course, but …
As far as I know, …
Right, …

3 I mean …
What I meant was …
What I'm trying to say is …
… or rather, …

4 ▶ 31 Listen to someone saying the expressions in Activity 3. Then practise saying them in pairs.

Discussion (Part 4)

▶ **EXAM** FOCUS p.207

5 Work in pairs. Take turns to ask and answer the questions. Use some of the expressions from Activity 3.

1 What sports do you most enjoy playing or watching?
2 Do you think anyone can become good at sport if they practise?
3 How important is sport for good health?
4 What are the advantages and disadvantages of team sports over individual sports?
5 Would you say you were a competitive person?

EXAM TIP

Try to keep talking. If you have no ideas, you could ask your partner what they think.

Conditional forms

▶ **GRAMMAR** REFERENCE p.166

1 **Look at the sentences. In which one is the situation: a) unlikely/imaginary? b) generally true? c) possible/likely?**

zero conditional:	When you get stressed, you start to lose it.
first conditional:	If you're tense, you'll make mistakes.
second conditional:	If he weren't so easy-going, he wouldn't run so fast.

2 **Underline the verb forms in the sentences in Activity 1. Then answer questions 1–3 about the form of conditional sentences.**

1 In the which type of conditional can *when* be used instead of *if*?

2 In the first conditional, which modals and verb forms can be used instead of *will*?

3 In the second conditional, which other modals can be used instead of *would*?

LANGUAGE TIP

Continuous forms can be used instead of simple forms.

If you're driving, will you give me a lift?

If you were thinking of taking up a new sport, which one would you choose?

3 **Decide how likely these sentences are, and use the words in brackets to make questions. Then work in pairs and ask each other the questions.**

1 If (*you/become*) a famous film star, who (*you/want*) to act with?

2 If (*you/win*) a lot of money, what (*you/spend*) it on?

3 If (*you/learn*) another language, which one (*you/ choose*)?

4 If (*you/have*) the money to go to any place in the world, where (*you/go*)?

5 If (*you/have*) the chance to do anything this evening, what (*you/do*)?

6 If (*the weather/be*) good this weekend, what (*you/do*)?

7 if (*you/get married*) next year, what kind of ceremony (*you/have*)?

8 If (*someone/follow*) you down the street, what (*you/do*)?

4 **Complete the sentences so they are true for you.**

1 If I didn't live in .... , I…

2 If I could change one thing in the world, …

3 If I found some money in the street, …

4 If I could meet three people, …

Speaking

5 **If you could live twenty-four hours in the life of anyone in history, who would you choose and why?**

Example:

If I could, I'd be Neil Armstrong in 1969. I'd love to be able to walk on the moon.

Multiple choice (Part 4)

▶ **EXAM** FOCUS p.205

1 Do you think that some people are born lucky? Talk about a time in your own life when you were lucky/unlucky.

2 ▶ 32 You're going to hear a journalist called Max Wilson talking about a book about luck in sport by Matthew Syed. Look at question 1 in Activity 3 and think of paraphrases for the options. Then listen to question 1. What paraphrases did you hear?

3 ▶ 33 Listen to the whole interview and, for questions 1–7, choose the best answer, A, B or C.

1 Max says that top sportspeople usually believe their success is due to
  A good fortune.
  B hard work.
  C natural skill.

2 According to Max, the examples of recent sporting achievements prove
  A that people in general have become stronger and fitter.
  B that standards are getting higher.
  C that technology is responsible for improved performance.

3 What does Max say about very talented young children?
  A It's easy to tell which will be the top performers.
  B They will succeed without special training.
  C As they get older their development may be slower.

4 In the book Matthew Syed says he had a greater chance of success because of
  A his parents' love of table tennis.
  B his competitive brother.
  C his own ambition.

5 What advantage is mentioned of the Omega Club when Matthew joined?
  A It was open all the time.
  B It had a lot of good players.
  C It had great facilities.

6 Matthew thinks the success of the Omega Club members was
  A hard to explain.
  B easy to predict.
  C a happy accident.

7 Max says that a ten-year investigation has shown that lucky people
  A believe they will succeed.
  B look for good opportunities.
  C depend less on talent.

4 Check your answers. What paraphrases did you notice?

EXAM TIP

Check your answers carefully the second time you listen.

5 Discuss whether it's too easy to blame bad luck when things go wrong.

Vocabulary

word building

1 Use the word given to form a word that fits the gap in the following sentences.

COMPETE

1 It is argued that encouraging children to be .... puts them under too much pressure.

2 There was disagreement between the .... teams about who should be the referee.

PERFECTION

3 Many athletes are .... and insist on getting it right every single time.

4 There are always slight .... in every gymnast's performance.

ATHLETICS

5 He's one of the best .... of his generation.

6 You need to be more .... to be a ballet dancer than a footballer.

2 How are the words you completed in Activity 1 pronounced? Mark the main stress.

Word formation (Part 3)

▶ **EXAM** FOCUS p.201

3 Read the text and decide which is the best summary. Don't worry about the gaps yet.

A superstitious athletes are the most successful

B reasons why athletes are superstitious

C the most common superstitions among athletes

> **EXAM TIP**
>
> Look carefully at the text around the gaps to see what part of speech the word should be.

4 Use the word given in capitals at the end of some of the lines to form a word that fits in the gap in the same line. There is an example at the beginning (0).

5 Find out if your partner has any lucky charms to bring good luck/keep them safe.

Sport

Superstitious athletes

Athletes develop superstitions by associating particular behaviour with good (0) ..*performance*.. Typical examples include insisting on wearing the same **PERFORM**
item of clothing, only eating certain food or always listening to the same song
before a match or a race. These superstitions usually have no
(1) .... with success but many athletes believe that they bring them **CONNECT**
good luck.

(2) .... sport at a professional level is extremely difficult and athletes **COMPETE**
are under pressure to achieve as close to (3) .... as they can possibly **PERFECT**
manage. Many athletes find this extremely (4) .... So anything that helps **STRESS**
them to feel more (5) .... isn't necessarily a bad thing and some athletes **RELAX**
maintain their lucky charms make them feel more (6) .... However, **CONFIDENCE**
these little superstitions could also be potentially (7) .... for athletes' **DANGER**
mental health because they can develop an unhealthy (8) .... on them. **DEPEND**
They should be focusing on improving their athletic ability instead of worrying
about superstitions. ■

Speaking

1 Complete the superstitions with the words in the box. Are they lucky or unlucky?

cat   knife   ladder   mirror   umbrella
wood

According to superstition it's lucky/unlucky

1 to walk under a ....·
2 to see a black .... in front of you.
3 to break a ....·
4 to touch ....·
5 to give someone a ....·
6 to open your .... in the house.

2 Discuss the questions with a partner.

1 Do you have the same superstitions in your country? Do you know any others?
2 What do you think superstitions are based on?
3 How lucky or unlucky are your favourite teams/sports heroes? Why?

Collocations with *luck*

3 Choose the correct word.

1 They had an amazing *piece/slice* of luck. The ref sent off the other team's best player.
2 With a *bit/little* of luck our team should win the Cup.
3 She's *had/got* nothing but bad luck since she was injured last year.
4 They *wished/told* me the best of luck before the match.
5 I couldn't *accept/believe* my luck. I'd been picked to play on the first team.
6 They'd been winning every match, but their luck *ran/went* out last week.

4 Match the verbs in the box with nouns 1–5. You can use more than one verb with some of the nouns.

achieve   beat   give up   lose   miss
reach   waste   win

1 an opportunity
2 an ambition
3 a competition
4 an opponent
5 a target

5 Complete the sentences with the correct form of the verbs from Activity 4. There may be more than one possible answer.

1 Great players never .... a chance to score a goal.
2 We were disappointed that we were knocked out before we .... the second round.
3 Well done everyone. You deserved to .... that match.
4 It's a pity she played so badly. She .... the opportunity to show everyone just how talented she is.
5 Only a lucky few ever .... their dream of becoming an Olympic medallist.
6 I don't mind .... to an opponent if I know he played better than me.
7 It was frustrating being .... so easily. I thought we had a good chance of winning.
8 She's the most competitive person I've ever met. She never .... even when she's losing badly.

Speaking

6 Find out what ambitions your partner has achieved/given up.

Third conditional

▶ **GRAMMAR** REFERENCE p.166

1 **Read the text at the bottom of the page and tick the sentence, A or B, which best summarises Tom's feelings.**

A If Tom hadn't had his monkey with him at the Olympic Games, he would have felt more nervous.

B If Tom hadn't had his monkey with him, he wouldn't have won a bronze medal at the Olympic Games.

2 **Which of these statements do you agree with?**

1 If Tom Daley hadn't had a lucky monkey, he might not have become a champion diver.

2 If Matthew Syed had lived in a different street, he wouldn't have become a table tennis champion.

3 Usain Bolt couldn't have been the world's fastest man if he hadn't grown up in Jamaica.

4 Serena Williams might have won fewer championships if her sister hadn't also been a tennis champion.

3 **Look at the rules below and choose the correct words.**

1 The third conditional is used to speculate about things in the *past/present*.

2 The 'if clause' *always comes first/can come first or second*.

3 *If* is always followed by the *past perfect/would have*.

4 *Might, could/may* and *will* can be used instead of *would*.

4 **Rewrite the sentences using the third conditional.**

1 Michael Johnson didn't win a fifth Olympic gold medal because he was injured.
Michael Johnson could have won ....

2 Ellie didn't train properly for the marathon so she wasn't able to finish the race.
If Ellie had ....

3 Lola and Marc met while they were doing a scuba diving course in Thailand.
Lola and Marc wouldn't ....

4 I went out jogging and fell over and broke my ankle on the ice.
If I hadn't ....

5 **Complete the sentences so that they are true about you.**

1 If I hadn't met ....

2 If I hadn't decided to ....

3 I'd have been very disappointed if
....

4 Things might have turned out differently if I
....

6 **Compare your answers in pairs. Did you learn anything new about your partner?**

Tom's monkey
Olympic diver Tom Daley, who won a gold medal at the 2008 European Championships at the age of just 13, has always had a lucky orange monkey. The monkey goes with him to all his events and sits on the poolside, and was even at the London Olympic Games, where Tom won a bronze medal. Tom has had a few setbacks during his career so he admits the monkey doesn't always bring good luck. But he believes having the monkey with him helps to calm his nerves.

Essay (Part 1)

structuring a paragraph

▶ WRITING REFERENCE p.180

1 Read the exam task. Then look at the the student's introduction and say whether sentences A and B are true or false.

> You have been discussing in class how to be a successful person. Now your teacher has asked you to write an essay, giving your opinion on the following statement.
>
> *Without failure there can be no success. Do you agree?*
>
> **Notes**
> Write about:
>
> 1 motivation
> 2 experience
> 3 problems of instant success
>   (your own idea)

> **Without failure there can be no success.**
> It's often said that it's impossible to succeed the first time you do something, and that the most successful people in life have many failures behind them.

A The introduction repeats the statement in the title but in different words.

B The writer states his/her opinion in the introduction.

2 Look at the student's second paragraph and put sentences A, B and C in the correct order.

> ᴬ Perhaps they appreciate their success more if it hasn't come easily. ᴮ In sport, for example, if top athletes lose a race or fail to score a goal, this may be just the motivation they need to inspire them. ᶜ Sometimes failure can make people more determined.

3 Read the rest of the essay and decide if you agree with the student's argument. What other examples could be used?

> ...... Many writers, for example, don't achieve success until they are quite old. This is because it takes a lot of time to learn how to write well. Making mistakes and learning from them is very important, whatever you do.
> ...... Young actors and singers often find it difficult to deal with instant success and the money and fame that comes with it. We all know many examples of people who have suffered because of this. It can have very tragic consequences.
>   To sum up, it is possible to have success without failure, but in my opinion, it may be better to fail first.

4 Which sentences best introduce the third and fourth paragraphs?

1 Success often requires a lot of experience.
2 You need to work hard and get a lot of experience.
3 People who are successful are often unhappy.
4 Being successful immediately can lead to failure in other ways.

EXAM TIP

It's important to give your opinion in the conclusion.

5 Read the exam task and write your own essay, using Activities 1–3 to help you.

> You have been discussing in class how to be a successful person. Now your teacher has asked you to write an **essay**, giving your opinion on the following statement.
>
> *Sporting heroes should try to be good role models. Do you agree?*
>
> You should write between **140** and **190** words.
>
> **Notes**
> Write about:
>
> 1 teamwork
> 2 influence on young people
> 3 _____ (your own idea)

1 Choose the correct word to complete the sentences.

1 To be successful you often need to overcome ....

   A goals   **C** motivation

   B setbacks   **D** deadlines

2 It's important to try and .... your potential.

   A succeed   **C** fulfil

   B aim   **D** commit

3 In order to achieve things you need to .... yourself goals.

   A set   **C** make

   B find   **D** expect

4 To perform well in sports you need to be able to cope .... pressure.

   A in   **C** for

   B on   **D** with

5 You should always try to focus .... achieving your goals.

   A with   **C** on

   B to   **D** in

6 Listen to good advice if you want to succeed .... life.

   A in   **C** for

   B on   **D** with

2 Correct the mistakes with the verb forms.

1 If I met Usain Bolt, I take a photograph of him.

2 We can get tickets for the match if we would book them today.

3 If you will practise harder, you could be a good player.

4 If you helped me more, I didn't have so many problems.

5 He can become world champion if he'd had a different coach.

6 He might have decided to join another team if the club wouldn't have offered him so much money.

7 She didn't become a world champion if she hadn't taken her trainer's advice.

8 They would have travelled to South Africa to see the final if they could afford it.

3 Use the word given in capitals at the end of some lines to form a word that fits in the space in the same line. There is an example at the beginning (0).

Imagine your success

Mental imagery is a technique which is often used by athletes to help improve their **(0)** _performance_ but it can be used by anyone who may be worried about   **PERFORM**

situations like giving a **(1)** .... or   **PRESENT**

having a job interview. It helps with any event which makes you feel **(2)** .... or   **COMFORT**

nervous.

This is how it works. Start your mental imagery training by imagining that you find the activity **(3)** .... and are   **ENJOY**

satisfied with your skills. Then practise doing the activity in your mind as

(4) .... as possible. See, feel and   **PRECISE**

experience yourself doing the activity

(5) .... , in the way you would like to   **SUCCESS**

do it in real life. This kind of mental

(6) .... is just as important as making   **PREPARE**

sure you are fit in other ways for the task ahead. Many people find it very

(7) .... to use their imagination in this   **HELP**

way before going to sleep at night.

Just before the event itself, spend some time alone going through your positive mental images. You may be surprised at

what a **(8)** .... difference this simple   **DRAMA**

technique can make to your confidence.

Virtual friends

10

Speaking

1 Discuss the questions in pairs.

1 How easy is it to be a good friend?

2 Why do people sometimes lose touch with friends?

2 Do the quiz.

LIFESTYLE

What kind of friend are you?

1 How many close friends would you say you have?
   A 1–3   **B** 4–8   **C** more than 8

2 Which of these things is the most damaging to friendship?
   A favouritism   **B** selfishness   **C** dishonesty

3 Do you think the best test of a close friend is
   A always being there to have fun with?
   B always being ready to do a favour?
   C always being able to pick up where you left off last time?

4 Where would you place friendship in relation to career and family?
   A more important than career and family
   B more important than career, less important than family
   C important, but less important than either career or family

5 Do you have someone you could call a best friend?
   A I used to.
   B Definitely.
   C No – I have lots of friends.

6 When you haven't seen a close friend for a long time, do you
   A not worry about it?
   B contact them via social networking?
   C feel guilty?

7 Which do you most value in a friendship?
   A loyalty   **B** generosity   **C** trust

8 The most important quality you need to be a good friend is to be
   A self-aware.
   B content with your own life.
   C lively and outgoing.

3 Look at the results on page 158 and add up your score. Discuss in groups whether the results describe you accurately or not.

Vocabulary

adjectives with *self*

4 Are these adjectives positive or negative? Work in pairs and use at least four to describe people you know. Give examples of their behaviour.

self-aware   self-centred   self-confident   self-conscious   self-important
selfless   self-satisfied   self-sufficient

5 Put the following features of friendship in order of importance.

- [ ] having a lot in common
- [ ] having a laugh together
- [ ] seeing eye to eye about things
- [ ] having the same tastes in music and films, etc.
- [ ] having shared experiences/memories
- [ ] being there for each other

6 Work in groups. Compare your lists and find someone who agrees with your order. What other features are important?

Multiple matching (Part 3)

▶ **EXAM** FOCUS p.205

7 You will hear five different people talking about their closest friend. Look at options A–H and say which are true about your relationship with your best friend(s).

EXAM TIP

Check that the option you have chosen summarises each speaker's main idea or opinion.

8 ▶ 34 Listen and choose from the list (A–H) what each speaker says about their relationship with their closest friend. Use the letters only once. There are three extra letters which you do not need to use.

A   We always try to help each other.
B   We disagree about a lot of things.
C   We have very different personalities.
D   We have only known each other for a short time.
E   We didn't like each other at first.
F   We enjoy doing the same things.
G   We don't see each other often enough.
H   We've got closer as we've got older.

Speaker 1 ☐
Speaker 2 ☐
Speaker 3 ☐
Speaker 4 ☐
Speaker 5 ☐

9 Listen again and note down the matching paraphrases for options A–H.

10 Describe your closest friend(s). Say

1   how you met.
2   what you do together.
3   why you like him/her/them.
4   what kind of person she/he is/they are.

Conditionals

alternatives to *if*

▶ **GRAMMAR** REFERENCE p.166

1 Look at the examples from the listening text and answer the questions.

> Unless we're very organised, it's hard to arrange to go out.

1 Do they need to be organised in order to see each other?

> Even if we haven't seen each other for a while, we can catch up really easily.

2 Does it matter if they don't see each other often?

> As long as we plan ahead, it's fine.

3 Is it essential for them to plan ahead?

> We don't go to football matches together. Otherwise, we'd end up arguing.

4 Would they argue if they went to a football match together?

2 Choose the correct word or phrase.

1 *Unless/As long as* you make an effort, it's too easy to lose touch with old friends.

2 I text my boyfriend every day. *Otherwise,/Provided that* he gets upset.

3 I want to invite all my friends to the party, *even if/whether* they can't all come.

4 *Provided that/Unless* I know some people who are going, I don't mind going to parties on my own.

5 I don't know *whether/if* or not to talk to him about the problem.

3 Which word or phrase from Activity 2

1 means *if not?*

2 is used instead of *if* before infinitives?

3 means *despite the fact that?*

4 is quite formal?

5 means *in a different situation?*

6 means the same as *as long as?*

Use of English

key word transformations (Part 4)

▶ **EXAM** FOCUS p.201

> **EXAM TIP**
>
> A range of grammatical structures and vocabulary may be tested. There will usually be two things you have to change in each answer.

4 For questions 1–6, complete the second sentence so that it has a similar meaning to the first sentence, using the word given. Do not change the word given. You must use between two and five words, including the word given.

1 I'll phone you tonight if it isn't too late when I get home.
UNLESS
I'll phone you tonight .... too late.

2 He will do anything for you, whether he likes you or not.
EVEN
He will do anything for you .... like you.

3 Unless it's raining, I'll wait for you outside the cinema.
LONG
As .... raining, I'll wait for you outside the cinema.

4 We couldn't go to the party because of the snow.
HAVE
If it hadn't been snowing, we .... to the party.

5 We should finish by four o'clock but it means we can't take a break for lunch.
PROVIDED
We should finish by four o'clock .... take a break for lunch.

6 Depending on the traffic, I might be a bit late.
WHETHER
I might be a bit late .... any traffic.

Vocabulary

easily confused adjectives

1 Complete the sentences with the adjectives in the box. More than one answer may be possible.

actual	present	current

1 We have no more information at the .... time.

2 I know she's in her early twenties but I don't know her .... age.

3 He's very interested in .... affairs.

typical	common	usual

4 He's not as lively as ....

5 On a .... Saturday night we would stay up late and watch a movie.

6 It's very .... to meet your future husband or wife at work.

particular	individual	unique

7 She doesn't get much .... attention from the teacher on the art course she's doing.

8 We decided to drive to the coast for no .... reason.

9 It's a .... opportunity to make new friends.

Multiple-choice cloze (Part 1)

▶ **EXAM** FOCUS p.200

2 For questions 1–8, decide which answer (A, B, C or D) best fits each gap. There is an example at the beginning (0).

EXAM TIP

Before filling in any of the gaps, always read the title and text quickly to get an idea of what it is about.

3 Work in pairs. Do you agree with what Andy says about making friends?

Speaking

4 Discuss which activities it's best to do with friends and which it's best to do alone, and why. Use the ideas in the box to help you.

going to the gym	playing computer games
shopping	watching TV

I **(0)** *B arrange* to meet my friend Andy in a café. Over a coffee we chat about music, **(1)** .... affairs and the ups and downs of our working lives. We don't **(2)** .... a lot of time talking about our feelings or our relationship, or the past. It's just not that kind of friendship. I **(3)** .... it that way, and I know Andy doesn't mind because I'm paying him to be my friend for a few hours.

Not so long ago, a friend was one **(4)** .... that money couldn't buy. Friendships were special. But not anymore. You can hire someone to show you around town, hang out at the gym or **(5)** .... you company while you shop. My friend Andy is an actor. He has never been paid to be someone's friend before but he understands why someone might **(6)** .... buying companionship. When he first came to London from Scotland a year and a half ago, he **(7)** .... socialising difficult. But Andy thinks it could be the desire for undemanding companionship, rather than loneliness, that is driving the growth in friend-hire: 'The average person doesn't want to have loads of **(8)** .... friends because it makes life too complicated.'

0	**A** organise	**B** arrange	**C** book	**D** fix
1	**A** common	**B** usual	**C** current	**D** actual
2	**A** have	**B** take	**C** lose	**D** spend
3	**A** choose	**B** wish	**C** select	**D** prefer
4	**A** fact	**B** matter	**C** thing	**D** point
5	**A** stay	**B** keep	**C** give	**D** face
6	**A** decide	**B** think	**C** consider	**D** encourage
7	**A** experienced	**B** realised	**C** discovered	**D** found
8	**A** real	**B** right	**C** present	**D** certain

Speaking

1 **Discuss the questions in groups.**

1 Where did you first meet most of your friends?

2 What proportion of your friends are
   A close friends?
   B acquaintances?
   C colleagues?
   D people you only communicate with online?

3 How important is social networking to you as a way of making friends?

VIRTUAL PEOPLE
REAL FRIENDS

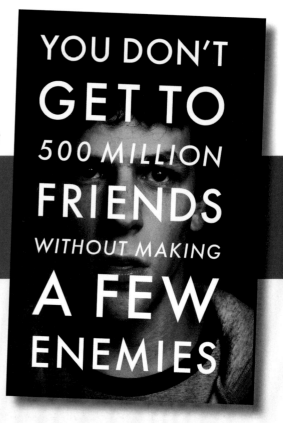

YOU DON'T GET TO 500 MILLION FRIENDS WITHOUT MAKING A FEW ENEMIES

The benefits of forming friendships with those we meet online are obvious, so why do people still make fun of the idea?

ANOTHER WEEK, another survey claiming to reveal great truths about ourselves. This one says that (shock horror!) people are increasingly turning 'online friends' into people they'd think worthy of calling real-life friends. Well, that's stating the obvious, I would have thought! If there's a more perfect place for making friends, I have yet to find it. However, when surveys like this are reported in the media, it's always with a slight air of 'It's a crazy, crazy world!' And whenever the subject crops up in conversation, it's clear that people look down on friends like these. In fact some members of my family still refer to my partner of six years as my 'internet boyfriend.'

It's the shocked reaction that surprises me, as if people on the internet were not 'real' at all. Certainly, people play a character online quite often – they may be a more confident or more argumentative version of their real selves – but what's the alternative? Is meeting people at work so much better than making friends in a virtual world? Perhaps, but for some a professional distance between their 'work' selves and their 'social' selves is necessary, especially if they tend to let their guard down and might say or do something they will later regret. And are people really much more themselves at a party than online?

Those people disapproving of online friendships argue that the concept of 'friendship' is used loosely in a world driven by technology, in which you might have a thousand online friends. They make a distinction between 'social connections' – acquaintances who are only a click away – and meaningful human interaction, which they say requires time and effort. They note that for many Facebook 'friends', conversation is a way of exchanging information quickly and efficiently rather than being a social activity. With its short sharp updates on what you're thinking 'right now', Facebook has been criticised for encouraging rushed and therefore shallow friendships.

This may all have an element of truth. However, for the first time in history, we're lucky enough to choose friends not by location or luck, but by those who have similar interests and senses of humour, or passionate feelings about the same things. And for people like me who might be a little shy – and there are plenty of us about – moving conversations from the net to a coffee shop is a much more natural process than people might expect. After having already made friends online, you can get rid of the social awkwardness that comes with trying to make a friend out of someone you don't know at all. You can enjoy their company when you eventually meet, knowing that you have enough in common to sustain the friendship. The benefit is clear – you cut out all the boring small talk. What could be better?

Obviously, there will always be concerns about the dangers of online friendship. There are always stories buzzing around such as 'man runs off with the woman he met on Second Life' or people who meet their 'soulmate' online and are never seen again. But people are people are people, whether online or not. As for 'real' friendship dying out, surely social networking is simply redefining our notion of what this is in the twenty-first century? The figures – half a billion Facebook users worldwide – speak for themselves. And technology has allowed countless numbers of these people to keep in close contact with their loved ones, however far away they are. Without it, many disabled or housebound people might go without social contact at all. Call me naive, call me a social misfit, I don't care. Virtual people make the best real friends. ∎

line 8

line 19

Multiple choice (Part 5)

▶ **EXAM** FOCUS p.202

2 Read the article about making friends online. For questions 1–6, choose the answer (A, B, C or D) which you think fits best according to the text.

EXAM TIP

The words or phrases in the text will be paraphrases or summaries of the option, NOT the exact words.

1 The writer thinks the findings of the survey described in the first paragraph are
A amusing.
B ridiculous.
C predictable.
D impressive.

2 What does *the subject* refer to in line 8?
A surveys
B the media
C real friends
D online friends

3 What does the phrase *let their guard down* mean in line 19?
A prefer to spend time alone
B find it difficult to hide emotion
C dislike spending free time with colleagues
D refuse to worry about possible consequences

4 According to the writer, online friendships are often criticised because
A their purpose is functional rather than social.
B the people have no shared history to hold them together.
C the more friends people have, the less each one is valued.
D the friendship can't be genuine until people meet face to face.

5 How does the writer feel about meeting up with her online friends?
A It's a waste of time.
B It can be difficult to arrange.
C It's easier than meeting complete strangers.
D It can often lead to even stronger friendships.

6 What is the writer's reaction to fears and warnings about online friendships?
A She accepts there will always be dangers however you make friends.
B She is nervous about the risks but thinks the benefits make it worthwhile.
C She believes that online relationships are safer than face to face friendships.
D She recommends online friendships only for people who can look after themselves.

Speaking

3 Work in pairs. Say whether you agree or disagree with the opinions from the text. Give reasons for your answers.

1 It is clear that people look down on 'online friends'.
2 People play a character online quite often.
3 Facebook encourages rushed and therefore shallow friendships.
4 Having already made friends online, you know that when you meet you have enough in common to sustain the friendship.
5 Social networking is simply redefining our notion of what friendship is in the twenty-first century.
6 Virtual people make the best real friends.

Vocabulary

compound adjectives: personality

4 Use the words in the box to make compound adjectives which describe people's characters.

| kind | level | like | old | quick | strong |

1 We enjoy the same kind of things; we're very ....-minded.
2 My brother hardly ever argues but my sister's always been ....-tempered.
3 As a child, he always got what he wanted; he was very ....-willed.
4 I have my head in the clouds, whereas my husband is very ....-headed.
5 Although he is so young, he has some ....-fashioned ideas.
6 I'm sure Jessica will help you. She's a ....-hearted person.

5 Work in pairs. Think of a friend who has one of these characteristics and describe their behaviour. Can you guess which characteristic your partner is describing?

Participles (-ing and -ed)
participle clauses

▶ **GRAMMAR** REFERENCE p.171

1 Look at extracts A–C and underline a present participle or past participle in each sentence. Which participles have an active meaning? Which have a passive meaning?

A Another week, another survey claiming to reveal great truths…

B Those people disapproving of online friendships…

C …in a world driven by technology…

2 Look at the extracts rewritten with relative pronouns. Which words are missed out with participles? Which words change?

A Another week, another survey which claims to reveal…

B Those people who disapprove of online friendships…

C …in a world which is driven by technology…

3 Replace the words in italics to make participle clauses.

Example:
The woman *who lives* next door is my best friend.
The woman *living* next door…

1 She is a kind-hearted woman, *who bursts* with energy.

2 Her sense of style, *which was developed* during her stay in France, is famous.

3 She recently twisted her ankle *while we were playing* tennis.

4 She has blonde hair, *which is cut* very short.

5 She gave me a fantastic picture, *which was painted* by her brother.

6 Everyone *who speaks* to her is impressed by her charm.

7 She has a job *in which she designs* clothes.

other uses of participles

4 Match extracts 1–4 from the text with other uses of participles A–D.

1 It's easy to criticise Facebook for *encouraging* rushed and therefore shallow friendships.

2 …which involves *sharing* your authentic self.

3 It's the *shocked* reaction that surprises me.

4 After *having* already *made* friends online.

A after certain verbs

B after conjunctions

C after prepositions

D as an adjective

5 Read the text quickly. Why are Ewan and Charlie such good friends?

6 Complete the text using the present or past participle form of the verbs in the box.

amaze	become	content	go
hate	have	say	talk

My best friend

Charley Boorman, actor, talks about his famous friend Ewan McGregor.

I first met Ewan while we were filming *The Serpent's Kiss*. I remember **(1)** .... up to him and introducing myself, by **(2)** .... 'Hi, I'm Charley. I hear you're into motorbikes.' After that we didn't stop **(3)** .... for the rest of the evening. Well, in fact, we haven't stopped for the last ten years!
After both **(4)** .... fathers for the first time, we had even more in common. When we decided to ride our motorbikes round the world, people said it would go one of two ways. Luckily for us, it went the good way and we had an **(5)** .... experience. People said we might end up **(6)** .... each other but we were able to help each other especially because we missed **(7)** .... our children around so much. We are both similar because we are happy and **(8)** .... with our lives and our families, and that has created a deep bond between us.

7 Talk about the friend or friends you have got a deep bond with. What creates bonds between friends of different ages?

Listening

1 ▶ 35 **Look at the exam task and listen to two students talking. Number the order in which they discuss the different stages.**

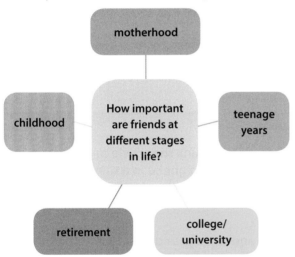

How important are friends at different stages in life?
- motherhood
- childhood
- teenage years
- retirement
- college/university

2 **Listen again and complete the extracts.**

1 OK, ... we begin?
2 We .... start .... …
3 .... you think?
4 .... …oh, sorry!
5 No, that's OK. ....
6 I was .... to say…
7 Would you .... that?
8 .... friends are important for men .... ?

3 **Which of the conversational strategies (A–C) do sentences 1–8 in Activity 2 fit into?**

A starting a discussion
B interrupting someone when you want a turn
C encouraging the other person to say something

Grammar

emphasis with *what*

▶ **GRAMMAR** REFERENCE p.168

4 **Write the sentences in another way, without using *what*. Start with the words in italics.**

1 What's really important to young kids is their *friends*.
2 What *you need* to have at that age is friends to go out with.

5 **How could you say sentences 1–4, using *what* for emphasis?**

1 I used to love going to theme parks.
2 It must be difficult staying at home all day with a baby.
3 It's interesting that men often take up sport as a way of making friends.
4 People need friends for every stage of their life.

Collaborative task (Part 3)

turn-taking

▶ **EXAM** FOCUS p.207

6 **Work in pairs and do the task with the mind map in Activity 1. You have about two minutes to do this.**

EXAM TIP

Take turns to speak and don't dominate. If you feel your partner is talking too much, interrupt politely by saying *Can I say something here?*

7 **Work in pairs and decide at which two stages in life people might need friends most. You have about a minute to do this.**

Speaking

1 Discuss the importance of friends throughout a person's life.

Article (Part 2)

Using a range of vocabulary

▶ **WRITING** REFERENCE p.185

2 Read the exam task and check you understand what you have to include in your article.

> You see this advertisement on an English language website.
>
> ### ARTICLES WANTED
>
> #### My closest friend.
>
> Where did you meet him/her? How long have you known him/her? What influence has she/he had on your life?
>
> Write us an article answering these questions. We will publish the best articles on our website.
>
> Write your **article** in **140–190** words.

3 Read the first two paragraphs of a model article and answer the questions about the techniques the writer has used to engage the reader.

1 Look at the words/structures in italics. What is the effect of using these?

2 Underline the 'more colourful' verbs which are used to express the following: *saw, walking with difficulty, ran, took, a lot.*

3 Which words are used to avoid repeating *friends* and *saw*? Think of similar words or expressions for *immediately, attracted by, unusual, have an argument, stupid, spoke.*

My closest friend

From the moment I saw Lucie, I knew we would be friends. She was so cool! How could I resist her?

It was my very first day at university *when* I first set eyes on her. I was struggling up the stairs when she rushed out of her room and grabbed one of my cases. *Not only did* she insist on carrying it for me, *but* she helped me unpack too. I was immediately attracted by her unusual clothes, mass of dark curly hair, bright eyes and energy. But *what* really made the friendship work *was* her warm friendly personality. We were *really* good mates until the end of our second year. Then we had a stupid argument and never spoke to each other *ever* again!

4 How do you think the article might continue? Discuss what might be in a third paragraph and think of a memorable concluding sentence.

5 Plan and write your own article using the guidelines 1–4.

1 Think about who you are going to write about and plan what will be in each paragraph.

2 Think of how you will make your introduction and conclusion effective, using some of the techniques from Activity 3 to interest and engage the readers.

3 Include a range of vocabulary.

4 Check your article for spelling, punctuation and grammar mistakes.

EXAM TIP

Instead of repeating the same words, use a near synonym or more extreme adjective to make your writing more interesting and demonstrate your range of vocabulary.

1 Choose the correct word/phrase to complete the sentences.

1 *As long as/Even if* he doesn't turn up, we can still go to the cinema.

2 *Provided that/Unless* the train's on time, I'll meet you at six outside the restaurant.

3 I still think he should apologise *whether/if* it's his fault or not.

4 Let's agree to disagree, *otherwise/even if* we'll have a big argument.

5 *As long as/Unless* it doesn't rain, I'll invite everyone for a barbecue in the evening.

6 We would never have met *if/whether* you hadn't got lost on your first day at university.

2 Choose the best answer, A, B, C or D.

1 I don't like people who are .... They're only interested in themselves.
   A self-aware **C** selfless
   B self-centred **D** self-confident

2 We don't .... a lot in common.
   A have **B** get **C** see **D** make

3 She's late again. That's .... of her.
   A usual **B** common **C** particular **D** typical

4 At the .... time there are nearly a billion users of Facebook worldwide.
   A actual **B** present **C** current **D** typical

5 Let's meet for a coffee at our .... place.
   A usual **B** typical **C** individual **D** unique

6 She's very level- .... and good at making decisions.
   A minded **B** willed **C** headed **D** hearted

7 There's a world .... difference between travelling by train and by plane.
   A from **B** of **C** in **D** to

8 My garden means the world .... me.
   A for **B** by **C** off **D** to

3 Join these sentences using an *-ing* or an *-ed* participle.

Example:
My favourite possession is this book. It was signed by the author.
My favourite possession is this book, signed by the author.

1 That woman is waving to us. She's one of my work colleagues.

2 That's the path. It leads to the sea.

3 I saw your brother. He was waiting for a train.

4 I found the money. It was hidden under my bed.

5 I'm living in a flat. It's owned by an old friend.

6 Shall we book the flight to Rome? It leaves at 6p.m. from Heathrow.

4 There is a mistake in each of these sentences Underline the mistakes and correct them.

1 He must have gone to France because I saw him a few minutes ago.

2 Tom has done so a lot of cycling that he is very fit.

3 We were warned driving slowly because of the icy roads.

4 I'm sure he'll phone as soon as he'll get there.

5 I ordered a fish risotto, that was delicious.

6 The boss wanted to know why was I resigning.

7 Next Sunday at midday, my daughter will get married.

8 I might go with him if I hadn't been so busy at work.

9 If we don't make a decision soon, they will be selling all the tickets.

10 My father suggested her that she went to work for him.

11 Here's the article I told you about, wrote by my sister.

12 I asked them don't speak in the library.

13 Louise may leave already but I'll check if you like.

14 I'll come, whether I have enough money.

15 If I weren't a teacher, I'll want to be a doctor.

5 Choose the correct word to complete the sentences.

1 I started to climb the mountain but after an hour, I *forgot/lost* my nerve.

2 His job takes him all *over/through* the world.

3 How do you *get/reach* to work every day?

4 *Work/Job* security is very important to think about.

5 Young people seem to be getting more *competing/competitive* at sports.

6 Shall we have a coffee and work *out/up* what to do?

7 One of the many strengths of the play is the amusingly written *set/script*.

8 The *growing/growth* in production seems to have slowed down in many places.

9 *Applications/Applicants* are all expected to have some previous experience.

10 Tom has decided to give up swimming in order to focus *on/in* athletics.

11 What are the chances of getting a direct *trip/flight* to Singapore next Tuesday?

12 I'm working overtime *in order to/that's why* save money for my holidays.

13 Digital technology appears to have taken *over/up* the world in the past five years.

14 I am not convinced that the government is *telling/informing* us the whole truth.

15 My son has just gone on a package *expedition/tour* with his two best friends.

PROGRESS TEST 2

Multiple-choice cloze (Part 1)

6 For questions 1–8, read the text below and decide which answer (A, B, C or D) best fits each gap. There is an example at the beginning.

Journey into space

When the first man landed on the moon, twelve-year-old Claudie Haigneré was on holiday on a French campsite. The first Frenchwoman in space recalls that day: 'My father, who was always **(0)** ..*curious*.. about the world, **(1)** .... us that something really extraordinary was about to happen. It was a beautiful evening, so we sat under the stars and watched TV. To see the moon so **(2)** .... away in the sky and then to see a man climb down a ladder onto the **(3)** .... of it was just incredible.'

After the moon landing, Haigneré read and watched whatever she could about space. **(4)** .... there herself seemed unimaginable. However, much later she heard that France's space centre was **(5)** .... for astronauts. It was an opportunity that Haigneré couldn't **(6)** .... Of 1,000 candidates, seven were chosen: six men and Haigneré.

Haigneré eventually went into space twice. What was it like being completely **(7)** .... from life on Earth? 'I usually had no time to sit and watch the earth turn. However, once I decided to **(8)** .... some time to enjoy the spectacle; it was extraordinary.'

0	**A** curious	**B** surprised	**C** interested	**D** fascinated
1	**A** said	**B** told	**C** explained	**D** suggested
2	**A** far	**B** long	**C** remote	**D** outside
3	**A** top	**B** side	**C** level	**D** surface
4	**A** Making	**B** Finding	**C** Reaching	**D** Travelling
5	**A** asking	**B** looking	**C** offering	**D** requesting
6	**A** miss	**B** lose	**C** wait	**D** avoid
7	**A** put off	**B** cut off	**C** set out	**D** got away
8	**A** do	**B** get	**C** take	**D** spend

Open cloze (Part 2)

7 For questions 9–16, read the text below and think of the word that best fits each gap. Use only one word in each gap. There is an example at the beginning.

Success

I have **(0)** ....*never*.... met anyone successful who didn't have a plan. I believe this is an essential key to success. Knowing what you want to **(9)** .... achieved in ten years' time, **(10)** .... if it doesn't seem a realistic goal for today, will give you the passion and drive needed to reach your ultimate goals. **(11)** .... you can answer the question 'What do I want to do?' clearly and confidently, then you have little chance **(12)** .... achieving anything significant.

For young people it's very important to remember that you'll **(13)** .... spending the rest of your life working. You'll spend more time at work than you will with friends and family, so it's incredibly important to identify what it is you really want to aim **(14)** ....

On the **(15)** .... hand, just because you're passionate about what you want to do, it doesn't necessarily mean you'll be any good at it. You need to recognise your capabilities and accept your limitations. There are certain skills you can learn but real talent is **(16)** .... that people are born with and it's impossible to learn this.

Word formation (Part 3)

8 **For questions 17–24, read the text below. Use the word given in capitals at the end of some of the lines to form a word that fits the gap in the same line. There is an example at the beginning.**

Tired of waiting

Although Simon is going to university this autumn to study
(0) _journalism_ , he has been   **JOURNAL**
working as a waiter for six months to pay for a holiday. At first, he says,
he was absolutely **(17)** .... at   **USE**
the job. It took him far longer than he'd expected to be able to do
it **(18)** .... .This was partly   **SUCCESS**
because he was given no formal
(19) .... at all. He says that   **TRAIN**
the job would not have been his
first **(20)** .... but it had been   **CHOOSE**
difficult to find any kind of temporary
(21) .... at all, so he'd had to   **EMPLOY**
take what he could get.

The salary is not good either, especially in view of the number
of hours he works. Waiters can't rely on being given a share of the
service charges because they aren't passed on by the
(22) .... of some restaurants.   **MANAGE**
So he just has to hope for generous tips instead.

He would never consider working in a restaurant again,
mainly because of the rude and
(23) .... attitude of many   **PLEASE**
chefs towards waiters. However,
he admits there were very few
(24) .... about the food.   **COMPLAIN**

Key word transformations (Part 4)

9 **For questions 25–30, complete the second sentence so that it has a similar meaning to the first sentence, using the word given. Do not change the word given. You must use between two and five words, including the word given. Here is an example.**

Example:
We're going to camp whether or not it's raining.
EVEN
We're going to camp .._even if it's_.. *raining.*

25 He'll be there at six unless he's held up at work.
PROVIDED
He'll be there at six, ... held up at work.

26 I'm unsure if I should invite Rob to the gig.
NOT
I'm unsure .... I should invite Rob to the gig.

27 There were so many people at the station that I couldn't find my friend.
SUCH
There were .... people at the station that I couldn't find my friend.

28 'I'm really sorry I broke your camera, Mum', Ellie said.
APOLOGISED
Ellie .... mum's camera.

29 'Why don't we go camping in Greece?' said Micky.
SUGGESTED
Micky .... camping in Greece.

30 'You shouldn't swim here,' the instructor told us.
WARNED
The instructor .... here.

Living on the edge

Gapped text (Part 6)

▶ **EXAM** FOCUS p.202

1 Look at the photo. What is your opinion about young people going on adventures like this? What are the risks and benefits for them?

2 Read the title and introduction to the article about a young mountaineer.

1 What kind of person do you think he is?

2 Read the main text quickly. Was there anything that surprised you about Jordan?

EXAM TIP

If you are not sure which sentence fits the gap, try the next gap and go back to the other one later.

3 Six sentences have been removed from the article. Choose from the sentences A–G the one which fits each gap (1–6). There is one extra sentence which you do not need to use.

Speaking

4 Work in pairs and discuss the questions.

1 What do you think about Jordan's achievement? Do you think his father was right to encourage him?

2 Do parents always encourage their children to achieve for the right reasons?

3 At what age do you think young people are ready to take decisions about their lives?

Vocabulary

using prefixes to work out meaning

5 Look at the words in the box, which are also underlined in the text, and match the prefixes to meanings 1–6.

<u>inter</u>national	<u>pre</u>-schoolers	<u>tri</u>cycle	<u>dis</u>order
<u>im</u>mobility	<u>hyper</u>-competitive	<u>over</u>time	<u>re</u>-occur

1 not **3** before **5** three

2 again **4** more than usual/too much **6** involving two or more different things

6 Work in pairs. Choose three prefixes and ask each other questions using them. **Example:** *Have you ever done a <u>triathlon</u>?*

Adjectives and verbs with prepositions

1 **Choose the adjective which does NOT fit in the sentence.**

1 She's very *committed/involved/dedicated/devoted* to teaching young people about safety.

2 She was very *concerned/worried/timid/anxious* about taking part in the race.

3 He felt *sure/convinced/determined/confident* of his ability to win.

4 He's *thrilled/excited/enthusiastic/keen* about joining the skydiving team.

2 **Use four of the adjectives to write sentences that are true for you. Then discuss your sentences with a partner.**

3 **Complete the sentences with the prepositions in the box. You can use them more than once.**

about	from	in	on	to	with

1 He complained .... the inaccurate map of the area.

2 She always insists .... the best diving equipment.

3 My father admitted .... feeling nervous.

4 He was involved .... a skiing accident.

5 He was prevented .... competing because of an injury.

6 She has to deal .... many dangerous situations.

7 You have to rely .... your partner when you're climbing.

8 He's determined .... enter the race.

9 My boss congratulated me .... my achievement.

10 He's very keen .... skydiving.

Phrasal verbs with *off*

4 **Replace the words in italics with the phrasal verbs in the box.**

back off	call sth off	cut off	go off
put sth off	see sb off	tell sb off	wear off

1 They *delayed* the start of the climb because of the storm.

2 Even though he was terrified of the dog he didn't *move away*.

3 The trip was *cancelled* because the weather was too bad.

4 We were *shouted at* by the guide for not following the safety rules.

5 A lot of people came to the port to *say goodbye to us* before we started the yacht race.

6 There was a loud bang and we realised one of the fireworks had *exploded* by accident.

7 When I hit my knee on the rock it hurt really badly but the pain gradually *went away*.

8 The village was *separated* from the outside world by the flood.

Speaking

5 **Find out if your partner has**

1 ever been cut off by snow or flooding.

2 ever called off something important.

3 ever been told off by a neighbour.

4 put anything off recently.

DANGER AVALANCHES

Hypothetical meaning

wish and *if only*

▶ **GRAMMAR** REFERENCE p.169

1 ▶ 37 **Listen to a man talking about skateboarding. Why did he give it up?**

A His wife wanted him to.

B He had too many accidents.

C He felt he was too old.

2 **Look at the examples and answer the questions.**

1 *If only I hadn't given up skating.*
Did he give up skateboarding? Is he sorry he gave up?

2 *If only I could start again.*
Would he like to start skateboarding again? Is this possible?

3 *I wish I was twenty years younger.*
Would he like to be younger? Is this possible?

4 *I wish my wife wouldn't tell me I need a new hobby all the time.*
Does his wife tell him he needs a new hobby? Does he mind?

3 **Look at the examples in Activity 2 and match the two parts of the sentences.**

1 We use *wish/if only* + past simple

2 We use *wish/if only* + *could*

3 We use *wish/if only* + *would*

4 We use *wish/if only* + past perfect

when we would like something to…

A have been different in the past.

B be different about other people in the present/future.

C change in the present/future about ourselves.

D be different about ourselves now.

LANGUAGE TIP

- Use *if only* when your feelings of regret are strong.
- *I wish/If only* can be followed by *was/were* in spoken English, but *were* is used in formal written English, e.g. **I wish I were** able to help you.

---

4 **Complete the sentences to make true wishes about yourself. Then say which of your partner's wishes are also true for you.**

1 I wish I could ....

2 I wish I didn't have ....

3 I wish my parents would ....

4 I wish I'd never ....

other expressions with hypothetical meaning

5 **Choose the correct alternative so that the second sentence means the same as the first.**

1 Suppose we didn't go to work tomorrow…
We *have decided not to go/are thinking about not going* to work tomorrow.

2 I met my friend Alison last night and it was as though we'd only seen each other the day before.
It felt like I *had/hadn't* seen my friend Alison very recently.

3 I'd rather you didn't go climbing this weekend.
I don't want you/You're not allowed to go climbing this weekend.

4 It's time we stopped for a rest.
Let's have/We don't have time for a rest now.

6 **Complete the sentences with the correct form of the verbs in brackets.**

1 Suppose we .... (*go*) there next week instead of tomorrow?

2 I felt as if someone .... (*gave*) me a million dollars!

3 I'd rather you .... (*not take*) so many risks.

4 It's time you .... (*realise*) how dangerous rugby can be.

7 **Work in pairs.**

Student A, turn to page 159 and follow the instructions.

Student B, turn to page 158 and follow the instructions.

Long turn (Part 2)

responding to your partner's photographs

▶ **EXAM** FOCUS p.206

1 Look at the photographs. Which of the sports would you least like to do?

2 ▶ 38 Listen to a student called Layla doing the task below and answer the questions.

> These photographs show people taking risks in different situations. I'd like you to compare the two photographs and say which person you think is taking the most risks.

1 Does Layla cover both parts of the task adequately?

2 Do you agree with her opinion? Why/Why not?

3 Listen again. What words and phrases does Layla use to

1 talk about the similarities and differences between the photos?

2 give her own opinion?

3 describe the people?

4 ▶ 39 After your partner has finished speaking, the examiner will ask you a question. Listen and say whether you agree with Leo.

EXAM TIP

When you answer the follow-up question, you only have to speak for about thirty seconds. Try not to repeat what your partner has said.

5 Work in pairs.

Student A, look at the photos on page 153 and do the exam task in Activity 2.

Student B, which of these jobs would you prefer to do?

6 Student B, look at the photos on page 155 and do the exam task in Activity 2.

Student A, would you enjoy doing dangerous sports like these?

Speaking

1 **Work in pairs and discuss the questions.**

1 Do you ever read reviews (e.g. before you watch a film/DVD, go to a restaurant, buy something online)?

2 Have you ever read a review that you completely disagreed with?

Review (Part 2)

expressing personal opinions

▶ **WRITING** REFERENCE p.186

2 **Read the exam task. What kind of information do people want to know when they read a film review?**

> You see this announcement in an English language magazine.
>
> > ## Film reviews wanted
> >
> > **Have you seen a film recently, in the cinema or on DVD, that you really liked?**
> > Write a review, describing it and saying why you would recommend it to other people of your age.
>
> Write your **review** in **140–190** words.

3 **Read the model review and match each paragraph with a topic.**

A summary of plot and comment on the acting

B factual details about the film

C overall opinion/recommendation

D details of the film-making

127 Hours

127 Hours is a survival drama film, based on a true story and set in an isolated part of Utah in America. Now out on DVD, it is co-written and directed by Danny Boyle.

The film stars James Franco, who is totally convincing as the real-life mountaineer, Aron Ralston, trapped for five days when his arm got jammed under a huge rock. As food and water begin to run out, he has to make a terrible decision if he isn't going to die. Then he walks for seven miles before he is eventually rescued.

With his unique creative and visual style, Boyle lets the camera do a lot of the talking with the fascinating shots of the Canyon and each and every expression of the unfortunate Aron. The rhythmic music is every bit as wonderful, and should have won the award it was nominated for.

Personally, I haven't been so gripped by anything for a long time. I hadn't expected to find it so totally inspirational. It may well put you off extreme sports for life, but you will come out wondering 'What would I have done in that situation?'

4 **Read the review again and tick the things that are mentioned.**

- [ ] cast
- [ ] music
- [ ] director
- [ ] producer
- [ ] story
- [ ] script
- [ ] costumes
- [ ] cinematography
- [ ] location

5 **Put the words in the box under the headings 1–5. Some words may go under more than one heading.**

complicated	confusing	convincing
disappointing	entertaining	exciting
fast-paced	frightening	impressive
outstanding	stunning	witty

1 Performances   4 Plot

2 Cast   5 Script

3 Special effects

6 **Read the exam task and brainstorm ideas. Think about how to organise your review and what kind of language to include. Then write the review.**

EXAM TIP

Make it clear at the end of the review what your overall opinion is and whether or not you would recommend the film/product/experience to someone else.

> You see this announcement in an English language newspaper.
>
> > ## WANTED
> >
> > **Where do you shop in our area?**
> > We'd like to know your opinion of a shop in the area. Include the type of things sold, value for money, quality, the staff and service.
> > We will publish the best reviews every week.
>
> Write your **review** in **140–190** words.

7 **Read your review and check you have answered the question and included all the relevant information. Make sure you have used a range of language and organised your ideas.**

1 Complete the second sentence so that it has a similar meaning to the first sentence, using the word given. You must use between two and five words, including the word given.

1 Ella is sorry she didn't learn to snowboard when she was younger.
WISHES
Ella .... how to snowboard when she was younger.

2 I would prefer you to wear a helmet when you ride your bike.
RATHER
I .... a helmet when you ride your bike.

3 I think you should go home now.
TIME
I think .... home.

4 It felt as if my legs were made of wool.
THOUGH
My legs .... were made of wool.

5 I took the bus because the train is so expensive.
BEEN
If the .... so expensive, I wouldn't have taken the bus.

6 I didn't get up in time and now I'm late for work.
WOULD
I .... late for work if I'd got up in time.

2 Read the text and complete the gaps with the correct preposition.

3 Complete the sentences with the correct form of the word in capitals.

1 Taking her children on such a dangerous trip was very .... **RESPONSIBILITY**

2 Being caught in the storm at sea was a .... experience. **TERRIFY**

3 Meeting my hero was very .... **MEMORY**

4 People were very .... of his decision to climb the mountain in such bad weather. **CRITIC**

5 The expedition was a great .... **SUCCEED**

6 It takes determination and .... of character to sail around the world alone. **STRONG**

Jessica Watson arrives back in Sydney

Returning **(1)** .... her 200-day solo trip around the world, sixteen-year-old Jessica Watson said: 'I'm just a girl who believed **(2)** .... her dream. You don't have to be someone special to succeed **(3)** .... achieving something big,' she said. She was congratulated **(4)** .... her success by the Australian Premier.

Critics questioned whether she was experienced enough to take **(5)** .... the treacherous journey and whether her parents should have called it **(6)** .... , but she said: 'The one thing I won't accept is when someone calls this reckless. We spent years preparing **(7)** .... this trip.'

The first few months of the trip went well, although the lack **(8)** .... human contact inevitably had an impact **(9)** .... her state of mind at times. Jessica admitted **(10)** .... being 'pretty moody and a little homesick' and in April wrote on her blog: 'I think I am ready to come home now.'

But harder times were to come. In the final stages of her trip Jessica had to deal **(11)** .... waves as large as a four-storey building and towering 'like liquid mountains'. She had to strap herself into her bunk and put on a crash helmet to prevent herself **(12)** .... being injured in the wild seas.

Crime scene

12

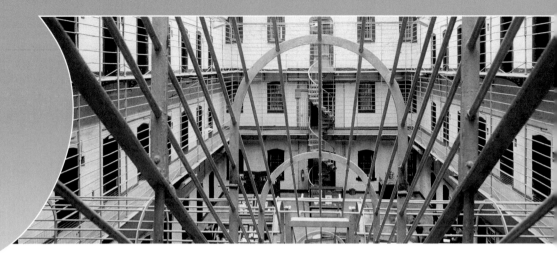

Speaking and vocabulary

1 **Discuss the questions in pairs.**

1 What would be the hardest thing about being in prison?

2 What would it be like to work as a prison officer?

2 **What is the purpose of a prison? Put these reasons in order of importance, then compare with a partner.**

☐ to protect the public

☐ to punish criminals

☐ to discourage other people from committing crimes

☐ to rehabilitate criminals into society

3 **Choose what you think is the most suitable punishment (A–D) for people 1–4.**

1 someone caught shoplifting for the first time

2 an armed robber caught stealing from a jewellery shop

3 a member of a terrorist organisation

4 someone caught driving dangerously

A paying a fine

B doing community service (e.g. street cleaning)

C serving a prison sentence

D having an overnight curfew and wearing an electronic tag

Sentence completion (Part 2)

▶ **EXAM** FOCUS p.204

4 **You will hear a journalist called Nick talking about places which used to be prisons, where paying guests can now stay. How would you feel about staying in a former prison?**

5 ▶ 40 **Listen and complete the sentences.**

6 **Work in pairs and discuss the question.**

Which of the former prisons would you prefer to stay in?

⌄ CHECK-**IN**

Prison hotels

The growth in (1) .... has encouraged former prisons to become hotels.

Most of the guests at Karosta prison are on (2) .... trips.

Each guest's (3) .... is inserted in a prison document.

Only (4) .... is available to drink at dinner.

When they are in their cells, guests must remain (5) ...., unless given permission to do otherwise.

Nick says the advertisement's description of the (6) .... at the prison is accurate.

For a three-day trip to Latvia which includes a one night stay at Karosta, go to www. (7) .... tours.com.

Nick does not recommend the (8) .... in cell rooms at the Alcatraz Hotel.

In the Alcatraz Hotel, the (9) .... are very different from those in a real prison.

One night in a single cell room at the Alcatraz Hotel costs (10) .... euros.

Vocabulary

crime

7 Complete the sentences with the words in the box. You can use them more than once.

arrest	suspect	witness	fine	sentence

1 The police made the .... only a few hours after the crime was committed.
2 A .... has to give evidence in court about what he saw.
3 The police began to .... the woman's husband of committing the crime.
4 Everyone thought the judge had given a very harsh ....
5 The police asked each .... who they were with on the night of the crime.
6 I'd hate to .... an accident.
7 I had to pay a large .... for speeding on the motorway.
8 The police were able to .... the burglar at the scene of the crime.
9 In some cases it's better to .... people than send them to prison.
10 At the end of a trial the judge has to .... the defendant, if the jury decides he or she is guilty.

8 Look at Activity 7 and answer the questions.

1 Are the noun and verb forms the same?
2 Is there any difference in pronunciation between the verb and noun?
3 Do any of the words have other meanings?

9 Use the vocabulary in Activity 7 to describe recent crime stories in the news.

collocations with *catch, follow, reach*

10 Complete the sentences with the correct form of the verbs in the box.

catch	follow	reach

1 Sometimes it's hard for a jury to .... *an agreement* or *a verdict*.
2 Local crime rates dropped again last year; this .... *a trend* that has continued for three years.
3 The criminals were .... *in the act of* breaking into the car and arrested at the scene of the crime.
4 I had to stop running to .... *my breath*, and the criminals got away.
5 The police haven't succeeded in .... *their target* for crime convictions this year.
6 The police are .... *a lead* which they think will help solve the crime.

Modal verbs

obligation, prohibition and necessity

▶ **GRAMMAR** REFERENCE p.170

1 **Read the statements and decide who said each one: a) a police officer, b) a prison officer or c) a prisoner?**

1 We *have to* inspect all mail sent to prisoners.

2 We *mustn't* talk to journalists about cases we are investigating.

3 We *don't have to* work or go to classes if we don't want to.

4 We *are not allowed to* have more than three visitors at a time.

5 I *must* try and stay positive until I am freed.

6 I *needn't have* spent so long preparing for the trial because in the end the defendant pleaded guilty.

2 **Which of the statements in Activity 1 refer to**

A an obligation the speaker feels is necessary?

B an obligation someone else says is necessary?

C things that aren't permitted?

D a lack of necessity/obligation?

E something that was done but wasn't necessary?

LANGUAGE TIP

Must is only used in the present. To talk about obligation in the past or future, use *have to*.

We **had to wear** a school uniform until we were sixteen;
I **will have to save more** if I want to buy a car.

3 **Choose the correct modal verb.**

1 If you are arrested you *don't have to/are not allowed to* answer all the police's questions.

2 Witnesses *mustn't/don't have to* tell lies in court.

3 We *must/had to* stay in our prison cells for up to twenty-three hours per day. It was awful.

4 We *must/have to* carry our identity cards at all times.

4 **Complete the second sentence so that it has a similar meaning to the first sentence, using the word given. You must use between two and five words, including the word given.**

1 It was good to see you but it wasn't necessary for you to visit me in prison.
NEED
You .... visited me in prison but it was good to see you.

2 You mustn't open the door to strangers.
ALLOWED
You .... the door to strangers.

3 It is prohibited for members of the jury to talk to the press.
MUST
Members of the jury .... to the press.

4 It isn't necessary for suspects to answer police questions.
HAVE
Suspects .... answer police questions.

5 He is responsible for collecting evidence at the scene of a crime.
HAS
He .... evidence at the scene of a crime.

6 Was it necessary for him to get advice from a lawyer?
NEED
Did .... advice from a lawyer?

Speaking

5 **Discuss what members of the jury/crime scene investigators/prison officers**

1 have to do.

2 mustn't do/aren't allowed to do.

3 are allowed to do.

4 needn't do/don't have to do.

Vocabulary and speaking

cybercrime

1 **Work in pairs and discuss the questions.**

1 In what ways do you think the internet can be a dangerous place?

2 How seriously do you take cybercrime?

3 What can people do to protect themselves against cybercrime?

2 **What do activities 1–5 involve? Match them with A–E.**

1 identity fraud

2 cyber bullying

3 identity theft

4 hacking

5 libel

A publishing something that is harmful to someone's reputation

B illegally gaining access to a computer or network

C pretending to be someone else

D deliberately hurting or embarrassing someone by email, text or on social networking sites

E stealing personal details for criminal purposes

3 **Which of activities 1–5 do you think is a) the most serious? b) the most common?**

4 **What do you think of people who**

1 download music/films illegally?

2 post a picture of someone without their consent on Facebook?

3 give false information online?

5 **What could the possible consequences of doing these things be? Think about**

1 the individuals.

2 society.

3 the industries involved.

Discussion (Part 4)

▶ **EXAM** FOCUS p.207

6 **Join another pair. Look at the examiner's questions 1–4 and, with your partner, take turns to answer them. The other students must listen carefully and note down whether you:**

A only gave very short answers/spoke too much.

B tried to include each other in the discussion.

C used a variety of phrases for agreeing/disagreeing.

1 Which is more important to you, your phone or your computer?

2 Do you think people rely too much on computers?

3 How would you feel if you couldn't access the internet for a month?

4 Do you think the internet is the best way to shop?

Then swap roles.

EXAM TIP

You can expand your ideas by giving specific examples (e.g. examples of people you know who rely too much on computers).

7 **Discuss your feedback in groups.**

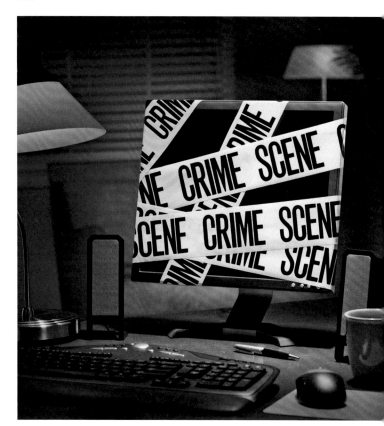

Speaking

1 Discuss the questions.

1 Why do you think crime fiction is one of the best-selling genres in many countries?

2 Which crime novels, films or TV programmes are popular in your country?

Multiple choice (Part 5)

▶ **EXAM** FOCUS p.202

2 You are going to read an extract from a crime novel. For questions 1–6, choose the answer (A, B, C or D) which you think fits best according to the text.

EXAM TIP

Make sure you read all the options carefully before making your decision.

1 The writer mentions Martin's unwillingness to kill flies to show that he

  A has a lot of patience.

  B wishes he was braver.

  C avoids being aggressive.

  D is fond of small creatures.

2 The people in the queue didn't try to stop the violence because they

  A were afraid of getting involved in it.

  B realised it was none of their business.

  C wanted to know what would happen next.

  D didn't want to lose their place in the queue.

3 Martin threw his bag at the Honda driver

  A to protect himself from being hit by the bat.

  B because the Honda driver was damaging the victim's car.

  C because he had decided it was the only sensible solution.

  D to distract the Honda driver from killing the Peugeot driver.

4 *ducked* in line 39 means

  A found it exciting.

  B tried his best to catch it.

  C moved to avoid being hit.

  D could never see anything.

5 *that* in line 56 refers to

  A using magic.

  B closing his eyes.

  C trying to hide from people.

  D making himself anonymous.

6 Martin was astonished that

  A his bag had missed the Honda driver.

  B the Honda driver had decided to leave.

  C the Honda driver was unable to find him.

  D the crowd were supporting the Honda driver.

kate atkinson

Martin had never done anything like that in his life before. He didn't even kill flies in the house, instead he patiently stalked them, trapping them with a glass and a plate before letting them free. The meek shall inherit the earth. He was fifty and had never knowingly committed an act of violence against another living creature, although sometimes he thought that might be more to do with cowardice than pacifism.

He had stood in the queue, waiting for someone else to intervene in the scene unfolding before them, but the crowd were in audience mode, like promenaders at a particularly brutal piece of theatre, and they had no intention of spoiling the entertainment. Even Martin had wondered at first if it was another show – a faux impromptu piece intended either to shock or to reveal our immunity to being shocked because we lived in a global media community where we had become passive voyeurs of violence (and so on). That was the line of thought running through the detached, intellectual part of his brain. His primitive brain, on the other hand, was thinking, Oh, this is horrible, really horrible, please make the bad man go away. He wasn't surprised to hear his father's voice in his head (*Pull yourself together, Martin*). His father had been dead for many years but Martin often still heard the bellow and yell of his parade-ground tones.

When the Honda driver finished breaking the windows of the silver Peugeot and walked towards the driver brandishing his weapon and preparing himself for a final victory blow, Martin realised that the man on the ground was probably going to die, was probably going to be *killed* by the crazed man with the bat right there in front of them unless someone did something and instinctively, without thinking about it at all – because if he'd thought about it he might not have done it – he slipped his bag off his shoulder and swung it, hammer throw fashion, at the head of the insane Honda driver

Speaking

3 **Discuss these questions.**

1 Do you think that Martin was right to get involved? What would you have done?

2 What examples of road rage have you experienced or witnessed?

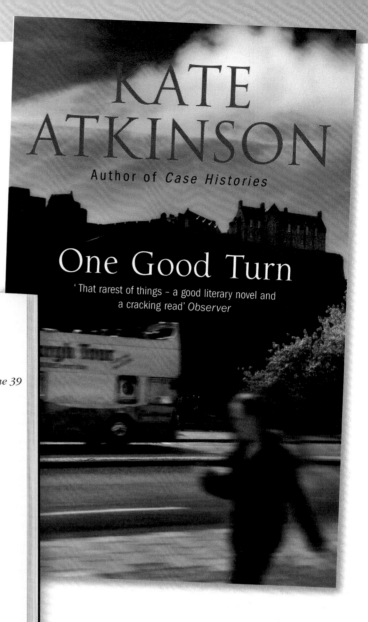

KATE ATKINSON
Author of *Case Histories*

One Good Turn

'That rarest of things – a good literary novel and a cracking read' *Observer*

---

one good turn

He missed the man's head, which didn't surprise im – he'd never been able to aim or catch, he was the ind of person who ducked when a ball was thrown in   *line 39* is direction – but his laptop was in the bag and the ard weighty edge of it caught the Honda driver on the oulder and sent him <u>spinning</u>.

The nearest Martin had been to a real crime scene reviously had been on a Society of Authors' trip around Leonard's police station. Apart from Martin, the roup consisted entirely of women. 'You're our token an,' one of them said to him, and he sensed a certain isappointment in the polite laughter of the others, as the least he could have done as their token man was be a little less like a woman.

Martin expected the Honda driver to pick himself p off the ground and search the crowd to find the lprit who had thrown a missile at him. Martin tried make himself an anonymous figure in the queue, ied to pretend he didn't exist. He closed his eyes. He d done that at school when he was <u>bullied</u>, <u>clinging</u>   *line 56* an ancient, desperate magic – they wouldn't hit him he couldn't see them. He imagined the Honda driver alking towards him, the baseball bat raised high, the c of annihilation waiting to happen.

To his amazement, when he opened his eyes, the Honda iver was climbing back into his car. As he drove away few people in the crowd gave him a slow hand-clap. artin wasn't sure if they were expressing disapproval the Honda driver's behaviour or disappointment at his ilure to <u>follow through</u>. Whichever, they were a hard owd to please.

Martin knelt on the ground and said, 'Are you OK?' to e Peugeot driver, but then he was politely but firmly t <u>aside</u> by the two policewomen who arrived and took ntrol of everything.

· 125 ·

Vocabulary

verbs

4 **Match meanings 1–8 to the verbs underlined in the text.**

1 do what is necessary to complete something

2 turn around quickly

3 follow something quietly in order to catch it

4 hold something or someone tightly

5 become involved in a difficult situation

6 hurt or frighten someone who is less powerful than you

7 wave something (e.g. a weapon) in a threatening way

8 move someone or something away

5 **Work in pairs. Choose three verbs from Activity 4 and use them to make two true sentences and one false sentence about your life. Take turns to read your sentences out. Can your partner guess which one is false?**

have/get something done

▶ **GRAMMAR** REFERENCE p.169

1 **Read the dialogue. Which of the phrases in italics refer to**

1 something over which people had no control?

2 something which happened as a result of an arrangement?

Zara: I heard there was a break-in at your office the other night. Did they take anything?

Dan: Luckily, not much. We *had some computers stolen* but that was about it.

Zara: What did the police do about it?

Dan: The usual. They *got the rooms fingerprinted* but I don't expect they'll catch anyone.

2 **Complete the rule to show how causative *have/get* is formed.**

have or .... + object + ... of the verb

3 **Read the dialogues 1–6 and complete the responses using the correct forms of the words in brackets.**

1 **A** This room looks different?
   B Yes, we .... (*have/just/paint*).

2 **A** This tooth has been aching for ages now.
   B Why don't you go to the dentist's and .... (*get/look at*)?

3 **A** My hair is so long it takes ages to wash and dry.
   B Why don't you .... (*have/cut*)?

4 **A** I think I must be getting a bit short-sighted!
   B Go to the optician's and .... (*get/test*).

5 **A** Did you build that shed yourself?
   B No, I .... last year (*get/a friend/make it*).

6 **A** What a beautiful family photograph.
   B Yes, we .... by a professional (*have/take*).

4 **Look at the list of some things victims have to do after a crime has been committed.**

> ☐ report the crime to the police
> ☐ change their locks
> ☐ repair broken windows
> ☐ buy a guard dog
> ☐ stop their credit cards
> ☐ clean the house
> ☐ find their insurance policy
> ☐ install an alarm

1 Put a tick (✓) next to the things people often do themselves.

2 Put a cross (✗) next to the things people would probably have done for them/get somebody to do for them.

3 Add anything else you can think of to the list.

4 Discuss your lists in groups. Have you ever had to do any of these things?

Vocabulary

phrasal verbs with *go*

1 Replace the words in italics with the correct form of the phrasal verbs in the box. There may be more than one possible answer for each question.

---

go off   go over   go on   go ahead
go down

---

1 The policeman had no idea what was *happening*.

2 They decided to *continue* with the original investigation.

3 Jack has *lost interest in* the idea of becoming a detective.

4 The computer network has *stopped working*.

5 The dog started shaking when the fireworks *exploded*.

6 I didn't keep the milk in the fridge and it *became sour*.

7 The lights *stopped working* for no apparent reason.

8 I finished early, so I *revised* what I'd written.

2 **Work in pairs and ask each other these questions.**

1 Have you ever gone off someone or something?

2 Have you ever gone ahead with something against someone's wishes?

3 Do you always go over your work before you hand it in?

4 Do you usually know what is going on in the world?

Open cloze (Part 2)

▶ **EXAM** FOCUS p.201

3 **Read the text quickly. In what way has tourism been affected by crime novels?**

4 **Read the text again and think of the word which best fits each gap. Use only one word in each gap. There is an example at the beginning.**

5 **Have you ever been on, or would you consider going on, a tour of a place where a book, film or TV show was set? Why/Why not?**

In the footsteps of the fictional detective

Detective novels have been extremely popular ever **(0)** *since* Sherlock Holmes first caught the public's imagination over a hundred years ago. However, nowadays this particular genre of novel seems to **(1)** _____ selling even more than ever. Novels **(2)** _____ *The Da Vinci Code*, for example, have sold millions of copies all **(3)** _____ the world and have been made into blockbuster films. In fact, *The Da Vinci Code* has become **(4)** _____ popular that walking tours are available in Paris in order **(5)** _____ people to be able to see the places which were mentioned in the novel.

One of the **(6)** _____ popular fictional detectives these days is Wallander, the main character in a series of novels written **(7)** _____ the Swedish author, Henning Mankell. For millions of people worldwide, **(8)** _____ small town of Ystad in Sweden is now synonymous with murder and the man who solves them. People flock there in huge numbers to visit, which proves that crime is a tourist attraction.

Report (Part 2)
Making recommendations

▶ **WRITING** REFERENCE p.184

1 **Read the exam task and a student's report. Then answer the questions.**

1 Is all the necessary information included?
2 Is there any irrelevant information?
3 Is the report written in an appropriate style?

> The college where you study has been given some money to spend on improving security, either by installing lockers for students to keep valuables in, or security cameras inside the building. Now the director of the college has asked you to write a report describing the benefits of both ideas and saying which one the money should be spent on and why.
>
> Write your **report** in **140–190** words.

Introduction
The purpose of this report is to recommend how the money provided for improving security at the college should be spent. It has been suggested that either lockers for students' valuables or security cameras should be installed.

Benefits of installing lockers
Currently there is nowhere for students to keep valuable possessions such as laptops or sports equipment. If lockers were installed, students would no longer have to carry all their valuable things with them around the college, which reduces the risk of them being stolen. I dropped my laptop in the canteen last year and broke it.

Benefits of installing security cameras
• would reduce the number of mobile phones and other valuables that are stolen each year
• would discourage people from stealing
• would make it easier to identify thieves

Recommendations
Although both ideas would be popular with students, I think the security cameras would be more successful at improving security and reducing crime. There also isn't enough space in the college for enough lockers to be installed. I would therefore recommend spending the money on putting security cameras inside the building. But another solution is to discourage students from bringing valuable things to school.

2 **Complete the sentences with the correct form of *spend*. Sometimes more than one answer is possible.**

1 I would therefore recommend *spending* the money on security cameras.
2 My recommendation would be .... more money on security cameras.
3 I recommend the college .... more money on security cameras.
4 It is recommended that the money .... on security cameras.

3 **Which verbs could be used to replace *recommend* in each sentence in Activity 2?**

4 **Work in pairs. Read the exam task and make notes under the headings *Advantages*, *Disadvantages* and *Recommendations*.**

> A large number of mobile phones have been stolen from your college recently. The director of the college wants to avoid this problem by banning mobile phone use in college and has asked you to write a report about this. You should explain what the advantages and disadvantages of this idea would be and make recommendations.
>
> Write your **report** in **140–190** words.

5 **Write your report in 140–190 words. Remember to check your work using the writing checklist on page 179.**

EXAM TIP
You should finish your report by giving one or two recommendations. It doesn't matter what solutions you suggest as long as your ideas are expressed appropriately.

1 Choose the correct option (A, B, C or D) to complete sentences 1–6.

1 The police .... an arrest and took the suspect to the station.
  A made   **B** did   **C** had   **D** got

2 Because it was his first offence, the judge let him .... with a warning.
  A up   **B** off   **C** down   **D** in

3 The police are .... a lead which they hope will help solve the crime.
  A reaching   **B** catching **C** following **D** inspecting

4 The jury took over a week to .... a 'guilty' verdict.
  A do   **B** make   **C** arrive   **D** reach

5 The defendant went .... a long trial before he was sentenced.
  A off   **B** over   **C** through   **D** by

6 As the burglar was breaking into the shop, the alarm .... off.
  A went   **B** came   **C** sounded   **D** let

2 Complete the second sentence so that it has a similar meaning to the first sentence, using the word given. You must use between two and five words.

1 We went to the lesson but it wasn't necessary because it was cancelled.   **NEED**
  We .... to the lesson because it was cancelled.

2 The policeman didn't give us permission to go into the courtroom.   **ALLOWED**
  We .... go into the courtroom.

3 During the lesson you aren't allowed to speak unless you raise your hand.   **MUSTN'T**
  During the lesson, you .... raising your hand.

4 Why don't you talk Harry into checking your brakes for you?   **GET**
  Why don't you .... your brakes for you?

5 I've asked the newsagent's to deliver the newspaper every day.   **DELIVERED**
  I've told the newsagent's that I want to .... every day.

6 I'm going to ask a friend of mine to make my wedding dress.   **HAVE**
  I'm going to .... by a friend of mine.

3 Complete the text, using the correct form of the word in capitals.

What happens when you report a crime?

A woman went into the police station to report a **(1)** .... , and   **THIEF**
was able to give a full **(2)** .... of the man who took her purse.   **DESCRIBE**
A witness also identified the man and told police that he had been
acting **(3)** .... , so it wasn't very long before the police were   **SUSPECT**
able to arrest the man. At the station, a request was made for a
(4) .... to be present while the interviews were taking place.   **LAW**
This was done, and in the meantime, the police discovered that the
man had several other **(5)** .... to be taken into account. In court,   **CONVICT**
the jury took a long time to reach a **(6)** .... But the man was   **DECIDE**
eventually found **(7)** .... and had to be sentenced. Surprisingly,   **GUILT**
despite his previous **(8)** .... record, the judge chose not to give   **CRIME**
the man a prison sentence, deciding instead to make him do six
months' community service.

Who are you again?

Multiple matching (Part 7)

▶ **EXAM** FOCUS p.203

1 **Look at the small photos and put the faces in the order that they most resemble the big photo below. Then answer the questions.**

1 Did you find this task easy or difficult? Did other people do better/worse than you?

2 How did you do the task? Did you have to study the features carefully?

EXAM TIP

Leave any questions you are not sure about and go back to them later. Always answer them as you will not lose marks for a wrong answer.

2 **You are going to read an article about people who suffer from 'face blindness'. For questions 2–10, choose from the people (A–D). The people may be chosen more than once.**

Which person

says that <u>location</u> is her biggest clue to recognising people?	1 C
is in difficulty when everyone dresses the same?	2
has problems if people change their appearance?	3
once failed to recognise a friend until he spoke?	4
fears that her disability might affect her work?	5
says she once mistook a stranger for her boyfriend?	6
suspects that people must think she is unfriendly?	7
has had problems identifying herself?	8
prefers to avoid large social gatherings?	9
believes the condition can be passed down the generations?	10

IDENTITY CRISIS

We can all forget a face but some people – around one in fifty – can't recognise their colleagues, friends, even their parents. It is a condition known as 'face blindness'.

A Emily's worst experience was arriving at a restaurant to meet the man she'd been going out with for a month. 'Seeing him sitting alone at the bar, I gave him a kiss on the cheek and we talked for a few minutes. Then an embarrassing thought struck me. "We've never met before, have we?" I asked. "I don't think so," he replied, "but you seemed pretty sure." This incident, along with many similar experiences, led me to realise that I am face-blind. I'm OK if I can rely on facial clues other than features, such as glasses or an unusual hairstyle, but it means I can be completely thrown if someone has their hair coloured, grows a beard or gets contact lenses.

B Andrea works in a design studio. It's a really good profession for me as people tend to express themselves through clothes and jewellery and it's easier to remember who usually wears a huge watch or very bright tops or whatever, rather than faces. So you can imagine how tricky it is at meetings when clients are all in suits and white shirts, looking identical. And when I'm the only one in the office and I have to open the door, I might say "Hello, how can I help you?" when I've done business with them ten times before. In fact, I worry that I'm going to lose my clients because of this. I'm also expected to meet clients outside work. I obviously try to get out of going to big parties because it's a nightmare with my condition. If I have to go, I always memorise what people are wearing when I'm first introduced to them.'

C Laura tells us about an experience she had recently. 'I was coming out of the cinema and a woman smiled at me. I assumed I must know her, but I usually depend on venue and this one didn't help me to work out whether she was a colleague, a parent at my son's school, or a friend. So what I did was smile faintly. Not too much, in case I was wrong. I then hoped desperately that if she spoke, a few moments' conversation would place her. Sure enough it did, I realised she is someone who sits in an office quite near to me. Embarrassing, but an everyday occurrence for people like me; and I probably come across as rather a cold person for never speaking first. If people have features that stand out from the crowd, such as gappy teeth or a birthmark, I'm not too bad. But I'm hopeless if you have regular features like my colleague. My daughter is just the same. So is my mother, which leads me to believe the disorder must run in families.'

D Chloe admits that when she's out, she now puts earplugs in and pretends she's listening to music. 'I came up with this plan because I've so often offended people by not recognising them. I once thought I was being followed by a man. I walked faster, ignoring him and it was only when his American accent triggered my memory that I realised it was a man I've known really well since university. Even worse, though, I've caught sight of myself in a shop window and not realised it was my own reflection!'

Speaking

3 **Discuss these questions.**

1 Which of the strategies mentioned in the article do you think would be the most effective in helping with face blindness?

2 What advantages and disadvantages would there be of being a 'super-recogniser' – someone who can recognise people again many years after they've seen them just for a moment?

Vocabulary

phrasal verbs with *come*

4 **Match the phrasal verbs with *come* in sentences 1–8 with the definitions A–H.**

1 I *came across* a pile of old letters while I was tidying up my office.

2 I probably *come across* as unfriendly to some people.

3 I *came up* with this plan because I've so often offended people.

4 I'm sure Paolo will *come round* to the idea sooner or later.

5 I think Jess has *come down with* flu.

6 If I *came into* money, I'd give some to medical research.

7 My exam results are *coming out* next week.

8 She's got her twentieth birthday *coming up* soon.

A find by chance
B happen
C give the impression/appear
D think of
E inherit
F get/catch something
G agree to something you're not sure about
H be made public

5 **Work in pairs. Ask each other questions using the phrasal verbs in Activity 4.**

Examples:
Do you think you come across as a different kind of person to who you really are?
Have you ever come down with an unusual illness or condition?

Modal verbs

ability

▶ **GRAMMAR** REFERENCE p.170

1 **Read the forum extracts. Which person is a) a 'super-recogniser'? b) face-blind?**

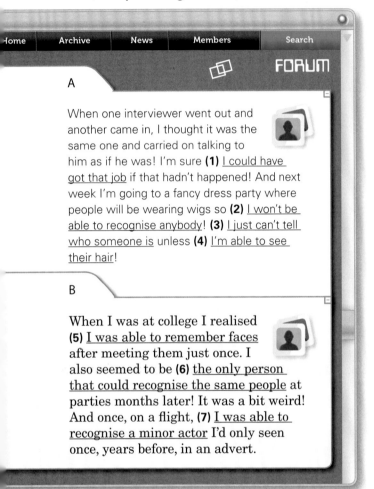

| Home | Archive | News | Members | Search |

FORUM

A

When one interviewer went out and another came in, I thought it was the same one and carried on talking to him as if he was! I'm sure **(1)** I could have got that job if that hadn't happened! And next week I'm going to a fancy dress party where people will be wearing wigs so **(2)** I won't be able to recognise anybody! **(3)** I just can't tell who someone is unless **(4)** I'm able to see their hair!

B

When I was at college I realised **(5)** I was able to remember faces after meeting them just once. I also seemed to be **(6)** the only person that could recognise the same people at parties months later! It was a bit weird! And once, on a flight, **(7)** I was able to recognise a minor actor I'd only seen once, years before, in an advert.

2 **Which of the underlined phrases (1–7) are examples of the following?**

A general ability in the past ..*5*.. ....

B ability on a particular occasion in the past ....

C ability in the present ....

D ability in the future ....

E things which were possible but did not happen ....

LANGUAGE TIP

- We can also use *know how to* to talk about ability.
  *I don't **know how to** drive.*
- *Succeed in* and *manage to* give the idea of overcoming difficulty.
  *I finally **succeeded in** contacting Josh.*
  *He finally **managed to** find his way home.*

---

3 **Choose the correct verb form to complete the sentences. Both may be possible.**

1 After we'd tried everything, we *could/were able to* get the computer to work at last.

2 When we lived on the coast we *could/were able to* swim every day in the summer.

3 She must *can/be able to* leave earlier than that!

4 If you'd got here earlier we *could catch/could have caught* the fast train together.

5 I*'ve been unable to/can't* recognise faces since I had the accident last winter.

6 I hope *can/to be able to* finish this today.

4 **Complete the second sentence so that it has a similar meaning to the first sentence using the word given. You must use between two and five words, including the word given.**

1 I couldn't finish the competition because I wasn't feeling well.
WAS
I .... the competition because I wasn't feeling well.

2 When I was younger, I was the best football player in my year.
PLAY
When I was younger, I .... anyone else in my year.

3 As it's such a long way, I don't think I'll be able to run all of it.
SUCCEED
As it's such a long way, I don't think I'll .... all of it.

4 I didn't take the job, even though I was offered it.
COULD
I .... the job I was offered, but I didn't.

5 I knew how to cook before I went to university.
ABLE
I .... before I went to university.

5 **Complete the sentences with an expression of ability so they are true for you. Use the ideas in the box to help you.**

---

cook play a musical instrument
ride a horse/motorbike run a marathon
speak a language fluently

---

1 I used to …

2 Once, I …

3 One day, I hope …

4 I've never …

5 It would be nice …

6 I should …

Speaking

1 Look at the photos of people keeping a record of their memories and discuss the questions.

1 What kind of things do people often want to keep memories of?

2 Which of these two methods do you think is best? Why?

3 What other ways are there to record your memories?

Vocabulary

useful phrases for Part 2

2 Match expressions 1–6 with the reasons for using them (A–F).

1 Both of these photos …

2 What I meant was …

3 Did you say we had to …?

4 It's a kind of …

5 It might be a good way of …

6 One shows … while the other shows …

A making sure you understand

B correcting yourself/making something clearer

C talking about how things are similar

D talking about differences

E speculating

F saying something in a different way if you don't know the word

3 Work in pairs and think of as many other useful expressions as you can for each category.

Long turn (Part 2)

▶ **EXAM** FOCUS p.206

4 Work in pairs.

Student A: Compare the two pictures in Activity 1, and say why people might choose to record their memories like this. You should speak for about a minute.

Student B: Do you prefer to write down your memories or keep photographs?

5 Now turn to page 156 and complete the task.

6 Discuss how well you feel you did Activity 4.

1 Were you able to speak for a minute without pausing too much?

2 Did you use 'fillers' (e.g. *er…*, *well…*, *right…*) when you paused, rather than leave long silences?

3 Did you compare the photos rather than just describe them?

4 Did you give your personal opinion?

7 Tell your partner two things they did well and two things they could improve.

Expressions with *mind*

1 **Choose the correct meaning, A or B, for the expressions with *mind*.**

1 I just couldn't think what the answer was. *My mind had gone completely blank.*

    A I'd forgotten everything.

    B I wasn't sure of the answer.

2 I had no idea where I was. I thought I was *losing my mind.*

    A getting lost

    B going mad

3 OK, thanks for your suggestion. *I'll bear that in mind.*

    A I've changed my mind.

    B I'm going to remember that.

4 *I'm in two minds about* whether to go to the party.

    A I haven't decided yet.

    B I'm really looking forward to it.

5 *It had crossed my mind* that she would forget to come.

    A I was convinced.

    B It occurred to me.

6 I'm really sorry I didn't phone you back last night. *It slipped my mind.*

    A I forgot.

    B I was really busy.

7 I must *put his mind at rest* and tell him I've found his credit card.

    A make him lose his memory

    B stop him worrying

8 To *take her mind off* breaking up with her boyfriend, we threw a party.

    A make her forget

    B persuade her not to do it

Speaking

2 **Use the expressions with *mind* to talk about something**

1 you're not sure about.

2 you forgot recently.

3 you're worried about.

4 you think about often.

Verbs with similar meanings

3 **Choose the correct verb.**

1 I always *store/record/preserve/maintain* my favourite photos in a special box.

2 The photos helped her to *preserve/recall/reflect/maintain* the events of that day.

3 We *recalled/remembered/reflected/reminded* on what had gone wrong and how we could improve.

4 He *recalled/recorded/reminded/remembered* her of her grandfather.

4 **Complete the sentences with the correct form of the verbs. Sometimes more than one word is possible.**

believe	consider	judge	think

1 I don't .... in doing exercises to improve your memory.

2 I am in no position to .... whether they are doing the right thing.

3 I am .... writing a family history.

4 He is .... of becoming a journalist.

5 It is .... that memory declines as people get older.

6 I .... myself lucky that I have such a good memory.

7 You need to .... for yourself whether or not the job is a good opportunity.

8 They are .... about starting a family.

5 **Which answers in Activity 4 depend on you knowing**

1 whether the verb can be used with a particular preposition?

2 a fixed phrase?

LANGUAGE TIP

- *think of/about* can mean *consider*.
  I'm **thinking of/about** doing a journalism course.
- *think of* is used to ask about someone's opinion.
  What did you **think of** the film?
- *think about* is used to talk about the action of thinking.
  I'm **thinking about** how to solve the problem.

Multiple-choice cloze (Part 1)

▶ **EXAM** FOCUS p.200

1 **Read the text quickly (don't worry about the gaps yet). What problem does the writer describe?**

A Not having enough storage space for all his text messages.

B Making difficult choices about what to keep.

C Storing too much unnecessary information.

135

The lost art of forgetting

Of the (0) .A..approximately.. 1,500 text messages I have stored on my phone, around three quarters of them are worthless. Of the remaining quarter, most are significant in some way, but also not really worth (1) .... forever. And then there is maybe a small (2) .... of text messages that I really do want to save for future reference.

Instead of deleting the messages I no longer need, I tend to save them all. This is much quicker than having to (3) .... which ones to save. Storing all these messages isn't a problem because so far I've only used a fraction of the space (4) .... but it does mean it takes a long time to (5) .... for the important ones.

I see this as part of a (6) .... problem. In the digital age it's too easy to hang onto every little social exchange and every photo. We are no longer in a position to (7) .... whether something is valuable or worthless. We need to keep (8) .... ourselves that we can't remember everything.

EXAM TIP

When you have finished, read the whole text to make sure it makes sense and there are no gaps. If necessary, make a guess.

2 **For questions 1–8, decide which answer (A, B, C or D) best fits each gap. There is an example at the beginning (0).**

0	**A** approximately	**B** generally	**C** normally	**D** probably
1	**A** keeping	**B** maintaining	**C** holding	**D** gathering
2	**A** list	**B** total	**C** handful	**D** group
3	**A** sort out	**B** make up	**C** come across	**D** take up
4	**A** open	**B** available	**C** empty	**D** vacant
5	**A** discover	**B** seek	**C** identify	**D** search
6	**A** grander	**B** wider	**C** clearer	**D** looser
7	**A** believe	**B** regard	**C** judge	**D** think
8	**A** recalling	**B** reminding	**C** reflecting	**D** memorising

3 **Check your answers and make sure you understand why the incorrect options are incorrect.**

4 **Discuss in pairs: what do you do with old text messages?**

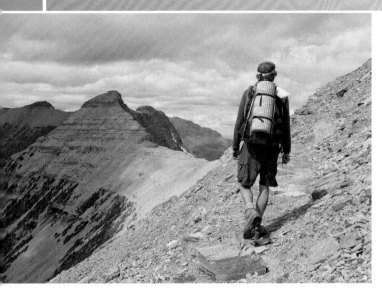

Multiple choice: short extracts (Part 1)

▶ **EXAM** FOCUS p.204

1 ▶ 41 **You will hear people talking in eight different situations. For each question, choose the best answer, A, B or C.**

EXAM TIP

Underline the key words in the question and make sure the option you choose answers this question.

1 You overhear a conversation between two friends. What did the woman find difficult when she was learning Chinese?

 A the writing

 B the grammar

 C the pronunciation

2 You hear a woman describing her work colleagues. What does she say about them?

 A They are unsociable.

 B They only talk about work.

 C They gossip about each other too much.

3 You hear a man telling a friend about travelling alone. What disadvantage does he mention?

 A There is no support when things go wrong.

 B There is no opportunity to share memories afterwards.

 C There is no one to discuss problems with at meal times.

4 You hear a student talking about his future plans. What is he thinking of doing when he leaves university?

 A getting a job in a zoo

 B becoming a journalist

 C working as a conservation volunteer

5 You overhear a woman leaving a message for her son. Why is she phoning him?

 A to change an arrangement

 B to remind him about an appointment

 C to apologise for being late

6 You hear two friends talking at a party. Why doesn't the woman enjoy parties?

 A She finds them tiring.

 B It's difficult to meet new people.

 C She can't hear what people are saying.

7 You hear a woman describing a problem she had when travelling. How does she feel about the problem?

 A sorry

 B angry

 C confused

8 You hear a man and a woman talking about an old photo. Why do they like the photo?

 A They think they look young.

 B It reminds them of a happy event.

 C They prefer the fashion at that time.

Speaking

2 **How do you feel about the following things?**

1 learning a language

2 going to parties

3 travelling alone

4 remembering phone and pin numbers

5 looking at old photos

Vocabulary

expressions with *time*

3 **Match sentences 1–4 with the responses A–D.**

1 I can't believe it's the end of July already.

2 Grandad had a computer before anyone else in his office, didn't he?

3 My dad has finally bought a new car.

4 My boss is always telling us to stop chatting.

A I know. Doesn't time fly?!

B He's right. Time is money!

C That's right. He was ahead of his time.

D At last! That's not before time!

4 **How far do you agree that**

1 time is money?

2 time flies?

Reflexive pronouns

▶ **GRAMMAR** REFERENCE p.173

1 **What's the difference in meaning between the following sentences?**

1 **A** Florence reminded herself that there was nothing to worry about.
  B Florence reminded her that there was nothing to worry about.
  C Florence herself reminded her that there was nothing to worry about.

2 **A** Suzy and Sam blamed themselves for losing the photographs.
  B Suzy and Sam blamed each other for losing the photographs.

3 **A** I went there myself.
  B I went there by myself.

LANGUAGE TIP

- Use reflexive pronouns with transitive verbs (verbs that take a direct object) when the subject and object are the same person. *I keep reminding **myself*** (NOT ~~me~~) *of the number.*
- Intransitive verbs (verbs which do not take a direct object), e.g. *remember, relax, feel*, do not need a reflexive pronoun.

---

2 **Complete the sentences with a pronoun (e.g. *me*), a reflexive pronoun (e.g. *myself*) or (-) when no pronoun is needed.**

1 At the party a man I didn't know recognised me from work and came and introduced .... to me.

2 We enjoyed .... a lot at the party.

3 My boyfriend is very forgetful, so I always remind .... to take his keys and wallet when he goes out.

4 My parents think because I forget things a lot, I don't know how to look after ....

5 My husband can't relax .... at parties because he's worried he'll forget someone's name.

6 Stop pulling my hair. You're hurting .... !

7 She blames .... for the flood because she forgot to turn off the taps.

8 My brother was so good at the piano that our parents always compared .... to Mozart!

3 **Decide where the reflexive pronoun can go in these sentences to give emphasis.**

1 The president of the bank apologised for losing my money.

2 I never have a problem remembering numbers.

3 Even Einstein occasionally made mistakes with numbers.

4 I think you should tell him.

4 **Work in pairs. Think of at least three pieces of advice to give people who have difficulty remembering names, numbers, English vocabulary or dates. Use the verbs in the box to help you.**

give	remind	send	tell	test	write

Example: *Keep reminding yourself of the number.*

5 **Share your advice with the class. Did you have anything on your list that nobody else thought of?**

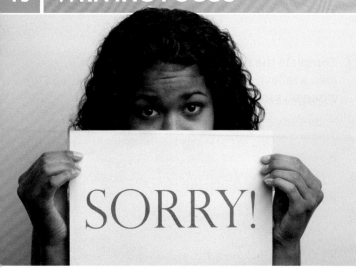

Speaking

1 **Discuss the questions with a partner.**

1 Do you always apologise in these situations?

   A being late
   B forgetting a friend's birthday
   C forgetting your homework
   D losing your temper
   E breaking something
   F having an argument

2 When you know you've done something wrong, is it better to deny it or take responsibility?

Informal email (Part 2)

using a range of functional language

▶ **WRITING** REFERENCE p.182

2 **Choose the correct word.**

Apologising

1 I'm afraid I *offer/owe* you an apology.

2 I *can/can't* apologise enough for *forget/forgetting* your birthday.

3 I'm *extremely/absolutely* sorry for …

4 I *would/must* apologise for …

5 Please could you also *give/make* my apologies to (name of person)?

Explaining and giving excuses

6 I'm afraid the problem couldn't be *avoided/denied*.

7 I can't get *out of/away from* going to my grandmother's party.

8 I'm afraid the decision wasn't *up to/out of* me.

9 It isn't my *fault/blame* that I was late.

Showing concern

10 I hope you *won't/shouldn't* mind too much.

11 I hope you won't be *terribly/completely* disappointed.

12 I hope it won't *cause/put* you any inconvenience.

3 **Which phrases in Activity 2 can you use in an informal email?**

4 **Look at the phrasal verbs in questions 7 and 8 in Activity 2 and answer the questions.**

1 Which one means *not my responsibility* and which one means *impossible to avoid*?

2 Are phrasal verbs more frequently used in formal or informal writing?

5 **Which of the intensifying adverbs in the box can you use with both *sorry* and *disappointed*?**

absolutely awfully deeply enormously
extremely incredibly terribly totally

LANGUAGE TIP

Fixed phrases or collocations (e.g. *owe someone an apology*) are often used to apologise, make excuses, show concern, etc.

6 **Work in pairs. Read the exam task and discuss the kind of information you should include and in which paragraph.**

You receive an email from your English-speaking friend Sam. Write an **email** to Sam, apologising and explaining that you can't look after his dog as there is something important you've forgotten you had to do. Write **140–190** words.

> Thanks so much for offering to look after my dog while I'm away. I really appreciate it. I know that Bonzo will love staying with you and be really well looked after. Just to confirm – I'll be away from 11–14 August.
> Thanks again
> Sam

7 **Write your email. Then check your work for spelling, grammar and punctuation mistakes and check you have written 140–190 words.**

EXAM TIP

You can use phrasal verbs and intensifying adverbs, e.g. *extremely*, *absolutely*, in informal writing.

1 Complete the text with the words in the box. You will need to use some words more than once.

ability	able	could	couldn't
know	managed	unable	

WOMAN **139**

Learning to live again

Six years ago, Claire Robertson woke from a coma, surrounded by her husband and children. She had no idea who they were.

One day I woke up in hospital surrounded by my husband and four children. I **(1)** .... recognise any of them. I had lost my memory. The first person I was **(2)** .... to recognise was my youngest son. This was after I had been in hospital for over five weeks. He spoke to me from behind a curtain and it was his voice that I was **(3)** .... to recognise.
I had to believe that my husband was who he said he was but I was **(4)** .... to remember anything about him or our previous life together. I was convinced that I **(5)** .... never have been married to him or lived in our house. I didn't **(6)** .... how to find my way around the house and I'd lost the **(7)** .... to cook.
Things started to get better when I began to write things down. And slowly I've **(8)** .... to piece together some memories. But much of the time I am still a stranger in my own world. I'm **(9)** .... to watch family videos, which remind me of the twenty years I've lost, without crying. Still, I'm very grateful for the love of my family. I **(10)** .... have got this far without them.

2 Choose the correct word to complete the sentences, A, B or C.

1 She comes .... as being very shy.
   A across   **B** up   **C** round
2 We came .... the idea after a lot of consideration.
   A out   **B** up with   **C** across
3 I'd never come .... him before but he seemed to know who I was.
   A out   **B** across   **C** up
4 We've got a revision test coming .... soon.
   A down   **B** up   **C** over
5 My parents eventually came .... to the idea of having a party at home for my eighteenth.
   A out   **B** up   **C** round
6 She's always coming .... with coughs and colds.
   A up   **B** down   **C** across
7 His secret will come .... one of these days.
   A out   **B** round   **C** up
8 The film comes .... on Friday. We'll need to book tickets.
   A across   **B** up with   **C** out

3 Complete the second sentence so that it has a similar meaning to the first sentence, using no more than five words, including the word given.

1 'We did it on our own without any help,' they said proudly.
   THEMSELVES
   They said they ...., without any help.
2 'The accident was all my fault,' she cried.
   BLAMED
   She .... accident.
3 'I always put a note in my diary about my friends' birthdays,' she said.
   REMINDS
   She said she always .... her friends' birthdays by putting a note in her diary.
4 'I am very sorry I'm late,' he said.
   APOLOGISED
   He .... late.
5 'I might become a doctor. I haven't decided yet,' She said.
   THINKING
   She said that she .... a doctor.
6 'I believe I am a very lucky person,' he said.
   CONSIDERS
   He .... a very lucky person.

Say what you mean

Speaking

1 **Work in pairs and discuss the questions.**

1 How much variation is there in people's speech in different parts of your country?
2 Are there any accents you find particularly attractive?
3 How easy is it to change your accent? Why might some people want to do this?

2 **When people make these gestures, what are they trying to communicate?**

1 shrugging their shoulders
2 raising their eyebrows
3 shaking their head
4 crossing their fingers
5 rolling their eyes

3 **What gestures do you frequently use when speaking? Do you think gestures mean the same in all languages? Why do some cultures use gestures more?**

Multiple matching (Part 3)

▶ **EXAM** FOCUS p.205

4 ▶ 42 **You will hear five different speakers talking about communicating with people. For speakers 1–5, choose from the list (A–H) what each person says. Use the letters only once. There are three extra letters which you do not need to use.**

A It's a mistake to think that all women are good communicators.
B Some people give the wrong impression by the way they speak.
C Some accents are considered more attractive than others.
D Most people change the way they speak in different situations.
E Speaking in a particular way brings many advantages.
F It is impossible for people to change the way they speak.
G The gestures people use give away important information about them.
H The way people speak is an important part of their identity.

Speaker 1 ☐
Speaker 2 ☐
Speaker 3 ☐
Speaker 4 ☐
Speaker 5 ☐

EXAM TIP

During the second listening check your answers carefully. Make sure you do not put the same answer twice.

5 Work in pairs and discuss how true you think these statements are.

1 Women are better listeners than men.

2 Men are better at public speaking.

3 Women are better at expressing their emotions than men.

4 Men don't really talk about personal issues with their friends.

say, speak, talk and *tell*

6 Complete the sentences with the correct form of the verbs.

say	speak	talk	tell

1 I don't .... a word of Chinese but I want to learn.

2 Everyone .... I have a big mouth and I shouldn't talk so much.

3 Don't .... me you haven't sent the invitations yet!

4 Why don't you just .... there's been a misunderstanding? I'm sure she'll forgive you.

5 That was a very silly thing to .... to her.

6 We're not very good at .... about our feelings.

7 Which of the words in the box go with *tell* or *talk*? Copy and complete the table below.

the difference	a joke	lies	rubbish
(someone) a secret	sense		a story
the truth	to yourself		

tell	talk

8 Choose the correct verb to complete the expressions. Then match the examples with the meanings A–F.

1 It goes without *speaking/saying* that it's easier to learn a language when you're young.

2 Actions *speak/say* louder than words.

3 Just *say/speak* the word if you need anything.

4 He hasn't got much to *say/speak* for himself.

5 Generally *speaking/saying*, I think women are better communicators than men.

6 I have more respect for a politician who *says/speaks* their mind.

A says what they are thinking

B on the whole

C don't hesitate to ask

D everyone knows this

E says very little

F what you do is more important than what you say

Ways of speaking

9 Complete the sentences with the correct form of the verbs in the box.

mumble	mutter	whisper	yell

1 My teacher .... at me in front of the whole class because I'd forgotten my homework again.

2 You can only .... in the library.

3 My dad .... to himself when he doesn't agree with politicians on the TV.

4 Some people in my class always .... the answers and I can't understand what they're saying.

10 Work with a partner. Think of some situations when

1 actions speak louder than words.

2 it's best to speak your mind.

3 it's acceptable to yell at someone.

4 it's rude to whisper.

it is, there is

▶ **GRAMMAR** REFERENCE p.170

1 **Choose the correct pronoun. Both answers may be possible.**

1 *It/There* will be very hot so you don't have to wear a jacket and tie.

2 *It/There* always used to be arguments about who paid the bill when we ate out.

3 *It/There* seems to be a lack of communication.

4 *It/There* once used to be unacceptable to eat in the street.

5 *It/There* might be a good idea to find out what the customs are before you visit a country.

6 *It/There* is a long time until dinner so have a snack now.

2 **Complete these sentences with *it* or *there* and a form of *be* if necessary.**

1 .... not unusual to have dinner at 10.30p.m.

2 .... common for men to greet each other with a kiss on the cheek.

3 .... might sometimes be applause when a guest arrives.

4 .... no need to tip the waiters in restaurants.

3 **In which countries are the customs in Activity 2 true? There may be more than one answer.**

Argentina   China   Japan   Saudi Arabia

4 **Use sentences with *it* and *there* to describe customs in your country.**

Key word transformations (Part 4)

▶ **EXAM** FOCUS p.201

5 **For questions 1–6, complete the second sentence so that it has a similar meaning to the first sentence, using the word given. Do not change the word given. You must use between two and five words, including the word given.**

1 I had a wonderful time and I really enjoyed seeing everyone again. **GREAT**
I had a wonderful time and .... everyone again.

2 The weather forecast has predicted more snow. **GOING**
According to the weather forecast, ... more snow.

3 She said she was really pleased you could all come. **WONDERFUL**
She said .... you could all come.

4 The park used to have a playground for children. **BE**
In the park .... a playground for children.

5 He said I didn't need to make an appointment. **NO**
He said .... for me to make an appointment.

6 I would suggest taking your coat. **MIGHT**
I think that .... a good idea to take your coat.

Interview (Part 1)

▶ **EXAM** FOCUS p.206

1 Tick the things you should do in Part 1 of the Speaking test.

1 ask the examiner questions ☐
2 speak to both examiners ☐
3 answer personal questions ☐
4 give opinions about things ☐
5 talk to your partner ☐
6 answer the same questions as your partner ☐

2 Check your answers by looking at the Exam focus on page 206.

3 Choose a topic and write three questions about it to ask other students. Use the ideas in the box to help you.

family	free time	future plans	holidays
home town	likes and dislikes		work/studies

4 Work in groups. Practise asking and answering each other's questions.

Long turn (Part 2)

▶ **EXAM** FOCUS p.206

5 Look at the photos and the exam task. Which of the following will you need to do?

1 compare ☐
2 speculate ☐
3 describe in detail ☐
4 give a personal reaction ☐
5 discuss advantages and disadvantages ☐
6 give examples ☐
7 use paraphrases ☐
8 agree and disagree ☐

6 Work in pairs.

Student A: Do the task on this page.

Student B: Turn to page 156. Take turns to do your task. Try to speak for a minute each.

> **Student A**: Here are your photographs. They show people trying to communicate a message. Compare the photographs and say which of these ways of communicating messages is most effective.

EXAM TIP

The examiner will tell you the task but it is also written on the paper with the pictures, so you can remind yourself of it.

Speaking and vocabulary

1 How do dogs communicate with each other and with humans? Use some of this vocabulary.

bark	growl	lick	sniff	wag their tail
mark their territory		raise the hair on their backs		

Gapped text (Part 6)

▶ **EXAM** FOCUS p.202

2 You are going to read an article about how dogs communicate. Six sentences have been removed from the article. Choose from the sentences A–G the one which fits each gap (1–6). There is one extra sentence which you do not need to use.

EXAM TIP

When you have finished, read through the text to check that it makes sense and that you haven't used a sentence more than once.

---

3 Compare your answers. Which words or expressions in the text helped you to decide?

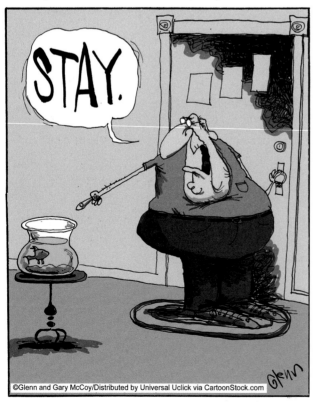
©Glenn and Gary McCoy/Distributed by Universal Uclick via CartoonStock.com

Speaking

4 Discuss these questions in groups.

1 In what ways have any pets you have had communicated with you?

2 In what ways do animals have a good or bad effect on our lives? Use the topics below to help you think.

entertainment	environment	food
health	sport	transport

Vocabulary

idioms: animals

5 Read sentences 1–8. Then try to work out the meaning of the idioms in sentences A–H and match them with 1–8.

1 Why don't we have the meeting during lunch?

2 I've never seen Anna so nervous.

3 Tom's party was meant to be a secret.

4 My boss is actually quite nice when you get to know her.

5 Nobody even knew Kate was going out with anyone.

6 My kids never care when I tell them off.

7 When she went to university there were lots of other people just as clever as her.

8 The team was really thirsty after playing tennis in that heat.

A Her *bark is worse than her bite*.

B However, Lucy *let the cat out of the bag* by letting him see the invitation.

C So she really *put the cat among the pigeons* by announcing she was getting married.

D This was a shock, because she was *a big fish in a little pond* at school.

E She's *having kittens* about what to do next.

F That way we could *kill two birds with one stone*.

G It's like *water off a duck's back*.

H At the end, they *made a beeline* for the café.

6 Work in pairs. Make sentences about your own lives using some of the idioms in Activity 5.

Inside a dog's world

Alexandra Horowitz, a psychologist who studies dog behaviour, describes dogs as 'anthropologists among us', and in her engaging book *Inside of a Dog*, she studies them with the same intensity and affection that they devote to us. Even in the middle of a busy modern city, we're surrounded by all kinds of animals that share our space and our food, but only one of them bothers to study us.

To rats, crows and cockroaches, we're mostly an irritation and sometimes a threat. Dogs are different. [1] They also try to control us, persuading us to provide them with food and shelter. People are used as tools to solve the puzzles of closed doors and empty water dishes.

Most interestingly, dogs confirm our prejudices about other people. [2] But in fact, when their dog greets a stranger with a wagging tail or a growl, he is copying his owner's unconscious signals, which he has gradually worked out through smells and body language.

If we want to understand the life of any animal, we need to think about it from their perspective. We need to know what it can sense and how it responds to this. And, whereas humans see the world, a dog smells it. [3] Instead they bravely stride up to an unknown object and take a nice deep sniff. When a dog turns its head towards you, it is to let his nose 'look' at you. The eyes just come along for the ride.

Sniffing objects gets smells to the brain via receptor cells in the nose. Humans have around six million of these. Six million seems an enormous amount but some dogs have more than 300 million, which explains their remarkable sense of smell. They put this to great use socially, especially by lifting a leg at every lamp post to convey a message. [4] Instead, the purpose is for them to leave information about themselves; how often they walk by that spot, their recent victories and how interested they are in mating. In this way, the pile of scents becomes a kind of noticeboard.

All mammals tend to produce the same kinds of sounds to express certain meanings and dogs take advantage of this when they communicate with humans. They are able to vary the length, range, pitch and frequency of their barks in different situations. [5] It has been suggested that dogs learnt to develop a wider vocal range as they became domesticated.

[6] Look a dog in the eyes, and you get a definite feeling that he's looking back. When information, reassurance or guidance is needed, they seem to inspect our faces. In fact, we are known by our dogs probably far better than we know them. They are amazingly skilful at spying on our every move, knowing about our comings and goings and whether we are anxious or sad. They are students of our behaviour and what makes them especially good is that they never tire of watching out for changes in our expressions and moods.

A All dog owners think that their pet is a good judge of character.

B Because of this, forgetting what we think we know about dogs is the best way to begin to understand them.

C But what about a dog's ability to see and understand?

D However, contrary to popular belief, the main point of this kind of communication is not to mark their territory.

E As a result, most people can tell whether a dog is happy, lonely or aggressive just by listening.

F Unlike wolves, they inspect our actions, interpret our emotions and, over time, learn how to please us.

G Dogs don't touch new things or stare at them as we do.

Subject/Verb agreement

▶ **GRAMMAR** REFERENCE p.175

1 **Look at examples 1–7 from the article on page 145 and choose the correct option.**

1 Only one of these animals *bother/bothers* to study us.

2 People *is/are* used as tools to solve the puzzles of closed doors and empty water dishes.

3 All dog owners *think/thinks* that their dog is a good judge of character.

4 Sniffing objects *get/gets* smells to the dog via receptor cells in the nose.

5 Six million *seem/seems* an enormous amount.

6 The good news *is/are* that this behaviour now seems to act as a greeting.

7 When information, reassurance or guidance *is/are* needed, dogs seem to inspect our faces.

2 **Match the examples in Activity 1 with the following rules.**

A singular verb is used after

A nouns which end in *s* but are not plural.

B expressions of quantity, measurement, time and distance.

C words/expressions such as *everyone, anything, hardly anyone, only one of, more than one.*

D abstract/uncountable nouns.

E an *-ing* clause as the subject.

A plural verb is used after

F nouns which are plural but don't end in *s.*

G words/expressions such as *both of, all, plenty of, the majority of.*

3 **Choose the correct alternative in each of these sentences. Both may be possible.**

1 The police *has/have* charged him with animal cruelty.

2 We gave her advice on looking after her dog but she didn't take *it/them.*

3 1,000 pounds *is/are* a lot of money to pay for a puppy.

4 Both my sisters *understand/understands* what a commitment having a pony can be.

5 Everyone *has/have* fallen in love with my new kitten.

6 Neither of them *know/knows* how to train a dog properly.

7 Our family *has/have* always had a variety of different pets.

8 There *is/are* a couple of dog bowls over there.

4 **Complete the animal facts with the correct form of the verb in brackets.**

Did you know?

- Despite the saying 'as blind as a bat', the majority of bats **(1)** .... (*be*) able to see perfectly well.

- The name 'mouse' comes from the Sanskrit for 'little thief'. People **(2)** .... (*have*) provided food for them ever since farming began. However, although everyone **(3)** .... (*seem*) to believe that mice like cheese, most **(4)** .... (*prefer*) chocolate.

- Rabbits are the world's third most popular pet. All modern rabbits **(5)** .... (*have*) been bred from the European wild rabbit.

- 85 percent of cats' time **(6)** .... (*be*) spent doing nothing.

- Medical advice **(7)** .... (*have*) suggested that owning a pet is good for your health.

- Current news **(8)** .... (*be*) claiming that dogs can be successful at detecting cancer.

5 **Complete these sentences so that they are true for you.**

1 Some of my friends …

2 The news these days …

3 People who live in towns …

4 The majority of football fans …

5 The staff at the school I go/went to …

6 Most of my family …

Open cloze (Part 2)

▶ **EXAM** FOCUS p.201

1 **Read the article and answer the questions in pairs.**

1 What is unusual about Kanzi?

2 In what way do scientists disagree about why animals can't speak?

3 Which group of animals are scientists particularly interested in studying, and why?

2 **For questions 1–8, read the text and think of the word which best fits each gap. There is an example at the beginning.**

The animal world's communication kings

The majority of mammals **(0)** _are_ able to understand some language, even though they can't 'talk back'. Kanzi, a bonobo ape, can recognise about 3,000 words, which **(1)** _____ a very impressive number and more than any other mammal understands, apart **(2)** _____ humans. So why is it that most mammals can understand but not speak? Scientists are divided on the issue. **(3)** _____ some believe that it is due to physical factors like tongue control, others are convinced that the key could be genetic.

Despite their inability to talk, some animals – around six species in all – can hear a sound, copy it and then reproduce it **(4)** _____ order to interact socially. Interestingly, the animals that can do this are dissimilar both to humans and to **(5)** _____ other. This diverse group includes animals **(6)** _____ as parrots and whales. Scientists have been studying the brain pathways of this group of animals with great interest. As a result **(7)** _____ this research, they hope that they will soon gain some insight **(8)** _____ our own unique talent for language.

3 **Check your answers. Which answers relate to subject/verb agreement?**

4 **Discuss these questions.**

1 Which method of animal communication do you think is the most interesting?

2 Which animals would you most like to be able to communicate with?

Essay (Part 1)

proofreading

▶ **WRITING** REFERENCE p.180

1 **Read the sentences 1–8. What type of spelling mistake (A–D) does each sentence contain? Correct the errors and compare your answers with another student.**

A missing letter   **C** wrong vowel

B extra letter   **D** wrong vowel order

1 I think that young people are definately spending too much time on social networking sites.

2 The goverment should do more to protect people's online privacy.

3 It's neccessary to see someone's face if you want to communicate with them properly.

4 Chatting online is a great way to make freinds.

5 Most of my friends are too dependant on their mobile phones – it's like an addiction.

6 It's suprising that so many people don't take online security very seriously.

7 It's rude when people anser their phone when they're having dinner with someone in a restaurant.

8 If I don't recieve many messages daily I feel depressed.

2 **Work in pairs. Look at the sentences in Activity 1 again and answer the questions.**

1 Do you think the spelling errors cause any confusion?

2 Which of the sentences do you agree with?

3 **Read the exam task and student's essay and follow the instructions.**

1 Correct the eight spelling mistakes in this essay.

2 Decide if you agree with the points made and compare your ideas with another student.

> In your class you have been talking about the importance of communication. Now your teacher has asked you to write an essay.
>
> Write your essay using **all** the notes and give reasons for your point of view.
>
> Young people are increasingly communicating using technology instead of talking face-to-face. Do you think this is a problem?
>
> **Notes**
> Write about:
>
> 1 relationships
> 2 communication skills
> 3 _security_ (your own idea)

Young people are increasingly communicating using technology instead of talking face-to-face. Do you think this is a problem?

I think there are both positive and negative points in the rise of young people's use of technology for communication purposes.

Firstly, it has become a lot easier to contact friends extremly quickly by phone or on social networking sites. This means making arrangments is easier, particularly during holidays when you can't communicate with your friends at college every day. I beleive this helps to make my relationships with friends stronger.

However, young people's safety has been put at risk becaus of the increase in this type of communication. The internet has become a place where bullies can post horrible and very hurtfull messages without having to identify themselves. This can affect vulnerable people very badly.

Another negative point is that young people's communication skills are sufering. They don't bother with the correct punctuation and often use abbreviations when texting. Sometimes this makes it hard to understand what they are trying to say.

Overall, I'm convinced that communicating using tecnology is very benefitial; it brings people closer together and helps young people to stay in touch with friends who live far away. But more needs to be done to make sure that young people's safety and privacy are protected.

4 **Work in pairs. Turn to page 160 and do the exam task.**

5 **Write your essay in 140–190 words and then check your work using the writing checklist on page 179.**

EXAM TIP

Remember to leave enough time to check your work for spelling, punctuation and grammar mistakes.

1 Choose the correct word.

1 *It/There* is unlikely to be time for questions after the presentation.

2 A high percentage of people *is/are* unable to remember their own mobile phone number.

3 *It/There* is some evidence that owning a pet is good for your health.

4 Both cats and dogs *is/are* unable to recognise human faces.

5 Only one of my brothers *has/have* a problem with remembering people's names.

6 Neither my brother nor my sister *like/likes* cats.

7 The police *has/have* found my grandmother's missing dog.

8 Information on ways to improve your memory *is/are* available on the website.

9 I think *there/it* should be possible to adapt to someone else's culture.

10 *It/There* may be a problem with our computer.

2 Choose the correct word to complete these sentences.

1 My students take no notice when I shout at them. It's like water off a duck's ....
   A head   **B** back   **C** feathers

2 Cycling to work means I get exercise too, so I'm killing two .... with one stone.
   A birds   **B** ducks   **C** rats

3 In her school sports club, Jo was a big fish in a little............
   A river   **B** lake   **C** pond

4 Dan put the cat among the .... when he resigned.
   A blackbirds **B** owls   **C** pigeons

5 Actions .... louder than words.
   A speak   **B** say   **C** talk

6 He's very quiet and never seems to have much to .... for himself.
   A speak   **B** say   **C** talk

7 I wish you would speak more clearly and not .... like that.
   A whisper   **B** mumble   **C** mutter

8 He really does .... rubbish sometimes.
   A say   **B** speak   **C** talk

3 Choose the correct word to complete the sentences. Sometimes more than one answer is possible.

ahead   down   in   into   of   off   on   over   through

1 We went .... the plan for his escape many times.

2 The climb was called .... because of bad weather.

3 The prison officers had to give .... to the prisoners' demands.

4 The effect of the medicine soon began to wear .... and my headache returned.

5 He insisted .... carrying all my equipment because I was so tired.

6 I've never been involved .... a serious accident.

7 She seems confident .... her ability to pass the test.

8 They had been .... a lot of difficult times so they deserved their success.

9 We were asked to hand .... our documents to the police for them to check.

10 The instructor told us .... for not using the equipment safely, like he taught us.

11 The search for the missing boy turned .... a murder hunt.

12 Against everyone's advice the team went .... with the bike race.

13 The computer network has gone .... so I can't send any emails this afternoon.

14 The police succeeded .... catching the thief very quickly and efficiently.

15 He was suspected .... the crime even though there were no witnesses.

4 There is a mistake in each of the following sentences. Underline the mistakes and correct them. There may be more than one possibility.

1 If Sarah had listened to her parents she will never have become a world champion.

2 If my father doesn't speak Russian, he wouldn't have got the job in Moscow.

3 If I had saved more money I would been able to go on holiday next month.

4 If I were younger I work much harder.

5 If only that car doesn't cost so much, I would buy it.

6 I wish my brother help me more with my homework.

7 Suppose we will not go to the party this evening.

8 I'd rather you come home before midnight.

9 You aren't allowed using Facebook in the college library.

10 It was a waste of time doing all that research. We needn't to do it.

11 They have just have their car stolen.

12 We're getting a friend looked after our house while we're away.

13 After trying several times we could finally get tickets for the show.

14 I need to remind me of my passwords.

15 You shouldn't blame myself for losing your wallet – it wasn't my fault.

PROGRESS TEST 3

Multiple-choice cloze (Part 1)   Open cloze (Part 2)

5 For questions 1–8, read the text below and decide which answer (A, B, C or D) best fits each gap. There is an example at the beginning.

Watch your (body) language

Most research now shows that as much as 70–80 percent of human interaction may be non-verbal. This kind of communication has been **(0)** _C widely_ studied since ancient times in an **(1)** .... to understand people's characters, and experts have endlessly **(2)** .... the significance of the way we move and position our bodies. **(3)** .... many feel that the study of body language can be over-simplistic, there is some evidence to show that some postures and movements indicate our emotional states of mind. The **(4)** .... people shake hands, for example, can be a good indicator of the power balance between them. Pulling the person towards you or grabbing hold of someone's elbow can show you want to **(5)** .... control. Personal space is another interesting area. The vast **(6)** .... of westerners feel uncomfortable if a friend stands closer than 45 centimetres, although this will **(7)** .... from country to country.
And finally, it is likely that, if someone is **(8)** .... to you, they will copy the way you stand or move. If you're trying to make somebody relax, it can also help to 'mirror' their movements in this way.

0	**A** highly	**B** deeply	**C** widely	**D** strongly
1	**A** act	**B** action	**C** attempt	**D** approach
2	**A** talked	**B** argued	**C** disagreed	**D** discussed
3	**A** But	**B** Although	**C** However	**D** Nevertheless
4	**A** way	**B** style	**C** custom	**D** manner
5	**A** be	**B** take	**C** bring	**D** stay
6	**A** number	**B** quantity	**C** majority	**D** amount
7	**A** vary	**B** alter	**C** compare	**D** contrast
8	**A** attracted	**B** appealed	**C** approved	**D** fascinated

6 For questions 9–16, read the text below and think of the word that best fits each gap. Use only one word in each gap. There is an example at the beginning.

Life without limits

Tim Shieff shouts from a rooftop nine metres **(0)** _above_ us. 'You should see the view from here! It's awesome!' Just a **(9)** .... seconds earlier Tim was down among the shoppers, on the streets of his hometown. Then he suddenly began climbing up a series of walls **(10)** .... he reached a rooftop world, **(11)** .... is invisible to the rest of the city's residents. Then, with a leap, he was over a 3.6 metre gap to the next building, landing on a flat roof and pausing for a one-armed handstand.
This is nothing extraordinary for Shieff. The 22-year-old is a world champion of freerunning, which he defines **(12)** .... 'the way you create a path without following the normal options presented to you'.
Shieff **(13)** .... to be a breakdancer, and now combines dance moves with those from gymnastics and acrobatics to create **(14)** .... own very individual style of movement. It was after he **(15)** .... seen the TV programme *Jump London* that he became inspired to discover rooftops.
Shieff agrees that it is a risky sport but adds that it is a calculated risk, based **(16)** .... years of practice, and he is always in control.

Word formation (Part 3)

7 For questions 17–24, read the text below. Use the word given in capitals at the end of some of the lines to form a word that fits the gap in the same line. There is an example at the beginning.

Memory Champions

Do you have what it takes to become a memory champion? You would need the
(0) *ability* to remember up **ABLE**
to 1000 numbers in a sequence in under an hour, plus several
other seemingly **(17)** .... **POSSIBILITY**
challenges.
The 'mind sport' of Memory was created in 1991. Today there
are **(18)** .... from thirty **COMPETITION**
countries participating in the sport with the aim of becoming the next World Memory Champion.
None of even the most
(19) .... memory **SUCCESS**
champions would claim to be **(20)** **SPECIAL**
.... gifted at memorising things. So how do they do it?
Well, apparently the brain is
better at remembering **(21)** **VISION**
.... images so memory champions spend a lot of time training their brains to translate abstract symbols into pictures. It's important to have a good
(22) .... in order to create **IMAGINE**
memorable images which the brain can store and then instantly recall at a later date.
Training your brain in this way
can be very **(23)** .... for **HELP**
anyone who needs to learn a lot of information in a short time.
Some people also believe that
this kind of training can be an **EFFECT**
(24) .... way of preventing memory loss as people get older.

Key word transformation (Part 4)

8 For questions 25–30, complete the second sentence so that it has a similar meaning to the first sentence, using the word given. Do not change the word given. You must use between two and five words, including the word given. Here is an example.

Example:
I'd strongly advise you not to get a dog just yet.
IF
I wouldn't get a dog just yet ....if I were...... you.

25 You mustn't cycle without wearing a helmet.
ALLOWED
You .... cycle without wearing a helmet.

26 Someone had already called the police so it wasn't necessary for you to call them.
NEED
Someone had already called the police so you .... them.

27 My parents would prefer me not to travel alone.
RATHER
My parents .... travel alone.

28 My grandfather would love to do extreme sports but he's too old.
WISHES
My grandfather .... extreme sports but he's too old.

29 'Don't forget to text me when you arrive,' Jake's mother said.
REMINDED
Jake's mother .... when he arrived.

30 I couldn't finish the race.
MANAGE
I .... finish the race.

Visuals for Speaking tests

Unit 3, Speaking focus, Activity 7
Student A

Your photos show people preparing or receiving gifts. Compare the photos and say what makes people happy about giving or receiving gifts.

> **What makes people happy about giving or receiving gifts?**

Unit 5, Speaking focus, Activity 5
Task 1

Student A: Look at the photos, which show people shopping for food. Compare the photos and say what the advantages and disadvantages are of shopping in these different ways.

Student B: Do you prefer to go shopping in town or shopping online?

> **What are the advantages and disadvantages of shopping in these different ways?**

Unit 11, Speaking focus, Activity 5

> **Which person is taking the most risks?**

Unit 7, Speaking focus, Activity 5

Task 1

Student A: Look at the photos, which show unusual places to live. Compare the photos and say why you think people might choose to live in these places .

Student B: Which of these places would you prefer to live in?

> **Why do you think people might choose to live in these places?**

Unit 3, Speaking focus, Activity 7

Student B

Your photos show people who love horses. Compare the photos and say what might make these people feel so strongly about their horses.

> **What might make these people feel so strongly about their horses?**

Unit 5, Speaking focus, Activity 5

Task 2

Student B: Look at the photos, which show people having dinner. Compare the photos and say what the people enjoy about eating in these different ways.

Student A: Do you prefer to eat in front of the TV or to sit at the table with other people?

> **What might the people enjoy about eating in these different ways?**

Unit 7, Speaking focus, Activity 5

Task 2

Student A: Look at the photos, which show unusual places to work. Compare the photos and say how difficult you think it would be to work in these places.

Student B: Are you an adventurous person?

How difficult do you think it would be to work in these places?

Unit 11, Speaking focus, Activity 6

Which person is taking the most risks?

Unit 13, Speaking focus, Activity 5

Student B: Compare the two different ways of remembering vocabulary and say what the people might find effective about doing these things.

Student A: How do you remember vocabulary best?

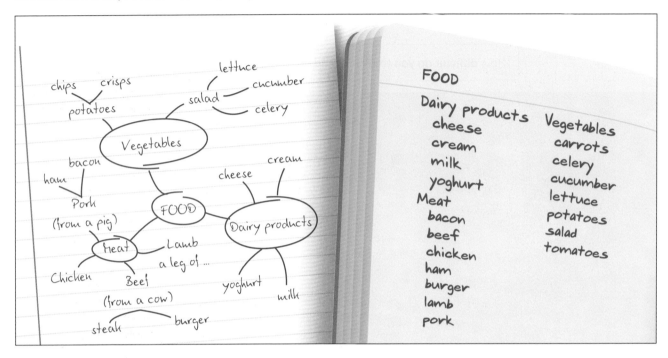

Unit 14, Speaking focus, Activity 6

Student B: Here are your photographs. They show people communicating in different ways. Compare the photographs and say which form of communication would be the most difficult to learn how to do.

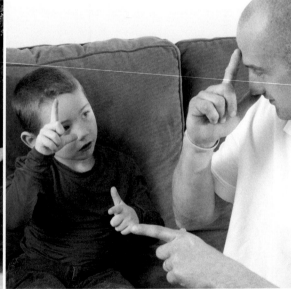

Communication activities

Unit 2, Use of English focus, Activity 3

PERSONALITY QUIZ

How to score:

Very likely = 5 points
Quite likely = 4 points
Neither likely nor unlikely = 3 points
Quite unlikely = 2 points
Very unlikely = 1 point

Find out

how *sociable* you are (add your scores for questions 1 and 5)
how *organised* you are (add your scores for questions 2 and 6)
how *creative* you are (add your scores for questions 3 and 4)

	7–10 points	5–6 points	1–4 points
Sociability My score =	You are adventurous and sociable. You enjoy going out and meeting new people. You're confident and fun to be with but you get bored easily.	You are a bit of both. Read both descriptions to find out more.	You are independent and shy. You need time to be alone. You take a long time to make new friends. You aren't easily led by other people.
Organisation My score =	You are organised and practical. You like to be in charge. You're very good at getting things done but you find it difficult to relax.	You are a bit of both. Read both descriptions to find out more.	You are relaxed and spontaneous. You don't like to plan ahead. You think there are more important things than being on time and meeting deadlines.
Creativity My score =	You are imaginative and creative. You're always full of ideas. You prefer to look at the big picture rather than focusing on detail.	You are a bit of both. Read both descriptions to find out more.	You are thoughtful and realistic. You pay attention to detail. You're cautious when making decisions. You always see both sides of an argument.

Unit 2, Writing focus, Activity 7

Read the exam task. Brainstorm ideas and decide whether you agree/partly agree/ disagree with the question. Look at the notes and decide which points to include in each paragraph. Then write your essay.

In your English class you have been talking about family relationships. Now your teacher has asked you to write an essay.

Write an essay using **all** the points and give reasons for your point of view. Write **140–190** words.

Is it better to have older or younger parents?

Notes
Write about:

1 things in common
2 experience
3 .... (your own idea)

Unit 10, Vocabulary and Listening focus, Activity 3

LIFESTYLE

Results: Add up your scores.

	1	2	3	4	5	6	7	8
3 points	A	C	C	A	B	C	C	A
2 points	B	A	B	C	A	A	B	B
1 point	C	B	A	B	C	B	A	C

Circle friendships
Score: 12 or less

You have, or want, a wide circle of friends, and people might say you have a gift for friendship. You seek to know people in many walks of life, with different lifestyles and characters. You like nothing more than being with them all but you may also worry that different friends of yours won't get on. This shows that you have many parts to your character, and different friends appeal to different parts. The risk of your friendship type is that you may not actually get to know any of your friends very well. They are drawn to your extrovert character though that can act as a barrier to intimacy.

Ladder friendships
Score: 13–18

You view life as a journey of change, evolution and progress. You therefore value friends who share your journey, or who are experiencing the same things as you. You like to encourage and help your friends get on in life and value it when they encourage and help you. You're very self-confident and enjoy meeting new people and make friends easily. But sometimes old friends will feel you've left them behind, though they will admit that you are an inspiring person to be with, someone who both challenges and excites them.

Soulmate friendships
Score: 19–24

You value a small number of close friends, perhaps just one, and regard other people in your life as acquaintances. The benefit of soulmate friendship is the chance of knowing someone well and allowing them to know you. You are loyal and completely trustworthy. You are self-sufficient and don't depend on friendship to maintain your self-esteem. The risk you face is of disappointment with friends, since it's quite hard to meet someone you connect with so strongly. In fact, you may well have had a close friend in the past, and now feel that you don't. You value friendship so much because you know the treasure it offers.

Unit 11, Grammar focus, Activity 7
Student B

Think of what you might say in the following situations. Use *I wish/if only* and other expressions with hypothetical meaning. Then roleplay the situations with your partner.

Situation 1: You are at a theme park with Student A. Student A wants to go on a new roller coaster ride at the theme park. You are afraid of heights and don't want to go on the ride. Try and persuade Student A to choose a different activity.

Situation 2: You are on a walking trip in the mountains with Student A. You are reading the map but you think you are lost. Suggest what action you should take.

Unit 8, Grammar focus, Activity 3

Match the underlined examples with the verb forms in the box.

going to   might   past simple   present continuous
present perfect   present simple   will   would

Interviewer: Lauren, how **(1)** did you hear about this job?

Lauren: Well, I **(2)** spotted the advert while I was on the internet. **(3)** I think it's something **(4)** I'd be good at.

Interviewer: Being an entertainment coordinator **(5)** will involve looking after very young children. **(6)** Have you had much experience of doing this?

Lauren: Well, **(7)** I look after my niece and nephew every month and **(8)** I'm taking them on a cycling holiday tomorrow.

Interviewer: Well, **(9)** you might be unlucky, I'm afraid, because **(10)** I've heard that **(11)** it's going to rain.

Lauren: Oh **(12)** I'm sure **(13)** we'll still have a lot of fun.

Interviewer: Well, **(14)** you sound very positive, and this is one of the qualities **(15)** we're looking for. Anyway, enjoy your weekend!

Lauren: Thanks.

Interviewer: Lauren, thanks for coming. **(16)** We'll write soon, but don't worry if **(17)** you don't hear anything for a few days.

Find the 'reported' versions of the underlined examples above in the email on page 84. Verbs 12–15 are not reported in the email.

Unit 11, Grammar focus, Activity 7
Student A

Think of what you might say in the following situations. Use *I wish/if only* and other expressions with hypothetical meaning. Then roleplay the situations with your partner.

Situation 1: You are at a theme park with Student B. You want to go on a new roller coaster ride.

Situation 2: You are lost in the mountains and Student B is reading the map. You know that you are better at reading maps than Student B. You are angry with yourself for getting into this situation.

Unit 7, Writing focus, Activity 5

Read the exam task. Brainstorm ideas and plan how you will organise it. Then write the essay.

In your English class, you have been talking about different kinds of holidays. Now your teacher has asked you to write an essay.

Write an essay using **all** the points and give reasons for your point of view. Write **140–190** words.

Is it better to have a holiday abroad or stay in your own country?

Notes
Write about:

1 cost
2 environmental issues
3 _____ (your own idea)

Unit 4, Listening focus, Activity 1

1B 2A 3C 4A 5C

Unit 8, Listening focus, Activity 3

In my work as a counsellor, I'm already seeing a huge increase in the number of victims of cyber bullying on social network sites and this is a trend that can only get worse. To deal with bullying or other problems that can occur online, social networking counsellors will support people in their cyber relationships using the same counselling skills we use today. The only difference is that, because we'll be online, it'll be easier for people to contact us when they need us – in the evenings, for example. This may mean that we'll have to change our working patterns and work out of office hours.

Unit 5, Grammar focus, Activity 7

Look at the table and choose the correct words in sentences 1–8.

	much	many	a lot of/lots of	some	a few/very few	hardly any	a little/a bit of/very little	any	no
In positive sentences		•	•	•	•	•	•		•
In negative sentences	•	•	•					•	
With countable nouns		•	•	•	•	•		•	•
With uncountable nouns	•		•	•		•	•	•	•

1 I don't eat *many/much* fresh fruit.
2 There aren't *a lot of/hardly any* healthy snacks in my local shop.
3 I drink *very few/very little* water.
4 We eat *hardly any/any* meat at home.
5 I drink *a lot of/many* orange juice.
6 I only eat *a little/a few* eggs a week.
7 There isn't *no/any* chocolate in my bag.
8 I always have *some/a few* rice with dinner.

Unit 14, Writing focus, Activity 4

Read the exam task. Brainstorm ideas for a third point.

In your English class you have been talking about ways in which animals can be useful to humans. Now your teacher has asked you to write an essay.

Write your essay using **all** the notes and giving reasons for your point of view. Write **140–190** words.

Dogs are the most useful animals to humans.
Do you agree?

Notes
Write about:

1 guard dogs
2 police dogs
3 .... (your own idea)

Grammar reference

Contents

1 Adverbs

1.1 Formation of adverbs from adjectives

1 Many adverbs are formed by adding *-ly* to the adjective form of the word, e.g. *clear* → *clearly*.
For adjectives ending in *-y*, drop the *y* and add *-ily*, e.g. *happy* → *happily*.
For adjectives ending in *-le*, drop the *e* and add *-y*, e.g. *gentle* → *gently*.
For adjectives ending in *-ic*, add *-ally*, e.g. *automatic* → *automatically*.

2 Some words ending in *-ly* are adjectives only, not adverbs, e.g. *cowardly, friendly, silly*. If an adverb is needed, a phrase must be used:
*They greeted us **in a friendly way/manner**.*

3 Some words ending in *-ly* can be used both as adjectives and adverbs, e.g. *hourly, daily, nightly*.
*Take the medicine twice **daily** (adv). There is a **daily** (adj) flight to the island.*

4 Some adverbs have the same form as adjectives, e.g. *early, fast, hard, still, straight, better, best, worse, worst*.
*He's got a **fast** (adj) car and he drives it **fast** (adv).*
*She has **straight** (adj) hair. He looked **straight** (adv) at me.*

5 Some adverbs have two forms, one like the adjective and the other form ending in *-ly*, e.g. *clear, close, direct, easy, free, hard, high, late*. There is usually a difference in meaning.
*Stand **clear** of the doors. (= keep away)*
*Try to speak more **clearly**. (= so we can understand)*
*He works very **hard**. (= he makes a lot of effort)*
*He had **hardly** any petrol left. (= almost none)*
*The balloon was **high** up in the sky. (= a long way up)*
*They think very **highly** of you. (= have a good opinion)*
*Children under twelve travel **free**. (= don't have to pay)*
*You can walk **freely** in the hotel grounds.*
(= without restrictions)
*The train arrived **late**. (= after the time it was expected)*
*He's not been very well **lately**. (= recently)*

1.2 Comparison of adverbs

The comparison of adverbs is similar to that of adjectives. See 4.5.

1.3 Adverbs of manner

These adverbs are used to say how the action of the verb is carried out.

1 Common adverbs of manner include *accurately, badly, carefully, patiently, straight* and *well*. They usually come in the middle of the sentence, after the main verb. If the verb has an object, the adverb comes after the object.
He spoke (the words) **clearly**.
She went **straight** *to the house.*

2 Prepositional phrases may also be used adverbially to answer the question *How?*
I ordered the book **over the internet**.
He shouted **in a loud voice**.

1.4 Adverbs of frequency

1 These adverbs are used to talk about how often we do things. We can put them in order from most often to least often like this:

always   ↑ most often
almost always
generally/normally/regularly/usually
frequently/often/sometimes
occasionally
almost /never/hardly ever/rarely/seldom
not ... ever/never   ↓ least often

2 In statements and questions, these adverbs come

- after *be* when it is the only verb in the sentence.
  I am **always** *a bit depressed in winter.*

- after the first auxiliary verb when there is more than one verb.
  I have **often** *seen her walking here.*

- before the main verb when there is only one verb.
  We **sometimes** *watch a video on Friday evenings.*

- in questions, after the subject.
  Don't you **usually** *work with Jenny?*

3 In negative sentences, *not* comes before *always, generally, normally, often, regularly* and *usually*.
We **don't often** *see him nowadays.*

4 With imperatives, *always* and *never* come at the beginning of the sentence.
Always *look on the bright side of life.*
Never *refuse an opportunity.*

1.5 Other types of adverbs used to describe frequency

1 These are common adverbs of frequency:
once
twice   } *a day/week/month/year*
five times
several times
every day/week/month/morning/afternoon/evening
every three/couple of/few years
on Monday/Wednesday/weekdays, etc.

2 These adverbs usually come at the end of the sentence, e.g. *I phone my sister* **several times a day**.
He goes jogging **every morning**.
They go abroad **every few years**.
However, they may come at the beginning for emphasis.
Several times a month, *I go to the cinema.*

1.6 Adverbs of attitude

These adverbs do not modify the verb, but express the speaker's opinion or attitude.

1 The following adverbs explain how he/she is feeling:
honestly, personally, seriously, etc.
Personally, *I think it's wrong to hunt animals.*
Seriously, *this is an important question.*

2 The following adverbs comment on how likely something is: *actually, certainly, clearly, definitely, maybe, obviously, perhaps, possibly, probably, surely, etc.*
Perhaps/Maybe *it will rain tomorrow.*
Surely *he is going to come?*
We'll **probably** *be late.*

3 The following adverbs explain the speaker's reaction to some event: *annoyingly, hopefully, luckily, naturally, surprisingly, understandably, etc.*
Hopefully, *we'll win the match.*
Annoyingly, *I forgot my phone.*

4 Adverbs of attitude usually come at the beginning of the sentence. However, the adverbs *certainly, definitely, possibly* and *probably* usually come in the middle of the sentence, after the verb *be*, before the main verb, or after the first auxiliary verb.
He is **definitely** *not a friend of mine.*
I'll **certainly** *be seeing her tomorrow.*

1.7 Modifiers and intensifiers

USE We can use adverbs to make adjectives, other adverbs and verbs stronger (intensifiers) or weaker (modifiers).

1 We can use these adverbs before gradable adjectives (i.e. adjectives that can be used in the comparative) and adverbs:

- *very, extremely, really, particularly, terribly* (emphatic)
- *quite, pretty, fairly, rather* (weaker than *very*)
- *a bit*

*I felt **terribly upset** when I heard the news.*
*He drives **rather fast**.*
*I thought the story was **a bit silly**.*

Watch out! *quite* has two meanings.
*The picture was **quite** good.* (= good but not very good)
*Her cooking was **quite** wonderful.* (= very, very good)

---

2 Adverbs such as *almost, barely, hardly, nearly* and *scarcely* have a negative meaning. They come in the middle of the sentence.

*I almost/**nearly** missed the train.*
*We could **barely** hear the speaker.*
*She **hardly** knew anyone at the party.*

3 Extreme or absolute (non-gradable) adjectives include: *amazing, boiling, disastrous, fantastic, freezing, impossible, marvellous, superb, wonderful*, etc. We can use the following adverbs with extreme adjectives: *absolutely, really, completely*.

*The special effects were **absolutely amazing**.*
*I've just read a **superb** new book about Egypt.*
*I love swimming in the sea, but it's **absolutely freezing** at this time of year.*

4 We can use these adverbs to emphasise both adjectives and verbs: *just, completely, totally* (= in every way).

*I **completely/totally** forgot about your birthday.*
*It's **completely impossible** to finish in time.*
*You look **just fantastic**.*
*Let's **just** go.*

2 Articles

2.1 The definite article: *the*

We use the definite article *the*

- when the person or thing referred to is unique.
  ***The sun** came out and soon we were dry.*
  ***The President** is giving a speech tonight.*
  the London Marathon**, **the Olympic Games

- to talk about specific things when the context makes it clear what we are referring to.
  *Your shoes are in **the cupboard**.*
  *Your dinner's in **the fridge**.*

- to talk about previously mentioned things.
  *A man and a woman walked into the room. **The man** was wearing sunglasses.*

- with superlatives.
  *He's **the bravest person** in the team.*

- to talk about a generic class of things.
  ***The bicycle** was invented about 200 years ago.*
  ***The tiger** is in danger of becoming extinct.*

- with oceans, seas, rivers and deserts.
  *He's sailed across **the Atlantic** and **the Pacific**.*
  *We went by canoe up **the Orinoco**.*
  *She said she'd driven across **the Sahara**.*

- with plural mountain ranges and island groups.
  *Are **the Andes** as high as **the Himalayas**?*
  ***The British Isles** include **the Isle of Wight** and **the Isle of Man**.*

- with continents and countries whose name includes a common noun.
  *He's from **the Czech Republic**, but he's living in the United States.*

- with areas.
  *There is a range of mountains in **the north**.*

- with hotels, cinemas, theatres.
  *They had afternoon tea at **the Ritz**.*
  *That new Polish film is on at **the Odeon**.*

- with newspapers.
  The Times**, **The Guardian**, **The Independent

- with national groups.
  ***The English** are a mixed race.*

2.2 The indefinite article: *a/an*

We use the indefinite article *a/an*

- with (singular) jobs, etc.
  *She's **an architect**.*
  *Is your sister **a football fan**, too?*

- with singular countable nouns (mentioned for the first time or when it doesn't matter which one).
  *I'd like **a sandwich** and **a glass of orange juice**.*
  What you need is a rest.

2.2 The indefinite article: *a/an* (continued)

We use the indefinite article *a/an*

- with these numbers: 100, 1,000, 1,000,000.
  *There were over **a hundred** people at the wedding.*
  *He made **a million** pounds in one year.*

- in exclamations about singular countable nouns.
  *What **an amazing view**!*

2.3 Zero article

1 We use no article (zero article) when talking about

- uncountable, plural and abstract nouns used in their general sense.
  *We had awful **weather** on holiday.*
  ***Happiness** isn't the only thing in life.*

- continents and countries.
  *They are going to visit **Africa**.*
  *Have you been to **Nepal**?*

- mountains and lakes.
  *They are going to climb **Mount Everest**.*
  *Is **Lake Titicaca** in Peru?*

- villages, towns and cities.
  ***San Marco** is a pleasant little fishing village.*
  ***Saffron Walden** is a small market town near Cambridge.*
  ***Auckland** is the biggest city in New Zealand.*

- streets, roads, etc.
  In London, there are some huge shops on Oxford Street.

- magazines.
  *Do you read **Time** magazine?*

- illnesses.
  *I've got **flu** and Sue's got **indigestion**.*

> **Watch out!** *I've got **a headache** and I think I'm getting **a cold**.*

2 Also use no article in the following expressions:
to/at/from school/university/college
at home
go home
in/to class
to/in/into/from church
to/in/into/out of prison/hospital/bed
to/at/from work
for/at/to breakfast/lunch/dinner
by car/bus/bicycle/plane/train/tube/boat
on foot
by accident/chance

3 *as* and *like*; *as if/as though*

3.1 *like*

1 *like* can be a preposition, meaning *similar to* or *in the same way as*.
*Do you look **like** your sister?*
***Like** John, I hate cooking.*

2 We use the question *What … like?* when we are asking for a description of a person, place or thing.
*'What's the restaurant **like**?' 'Oh, really good.'*

3 *like* can mean *such as/for example*.
*Let's buy him something nice **like/such as** a CD.*

4 *feel like* + object/*-ing* is used to talk about something that we want or want to do.
*I **feel like (eating)** some crisps.*

5 *seem/sound/look like* + object is used to introduce an idea we may not be completely sure about.
*It **seems like** a good idea.*

6 *like* is not used before an adjective on its own.
They seem happy. It feels cold.

3.2 *as*

1 *as* can be a preposition, coming before the name of a job or a role, or to describe the purpose of something.
*She works **as** a sales manager.*
***As** your father, I can't allow you to do this.*
*We use the loft **as** a play room for the kids.*
*I think of her **as** my best friend.*

2 *as* can be a conjunction, followed by subject + verb.
*You should do **as** your parents say.*
*I'll do **as** we agreed earlier.*

> **Watch out!** In colloquial English *like* is also used as a conjunction in this way, but this is regarded as incorrect by some people and is not used in formal writing.
> ***Like** I said, he's a really nice guy.* (colloquial)
> *I want you to do **like** I tell you.* (colloquial)

3.3 *as if/as though*

As if/as though are conjunctions followed by subject + verb.

- They are followed by the present or present perfect when referring to something likely.
  *He looks **as if he's crying**.*
  *It looks **as if it's stopped raining**.*

- To show that something is imaginary or unlikely, they can be followed by the past tense.
  *He looked **as if he had seen** a ghost!*
  *He behaves **as if he knew** more than us.*

> **Watch out!** In colloquial English *like* is also used instead of *as if/as though*.
> *You look **like** you're worried.* (colloquial)
> *It looks **like** we're going to win.* (colloquial)

4 Comparing

4.1 Types of comparison

There are three types of comparison

1 to a higher degree (comparative form + *than*)
*Mountain climbing is **more dangerous than** windsurfing.*
*The Andes mountains are **higher than** the Alps.*

2 to the same degree (*as … as*)
*Hiring a car would cost **just as much as** getting a taxi.*
*I don't enjoy swimming **as much as** I used to.*

3 to a lower degree (with *less + than* and *the least*)
*I am **less keen** on taking risks **than** I used to be.*
*Antarctica is **the least** densely populated continent.*

4.2 Comparative and superlative adjectives

1 With one-syllable adjectives
Add *-er* and *-est* to form the comparative and superlative of one-syllable adjectives.
*Which is the **highest** mountain in the world?*
For one-syllable adjectives ending in a vowel + a consonant, double the consonant, e.g.
hot → hotter → hottest.
For one-syllable adjectives ending in *-e*, add *-r* and *-st*, e.g.
fine → finer → finest.

2 With two-syllable adjectives ending in *-y* and *-ow*
For two-syllable adjectives ending in *-y* after a consonant, drop the *-y* and add *-ier* and *-iest.*
*Childhood is the **happiest** time of your life.*
For two-syllable adjectives ending in *-ow*, add *-er* and *-est.*
*The road became **narrower** as we went along.*
For other two-syllable adjectives see 4.3.

4.3 *more* and *most* + adjective

Use *more* and *most* with

- two-syllable adjectives (except for those listed in 4.2).
*Walking at high altitudes is **more tiring** than at sea level.*
*It was the **most boring** magazine I'd ever read.*

- adjectives with three or more syllables.
*This exam was **more difficult** than the last one.*
*This is the **most interesting** book I've read.*

4.4 Irregular comparative and superlative adjectives

These are the most common irregular forms:
good → better → best
bad → worse → worst
little → less → least
much → more → most
far → further/farther → furthest/farthest

*Jim is a **better** player than I am but John is **the best**.*
*It's **the worst** game I've ever seen.*
It's even worse than their last one.
*You live **further** from the station than I do but Pedro lives **the furthest** away.*

4.5 Comparing adverbs

1 Most adverbs of manner have two or more syllables. Therefore they form their comparatives and superlatives with *more* and *most*.
*If you speak **more clearly**, everyone will be able to hear you.*
*Sami works **the most quickly**.*

2 Adverbs with the same form as adjectives form their comparatives with *-er* and *-est.*
*I can run **fast**, but Toni can run even **faster**.*
*We were **the earliest** people to get to the party.*
*He'll need to work **harder** if he's going to pass the exam.*
*It'll take much **longer** if we walk – let's get the bus.*
*Who's **the quickest** at mental arithmetic?*
*We'll get there **sooner** if we walk.*

4.6 Irregular comparative adverbs

1 *badly* and *well* use the same comparative and superlative forms as *bad* and *good*.
*I did **worse** in maths than I'd expected, but **better** in English.*
*The weather's getting **better**, but I'm worried it will turn **worse** at the weekend.*

2 Other irregular forms include:
late → later → latest
much → more → most
little → less → least
*Tom arrived **later** than Peter but Mary arrived **last**.*
*I don't go to the cinema **much** but I go **more** than I used to.*
*She likes Saif **less** than Dean but she likes Ali **least** of all.*

4.7 Intensifying and modifying comparisons

modifiers	comparative/superlative	
(by) far	the most/least expensive the cheapest the most time	
much a lot far a bit	more/less expensive cheaper more time	than…
just almost/nearly not quite not nearly	as cheap/expensive as much time	as…

- We can use the following words to intensify and modify comparatives.

  far/much/a lot cheaper/less expensive
  very much bigger/better
  rather harder
  a bit/slightly/a little faster
  no worse than
  not any quicker
  just as good as
  almost/not quite as expensive as
  not nearly as cheap

> **Watch out!** You cannot use very on its own with comparatives.

5 Conditionals

5.1 Alternatives to *if*

- Common conditional linking words are: *if, as/so long as, unless, even if, whether, providing, provided (that), on condition that.*
- When the clause with the conditional linking word is at the beginning of the sentence, there is a comma. When the main clause begins the sentence, there is no comma.
  If you give me your number, I'll phone you tomorrow.
  As long as you take your mobile, I can phone you.
  I won't go **unless you come with me**. (= if you don't come with me)
  We're going on the walk **even if it rains**.
  I'll help you **provided that you don't tell**.
- *in case* is used to describe things we do as precautions against what might happen.
  I'll take the mobile **in case** I need to phone you.
- *otherwise* is used to describe what would happen if we did things differently. It usually begins a new sentence.
  I must leave by 3.30. **Otherwise** I'll get stuck in traffic.

5.2 Zero conditional

FORM *if* + present simple + present simple in the main clause

USE To describe a general truth
   If there **is** life on other planets, we **are not** alone.

Alternatives to *if*
Unless lions **are** frightened or hungry, they**'re not** dangerous.
When people are under stress, they often **perform** better.

5.3 First conditional

FORM *if* etc. + present simple + future in the main clause

USE • To describe what is possible or likely in the present or future
   I**'ll be** so disappointed **if we lose** the match **on Saturday**.

• You can also use *if*, etc. + present continuous/ present perfect + future/imperative in the main clause to talk about possibility/likelihood in the present/future.
   You **won't get** an interview **unless** you**'ve filled** in an application form.
   If you**'re watching** TV, you **will see** him on the news.

5.4 Second conditional

FORM *if* + past simple/continuous + *would/could*, etc. + past participle in the main clause

USE 1 To talk about something
   • that is contrary to the present facts, or seen as very unlikely to happen
     If I **was/were** twenty years younger, I**'d emigrate**.
     If I was/**were** Prime Minister, I**'d make** health care free.
   • which is very unlikely to happen in the future
     I **wouldn't apply** for that job **unless I thought** I had a good chance of getting it.

   2 To give advice.
     I**'d write** it out again **if I were you**.

5.5 Third conditional

FORM *if* + past perfect + *would/could/might have* + past participle in the main clause

USE To describe something in the past that could have happened but didn't, or that shouldn't have happened but did
   I **wouldn't have told** her that **if I'd known** she'd tell everyone else.
   She **could have got** there on time **if** she **hadn't missed** the bus.

5.6 Modal verbs in conditional sentences

Modal verbs *can, could, might,* etc. can be used in all types of conditional sentences.

*I **might send** him an email **if** I **can find** his address.*
***If** she had someone to look after the children, she **could go out** to work.*

5.7 Mixed conditionals

It is possible to have sentences that mix conditionals in

*   an *if* clause referring to the past with a main clause referring to the present or future.
    ***If** I **had invested** in that company ten years ago, I **would be** rich now.*
    ***If** we **hadn't been given** all that homework, we **could go** swimming.*

*   an *if* clause referring to the present or future with a main clause referring to the past.
    ***If** you **don't like** sweet things, you **shouldn't have ordered** that dessert.*
    ***If** you**'ve got** an exam tomorrow, you **ought to have started** revising by now.*

5.8 Polite expressions

1   *would* can be used after *if* in polite expressions.
    ***If** you **wouldn't mind** waiting here, I'll find someone to help.*

2   *if + should* is common in formal letters.
    ***If** you **should** require any further information, please do not hesitate to contact us.*

> **Watch out!** For even greater formality, *if* can be omitted, and *should* can begin the sentence.
> ***Should** you wish to contact me, I can be reached at the above address.*

6 Countable and uncountable nouns; expressions of quantity

6.1 Uncountable nouns

These have no plural. The following are common nouns that are usually uncountable: *accommodation, advice, behaviour, bread, copper* (and all other metals), *meat, sugar, English,* (and all other languages), *furniture, health, information, knowledge, luggage, maths* (and all other school subjects), *news, progress, research, rice* (and all other grains and cereals), *salt,* (and all other condiments, e.g. *pepper*), *scenery, spaghetti, traffic, transport, travel, trouble, water* (and all other liquids), *weather, work.*

> **Watch out!** Use *a slice,* and *a piece* with uncountable nouns for food.
> *I'll just have **a small slice** of cake.*
> *Would you like **another piece** of toast?*

6.2 Nouns which can be countable or uncountable

1   Nouns we can think of as a single thing or substance, e.g. *chicken, chocolate, egg, hair, iron, paper, stone*
    *There are only **two chocolates** left in the box.*
    *You've got **chocolate** on your T-shirt.*
    *We'll have to buy **a new iron**.*
    *Green vegetables are rich in **iron**.*
    *Have you read today's **paper**?*
    *I need to go and buy **some paper** for the printer.*
    *There's **a hair** in my soup.*
    *She's got short dark **hair**.*
    *The house is built of **stone**. (= rock)*
    *The necklace is made of semi-precious **stones**. (= gems)*

2   Nouns which are used to refer to particular varieties, e.g. *wine, country*
    *Would you like **some wine**? This is **a very good wine**.*
    *I'd like to have a house **in the country**. He's worked in **five different countries**.*

3   Words for some drinks, e.g. *coffee, beer*. The countable noun means *a glass of, a cup of, a bottle of,* etc.
    ***Coffee** is produced in Africa and South America.*
    *Shall we have **a coffee** and a piece of cake?*

4   *time, space, room*
    *There's **no time** to talk – we have to rush!*
    *I didn't have **a very good time** at the party.*
    There's no space left. You'll have to get another bag.
    *Fill in the **spaces** with the correct preposition.*
    There's room for seven people in this car.
    *This house has seven **rooms**.*

6.3 Expressions of quantity used with countable/uncountable nouns

1 *lots/a lot of* + plural countable and uncountable nouns (informal)
*I've got **lots/a lot of** homework, so I can't go out.*
*I've got **lots/a lot of** brothers and sisters.*

2 *much* + uncountable nouns
*We don't have **much homework**.*
***How much money** do you need?*

3 *many* + plural countable nouns
*How **many** bags have you got?*
*There are **many** interesting places in the world.*

> **Watch out!** In positive statements *lots/a lot of* is less formal and is more commonly used in spoken English.

4 *little, a little, a bit of* + uncountable nouns

A *a little, a bit* means *at least some*
*Just **a little rice**, please – not too much.*
*I've got a **bit of money**, but not enough to get a taxi.*

B *little* without *a* means *almost none*. This can be emphasised with *very*.
*The government has done **very little** to improve the situation.*

5 *few, a few* + plural countable nouns (= some but not many)

A Before *few* you can use
- the indefinite article *a*.
*There were quite **a few people** in the room.*
*There were only **a few people** staying at the hotel.*

- *the last, the first, the next, every.*
*Over **the next few weeks**, we have a lot to get ready.*
*For **the first few minutes**, you may feel a bit nervous.*
*I phone her **every few days**.*

B When *few* is used without *a*, it means *almost no*. This can be emphasised with *very*.
*(Very) **few** people know the secret.*

6 *some* + uncountable nouns and plural nouns (= between *a little* and *a lot*)
*There's **some** useful **information** on that website.*
There are some good scenes in that film.

> **Watch out!** If *some* is stressed, it often means *not many*.
> *I suppose he's written **some** good books.*

7 *hardly any* + uncountable nouns and plural countable nouns
*There were **hardly any customers** in the shop.*

8 *no, not any* + uncountable nouns and plural countable nouns
*There was **no milk** left./There **wasn't any milk** left.*
*There were **no students** on the bus./There **weren't any students** on the bus.*

7 Emphasis with *what*

This structure is a relative clause introduced by a *wh-* word. We use it to emphasise key information in a sentence. It is more common in spoken English, but is also used in writing.

People do not realise that these accidents can be avoided.
***What people do not realise is** that these accidents can be avoided.*

The authorities are collecting information.
***What the authorities are doing is** collecting information.*

You should learn to say no.
***What you should learn to do is** say no.*

Friends are important to young kids.
***What is important to young kids is** their friends.*

8 Habit in the past

8.1 Past habit: *used to*

FORM Positive statements: *used to* + infinitive
Negative statements: *did/didn't* + *use to* + infinitive
Questions: *Did you/she/they*, etc. *use to* + infinitive

USE We use *used to* to talk about past habits and states that do not occur now or no longer exist.
*We **used to** be driven to school, but now we walk.*
*What did people **use to** do before electricity was invented? Ken **used to** be shy, but he's more confident since he met Cindy.*

> **Watch out!**
> **1** *used to* is not used to say how often things happened or how long they took.
> **2** Be careful not to confuse *used to* with *be/get used to* + noun/-*ing*). This means *be/become accustomed to something* because you have been doing it for a while.
> *I'm **used to making** my own meals.*
> *I can't **get used to the cold winters**.*
> *Do you think we'll ever **get used to eating** dinner at 6.00?*

8.2 Past habit: *would*

Would is also used to talk about past habits and repeated actions but NOT about past states.
*When I was little, I **would/used to** play with my brother's toys.*
NOT *We ~~would~~ live in a small village.*

8.3 Past habit: past simple

This can also be used to describe past habits and states.
*When I **was** a child, I **walked** to school every day.*

9 have/get something done

FORM *have* + object + past participle (the most
common form)

get + object + past participle (also possible when
people are speaking informally)

USE **1** To say that someone else did something for you
because you wanted them to.

He **had his hair cut** *specially for the interview.*
He's got such big feet he **has to have** *shoes
specially* **made**.

Where can I **get these papers photocopied**?
He decided to **get the photograph enlarged**.

2 We also use *have something done* to say that
someone else did something to you even though
you didn't want them to.

He **had to have a kidney removed**.
She said she'd **had her necklace stolen**.

3 We use *get somebody to do/make somebody do
something* when we want to persuade or force
somebody to do something for us.

I **got my friend to drive me** *to the shops.*
The police **made the man hand over** *his car keys.*

10 Hypothetical meaning

10.1 *wish*

1 We use *wish* + past simple to express a wish that has not
come true in the present or to talk about wishes that
might come true in the future.
We use this structure when we want our situation (or
the situation of the person who is doing the wishing)
to be different.

I **wish** *Eleanor* **liked** *me.*
Don't you wish *you* **had** *a big car?*
I **wish** *she* **was/were** *going out with me.*
We all wish *the weather* **wasn't/weren't** *so bad.*

2 We use *wish* + *would/could* to refer to general wishes for
the future.

I **wish** *the sun* **would shine**.
I **wish** I **could be** *in the basketball team.*

3 *wish* + *would* is used to talk about wishes we have for
other people.

I **wish** *my sister* **would** *stop smoking.*
I **wish** *he* **wouldn't** *chew gum all the time.*

> **Watch out!** This form is not often used with *I* or *we*. To
> talk about wishes we have for ourselves we use *could*.
> I **wish** I **could** *have a holiday.*

4 We use *wish* + past perfect to refer to things we are sorry
about in the past.

I **wish** I **had been invited** *to the party.*
She wishes she hadn't told *him about Carlo.*

10.2 *if only*

If only is used with the same verb forms as *wish*, and is used
when your feelings are stronger. It is often used with an
exclamation mark (*!*). It is often used with *would/wouldn't* to
criticise someone else's behaviour.

If only I could *find the answer!*
If only they would *stop talking!*
If only I had never met *him!*

10.3 *it's time*

It's time is used with the past simple to talk about the
present or future. We mean that the action should have
been done before. For emphasis, we can also say *It's* **about**
time and *It's* **high** *time*.

It's (about) time you started *revising for the exam.*
It's (high) time we set off. *The train leaves in half an hour.*

10.4 *would rather*

1 We use *would rather* + past simple to say what we want
someone or something else to do in either the present
or the future.

I'd rather you didn't tell *anyone about all this.*
Would you rather I asked *someone else?*
I'd rather we didn't discuss *that, if you don't mind.*

2 We use *would rather* + past perfect to say what we
wanted to happen in the past.
I'd rather you hadn't told *her that.*
I'd rather you had asked *me first.*

> **Watch out!** *would rather* + infinitive without *to* is used
> to talk about our or other people's preferences in the
> present or future.
> **I'd rather go** *to the concert than to the opera.*
> **They'd rather go** *on foot.*

10.5 *suppose/what if?*

Suppose means *What if…?* It is used with

1 the present simple to describe something that may
possibly happen or may have happened.
Suppose *someone* **sees** *her with us.*
Suppose *someone* **hears** *you coming in.*

2 the past simple to talk about something that is just
imagination or which is unlikely to happen in the future.
Suppose *Eleanor* **knew** *you loved her. What would you do?*
Suppose *you* **won** *the prize. How would you feel?*

3 the past perfect to talk about something that could have
happened in the past but didn't.
Suppose *we* **hadn't told** *her. Would she have found out?*
Suppose *you* **had married** *Carlos. Would you have been
happy together?*

11 Indirect questions

1 Indirect forms are often used when you want to be polite. This may be because you don't know someone very well, or when you want to make a request and you feel uncertain about someone's reaction

2 The first part of the question often begins with a modal such as *would, could, I was wondering*. In the second part of the question the word order is the same as in a statement; auxiliaries such as *do/does/have/be* are not used and the subject and verb are not inverted.

   A Direct question:
     When does the film start?

   B Examples of indirect questions:
     *Could you tell me **when the film starts**?*
     *Do you know **when the film starts**?*
     *Would you mind telling me **when the film starts**?*
     *I was wondering **when the film starts**.*

12 *it is, there is*

1 We use *there is/there are* to begin a sentence describing whether or not something exists. It is often followed by an indefinite noun.
   ***There is** a little house at the foot of the hill.*
   ***There are** some trees growing along the side of the road.*
   ***There's** no point in worrying about it.*

2 We use *it is/was*, etc. to begin a sentence giving information about time, weather and distance.
   ***It is** a bright, sunny day.*
   ***It was** half past six in the morning.*
   ***It's** just over ten kilometres to the nearest town.*

3 We use *it is* as the subject of a sentence to refer forwards to a later clause with *that*, an infinitive or an *-ing* form.
   ***It is** a pity that no one can help.*
   ***It's** good to see you again.*
   ***It's** no use crying over spilt milk.*

13 Modal verbs and expressions with similar meanings

13.1 Possibility

1 We use *can* or *could* for theoretical possibility.
   ***Can** there **be** life on Mars?*
   ***Can** that **be** Peter over there?*
   *The weather **could be** better tomorrow. (= it's possible)*

2 We use *may, might, could* + infinitive to talk about likelihood in the present or future.
   *He **may be** in a meeting.*
   *She **might/could be** here already.*

3 We use *could/may/might* + *have* + past participle (perfect infinitive) to talk about the possibility that past events happened.
   *His face was familiar. We **may have met** somewhere before.*
   *He's not in the office. He **might have finished** work early.*
   *She **could have been** at the party, but I didn't see her.*

13.2 Certainty (deduction)

1 We use *must* to say that we are sure about something in the present or past.
   *You **must be** pleased with your exam results. (= present)*
   *He **must have touched up** the photograph. (= past)*

2 We use *can't* or *couldn't* in negative sentences. We do not use *mustn't*.
   *That **can't be** Keira Knightley. She's too old. (= present)*
   *They **can't have got lost**. They know the area really well. (= past)*
   *It **couldn't have been** Tom that I saw. (= past)*

13.3 Obligation, prohibition and necessity

1 We use *must/mustn't* and (*not*) *allowed to* to talk about present and future obligations/prohibitions imposed by the speaker, often on him/herself.
   *Payment **must** be made in cash.*
   *I **must** get some new shoes.*
   *You **must** read that book, it's excellent! (= recommendation)*
   ***Must** I really go now? (= appeal)*
   *You **mustn't** park here. (= prohibition)*
   *You **mustn't** eat so much. (= strong advice)*
   *You **aren't allowed to** wear trainers to school.*

2 We use *have to/have got to* to talk about present and future obligations that are imposed by someone other than the speaker.

> **Watch out!** *have got to* is more common in British than American English.
> *I **have (got) to take** my holiday in February.*
> ***Have** we **got to pay** to go in?*

3 We use *had to* to talk about past and reported obligations of all kinds.
   *They told us we **had to** leave our bags in the cloakroom.*
   *We **had to** stand up when the teacher came in.*
   *I knew I **had to** make a decision.*

4 We use *need to* to talk about obligation and necessity.
   *Do we **need to** type our work?*
   *You **need to** book tickets in advance.*

13.4 Lack of obligation or necessity

1 We use *needn't, don't need to, don't have to* to talk about a lack of obligation in the present or future.
   *You **don't need to/needn't meet** me at the station.*
   *We **don't have to wait**. We can go straight in.*

2 We use *needn't* + *have* + past participle to say that somebody did something, but that it was unnecessary.
   *You **needn't have gone** to all that trouble.*

3 We use *didn't need to* + infinitive to say that something wasn't necessary without saying whether the person did it or not.
   *You **didn't need to bring** any extra money.*
   *She **didn't need to cook** dinner for all of us!*

13.5 Ability

1 We use *can/could* to express general ability and typical behaviour of people or things.
*Temperatures **can rise** to over 30°C in the summer.*
Employers can be unwilling to employ people over fifty.
*My father **could be** very generous.* (= past)

2 We use *can/be able to* for present and future ability.
*I **can** understand French but I **can't** speak it very well.*
***Will** your parents **be able to** help you?*
*I like **being able to** cook my own meals.*

3 We use *can* for the future where there is a sense of opportunity.
*I **can come** tomorrow if you like.*
*You **can practise** your French when you go to Paris.*

4 We use *could/couldn't* and *was able to* to talk about general past ability.
*I **could swim** before I **could** walk.*
*I **was able to talk** when I was eighteen months.*
*Andrew's father **couldn't get** a job.*

5 We use *was/wasn't able to* to talk about past ability in a specific situation.
*Fortunately, he **was able to** swim to the shore.*

6 We use *could/couldn't* + perfect infinitive to talk about unfulfilled ability in the past.
*I **could have gone** to university, but I decided not to.*
*I **couldn't have been** a ballet dancer. I was too tall.*

7 Other expressions for ability:
*Do you **know how to** type?*
*He **succeeded in becoming** a professional footballer at eighteen.*
*We **managed to find** our way home.* (= suggests difficulty)

13.6 Advice: *should* and *ought to*, *be supposed to*

1 We use *ought to* and *should* to talk about obligations and duties in the future, present and past, or to give advice.
*You **ought to/should speak** English in class.*
***Shouldn't we tell** someone about the accident?*
***Oughtn't we to have invited** Mandy?* (= more formal)

2 We can use *be supposed to* when saying what someone should or should not do according to rules or regulations.
*You're **not supposed to park** here.*
*I'm **supposed to call** my mum when we leave the party.*

3 *should* + *have* + past participle is often used to criticise your own or other people's behaviour.
*I **should have told** you before.*
*You **shouldn't have promised** that.*

4 Other phrases for advice include
*You **could get** the next flight.*
***If I were you, I'd** phone him.*
***I'd advise** you **not to park** there.*

13.7 Asking for and giving permission

1 We use *can* and *are allowed to* to ask for and give permission.
***Can I borrow** your calculator for a few minutes?*
*Yes, you **can stay up** and watch the late night film.*
*You **can't wait** here. It's private.* (= not allowed to)
*You **are allowed to** borrow up to eight books.*

2 We use *could* to ask for permission when we are not sure what the answer will be.
A: ***Could I** open the window?*
B: *Yes, of course you **can**.*

> **Watch out!** *could* is NOT used for giving permission.

3 We use *may* to ask for or give permission in formal situations.
***May** I take that chair?*
*You **may** use pen or pencil.*

14 Participles (-*ing* and -*ed*)

14.1 Participles in relative clauses

We can use present participle (-*ing*) and past participle (-*ed*) clauses in place of relative pronouns to make writing more economical.

1 A present participle has an active meaning. It can replace relative clauses which have an active verb.
*This is the road **leading** to the school.* (= which leads…)
*There was a huge lamp **hanging** from the ceiling.* (= which hung…)

2 A past participle has a passive meaning. It can replace relative clauses which have a passive verb.
*The cathedral, **built** in the Middle Ages and recently **restored**, is well worth a visit.* (= which was built… which has recently been restored)

14.2 Other uses of participles (see also 22.1)

We also use participles

1 after certain verbs. *I enjoy **running**.*

2 after conjunctions. *Before **going** out, I locked the door.*

3 after prepositions. *She's really good **at swimming**.*

4 as adjectives. *That film was **amazing**.*
*I was **shocked** by his behaviour.*

5 as the subject of a sentence.
***Eating** too much is bad for you.*

6 to express reason, condition, or result in place of adverbs.
***Seeing** Jim in the distance, I called after him.*
(= because I saw Jim…)
***Having refused** the invitation, I then changed my mind.*
(= after I'd refused…)
***Seen** from a distance, the view is amazing.*
(= if/when you see it…)

15 Passive forms

15.1 Passive form and use

FORM To form the passive, use the appropriate tense of *be* + past participle.

present simple	Most phone calls **are made** on mobile phones.
present continuous	Calls **are being made** every day.
past simple	The first email **was sent** in the twentieth century.
past continuous	I thought I **was being asked** to help.
present perfect	Millions of text messages **have been sent**.
past perfect	Once personal computers **had been invented**, they spread quickly.
future *will*	She**'ll be given** her own room.
future perfect	The arrangements **will have been made** by the end of the week.
going to	The event **is going to be organised** by the manager.
modals	The machine **must have been** left switched on. Messages **may not be delivered** immediately.
-ing	Our dog doesn't like **being left** on his own.
present infinitive	They hope **to be chosen** to take part.
perfect infinitive	I was happy **to have been selected** for the team.

Watch out!

1 Verbs that do not take an object (e.g. *ache, arrive, sit down*) do not have passive forms. It is not possible to say *I was ached*.

2 For verbs with two objects, one of them a person, the passive sentence usually begins with the person. *Someone gave Mary a present.* → *Mary was given a present.* (NOT ~~A present was given to Mary.~~)

3 The verbs *make, hear, see, help* are followed by the infinitive without *to* in active sentences, but the infinitive with *to* in passive sentences. *They **made** him **go** home.* → *He **was made to go** home.*

4 *Let* does not have a passive form. We use *be allowed to* in the passive. *They don't **let** us talk in class.* → *We **are not allowed to** talk in class.*

USE The passive is used

- to talk about actions, events and processes when the action, event or process is seen as more important than the agent. This is often the case in formal or scientific writing.
  *The equipment **was checked** carefully.*
  *Rats **have been trained** to open boxes.*

- to put new information later in the sentence.
  *Hamlet **was written** by Shakespeare.*

15.2 *by* + agent

When we are interested in the agent, we use the preposition *by*.
*He was saved **by** his mobile phone.*
*The team were guided **by** a local climber.*

15.3 Passive reporting verbs

We often use reporting verbs such as *believe, claim, report, say, think* in the following impersonal passive structures when we don't know or don't wish to specify the subject.

- *it* + *be* + verb + *that*
  It is thought that the criminal is a local man. (= present)
  It was claimed that the minister had been involved. (= past)

- subject + *be* + reporting verb + infinitive
  The criminal is thought to be a local man. (= present)
  The minister was claimed to have been involved. (= past)

16 Relative clauses and pronouns

16.1 Relative pronouns

- The most common relative pronouns are:
  who (= subject) and *whom* (= object) to refer to people
  which to refer to things
  that to refer to either people or things
  whose the possessive of *who* and *which*
  when used after nouns referring to time
  where used after nouns referring to place
  why used to refer to reasons

Watch out!
The relative pronoun replaces the subject or the object.
*People **who** (~~they~~) live in glass houses shouldn't throw stones.*
*The vase, **which** I bought (~~it~~) years ago, is very valuable.*
What is not a relative pronoun.

16.2 Defining relative clauses

In defining relative clauses

1 the relative clause defines or identifies the person, thing, time, place or reason.
*Chris is the son of a woman **who works in television**.*
*That's the man **whose son is an actor**.*
*Winter was the time **when people tended to get insufficient fresh food**.*
*I know the place **where the play is set**.*
*I can't imagine **why he would want to leave you**.*

2 *that* can be used instead of *who* or *which*.
The girl that (who) lives next door rides a motorbike.
*The sports centre **that (which) is opening soon** will offer great new facilities.*

3 The relative pronoun can be left out if it is the object of the verb in the relative clause.
*The person (who/**that**) I spoke to yesterday said it was free.*
*Sue bought the watch (**which/that**) she'd seen.*

4 No commas are used before and after the relative clause.

16.3 Non-defining relative clauses

Relative clauses give extra information which CAN be omitted. Commas are used before and after the relative clause.
The pronoun *that* CANNOT be used instead of *who* or *which*.

*The museum, **where you can see Roman pottery**, is free.*
*The witness, **who refused to be named**, said the police had acted unwisely.*

16.4 Prepositions in relative clauses

Prepositions can come before the relative pronoun or at the end of the relative clause, depending on whether the sentence is formal or informal.

*The person **to whom I spoke** told me the hotel was fully booked.* **(formal)**
*John, **who I bought my car from**, has gone abroad.* **(informal)**

17 Reflexive pronouns

Reflexive pronouns (*myself, yourself, him/her/itself, ourselves, yourselves, themselves*) are used

* when the subject and object of a transitive verb are the same.
  *He stopped **himself** from saying something.*
  *I hurt **myself** when I fell over.*

* to mean 'without the help of others'.
  *I cleaned the car **myself**.*
  *We booked the holiday **ourselves**.*

* with *by* to mean alone/on your own.
  *Are you going to town **by yourself**?*

* with *enjoy, behave*, etc. when there is no object.
  *Enjoy **yourself**!*
  Behave yourselves!

* To add emphasis to the subject or object.
  *The President **himself** spoke to me.*
  *The actors were good but the film **itself** was boring.*

18 Reported statements, questions and imperatives/ Reporting verbs

18.1 Reported speech

This is when we report something that has been said or written.

1 If the report is after the time the thing was said or written, the verb form generally changes as follows

Direct speech	Reported speech
present simple/continuous *'I like your shoes, Kate,' said Jack.*	past simple/continuous *Jack said (that) he **liked** Kate's shoes.*
past simple/continuous *'I saw them advertised on TV,' said Kate.*	past simple/continuous or past perfect simple/continuous *Kate said (that) **she saw/had seen** them advertised on TV.*
present perfect simple/ continuous *'I've bought a hat,' Helen told me.*	past perfect simple/ continuous *Helen told me (that) she **had bought** a hat.*
will *'I'll take you there if you want,' she said.*	would *She said (that) she **would** take me there if I wanted.*
must (obligation) *'You must buy a ticket,' he said.*	had to *He said (that) we **had to** buy a ticket.*
can *'I can speak Spanish,' said Mel.*	could *Mel said (that) he **could** speak Spanish.*

2 The verb form does not need to change when

* the situation being reported is unchanged.
  *'Bananas **are** good for energy,' said the doctor.*
  *The doctor told us that bananas **are** good for energy.*

  *'The castle **is** 800 years old,' said the guide.*
  *The guide told us that the castle **is** 800 years old.*

* the thing reported contains the modals *would, could, might, ought to* and *should* or *must* for logical deduction.
  *'I **ought to** buy a new car,' she said.*
  *She said she **ought to** buy a new car.*

  *'I think he **must** be coming,' she said.*
  *She said she thought he **must** be coming.*

* the thing being reported contains the past perfect .
  *'He **had** already **been given** a prize,' she said.*
  *She said he **had** already **been given** a prize.*

3 Other changes that occur in reported speech are shown in the table below:

Direct speech	Reported speech
tomorrow	the next day, the day after, the following day
yesterday	the day before, the previous day
last week	the week before
here	there
this morning	that morning
today	that day
next Friday	the following Friday
ago	before

18.2 Reported statements

verb (+ that) + clause

'He works in television,' she said.
She **said (that) he worked** in television.
'I took the money,' she admitted.
She **admitted (that) she had taken** the money.

18.3 Reported questions

1 Reported *yes/no* questions
When there is no question word in the direct speech question, we use *if/whether*. Word order is the same as in the statement. The verb tense and other changes are the same as for other types of reported speech.
'Could I borrow your bike?' she asked.
She asked **if/whether** she could borrow my bike.

2 Reported *wh-* questions
The *wh-* word is followed by statement word order (subject followed by verb). All tense and other changes are the same as for other types of reported speech.
'Why did you leave that job?' she asked him.
She asked him **why he had left that job**.
'Where is the swimming pool?' he asked her.
He asked her **where the swimming pool was**.

18.4 Reported imperatives

verb + object + infinitive with *to*

'Please open your suitcase,' said the customs official.
The customs official **asked me to open** my suitcase.

'Don't walk on the grass!' said the official.
The official **told them not to walk** on the grass.

18.5 Reported recommendations

recommend (that) + clause; recommend + -ing
'I'd buy the red coat,' my friend said.
My friend **recommended buying/(that) I buy/bought** the red coat.

18.6 Reported suggestions

FORM suggest + -ing
suggest + that + past simple
suggest + that + (should) + infinitive without to
'Let's pay half each,' she said.
She **suggested paying half each**.
She **suggested we paid half each**.
She **suggested that we should pay half each**.

> **Watch out!** We can't say
> She suggested ~~to pay/suggested us to pay~~ half each.

18.7 Reporting verbs

1 verb + infinitive
agree, decide, offer, promise, refuse, threaten
We **agreed to go** to the meeting.

2 verb + object + infinitive
advise, beg, encourage, invite, persuade, remind, tell, warn
She **asked me** to tell the truth.

3 verb (+ that) + clause
accept, admit, claim, explain, recommend, say, suggest
She **says (that) we should be repaid the money**.

4 verb + object (+ that) + clause
promise, remind, tell, warn
He **told us (that) he would be on time**.

5 verb + -ing
admit, deny, recommend, suggest
He **admitted taking** the money.

6 verb + preposition + -ing
apologise for, insist on
She **apologised for being** late.

7 verb + object + preposition + -ing
accuse (of), blame (for), congratulate (on), discourage (from)
She **discouraged me from going** in for the competition.

8 verb + wh- word + infinitive
describe, explain, know, wonder
She **explained what to do**.

9 verb + object + wh- word + infinitive
ask, remind, tell
They **told us who to see**.

19 so, such, too, enough, very

19.1 so and such

FORM
- *so* + adjective/adverb/determiner (+ noun) (+ *that* clause)
  *The journey was **so dangerous that** they gave up after 200 miles.*
  *He has travelled **so widely that** he's forgotten what home is like.*
  *I had **so little information that** I couldn't make a sensible suggestion.*
  *It was **so hot!** (= emphatic)*

- *such* + (adjective) + noun (+ *that* clause)
  *The taxi took **such a long time** to come **that I decided to walk instead**.*
  *He had **such fun** at the party **that he didn't want to leave**.*
  *We had **such a** good time! (= emphatic)*

USE *so* and *such* are used to introduce a clause of result, or for emphasis.

19.2 too

FORM *too* + adjective/adverb/determiner (+ noun) (+ *to* infinitive)

USE *too* has a negative meaning – the speaker is not happy about the situation.
*It was **too hot** to sleep.*
*You**'re speaking too quickly** – I can't understand you I'm afraid.*
*That's **too much (money)**. I can't afford it.*

19.3 enough

FORM
- adjective/adverb + *enough* (+ *to* infinitive)
  *He's **rich enough to buy up** the whole town.*
  *You're not doing that work **carefully enough**.*

- *enough* + noun (+ *to* infinitive/+ *for* + noun)
  *Have you got **enough money to get a taxi**?*

USE *enough* has a positive meaning – the speaker regards the situation as possible.

19.4 very

FORM *very* + adjective/adverb/determiner (+ noun)

USE *very* is used for emphasis in either a positive or negative statement. It is sometimes used when we wish to avoid using a negative word.
*It's **very difficult** but I think I can do it.*
*He's working **very hard** – he's bound to pass.*
***Very few people** agree with her.*

20 Subject/Verb agreement

Verbs and their subjects usually 'agree'.
*Plants die if **they aren't** watered.*
*My **car is** very old.*

However, sometimes it's not clear whether the verb should be singular or plural.

1 A singular verb is used:
- with uncountable nouns which end in *s*, e.g. *maths, physics, genetics, aerobics, athletics, news*.
  ***Maths is** a very difficult subject.*
  *The **news is** bad, I'm afraid.*

- with expressions of quantity, time, distance, measurement.
  ***Twelve dollars is** too much to pay for a sandwich.*
  ***Ten kilometres is** a long distance to run.*
  ***Is three hours** long enough for you?*
  ***Two metres is** too high.*

- after words/expressions such as *everyone, anything, hardly anyone, more than, one of, neither of,* etc.
  ***Everyone was** waiting for the train to arrive.*
  ***One of them is** obviously wrong.*

- with abstract nouns.
  ***Happiness is** very difficult to measure.*

- when an *-ing* clause is the subject of a verb.
  ***Fishing is** a very popular activity.*

2 A plural verb is used with nouns that are plural but don't end in *-s* (e.g. *people, police*).
***Some people dislike** shopping.*
- after words/expressions such as *plenty of, a couple of, both of*.
  *I invited **both of them** back to play football.*

- after nouns which are always plural, e.g. *clothes, glasses, jeans, trousers, pliers, scissors*.
  *These **trousers don't fit** me.*

- to refer to a single item, use *a pair of*.
  *I need **a new pair of glasses**.*

3 Some collective nouns, (e.g. *staff, the team, the army, the public, the media, the United States*) can take a singular verb if we see them as a single unit or a plural form if we are referring to members of the group.
***My family is** very close.* (*family* = a single body)
***My family are** all living quite near to each other.* (*family* = a collection of individuals)

21 Verb forms

21.1 Present simple

We use the present simple

1 for routine or regular repeated actions (often with adverbs of frequency like *always, usually, often, sometimes, never, every Saturday morning, twice every week*).
*We **go** running **every evening**.*
*She **doesn't do** any work **at weekends**.*
*I **never get** home before eight o'clock in the evening.*

2 for present habits.
*I **generally park** outside the library.*

3 when we are talking about permanent situations.
*She **comes from** South America.*
*They **live** in London.*

4 with scientific facts.
*Water **freezes** at 0°C.*

5 with stative verbs (verbs which are not normally used in continuous forms) e.g. *be, have, depend, know, think, understand, disagree, like, want, hear, love, see, smell, taste*.
*They **don't have** a car.*
***Does** she **understand**?*
*I'm sorry, but I **disagree** completely.*
*That perfume **smells** too strong.*

6 when we are talking about the future as expressed in timetables, regulations and programmes.
*The plane **leaves** at 8.45a.m.*
*When **do** the holidays **begin**?*

7 in time clauses with a future meaning, e.g. *after, as soon as, if, until, when*.
*I'll see her **when/as soon as** she's free.*
*Give this to Susie **if** you **see** her.*
*Tom can't apply for the job **until** he **gets** the right qualifications.*

21.2 Present continuous

We use the present continuous when we use dynamic (action) verbs to talk about

1 actions happening now.
*I think **he's watching** TV.*

2 changing/developing situations.
*My broken leg **is getting** better.*

3 temporary situations.
*I **am staying** in this hotel for two weeks.*

4 annoying or surprising habits with *always*.
*She's **always losing** her keys.*
*He's **always buying** her flowers.*

5 plans and arrangements in the future.
***Are** you **going out** this evening?*

21.3 Present perfect simple

We use the present perfect simple

1 to talk about states, single or repeated actions over a long period of time up to the present (often with *ever/never, often/always*).
*I**'ve always wanted** to be an actor.*
***Have** you **ever been** to Australia?*
*I**'ve only used** my mobile phone **once** since I bought it.*
*She**'s read** that book **at least ten times**.*
*That's the first time I**'ve ever eaten** octopus.*
*It's the worst concert I**'ve ever been** to.*

2 to talk about recent single actions with a present result (often with *just, already, yet*).
*I**'ve already seen** that film and I don't want to see it again.*
***Have you finished** your essay **yet**?*
*Our friends **have** just arrived.*

> **Watch out!** In American English, it is acceptable to use the past simple in sentences like these.
> *I didn't have breakfast yet.*
> *I already saw that film.*

3 to talk about an unfinished period of time up to the present (often with *for/since, this week/month/year*).
*Tomoko **has lived** in England **for five years**.*
*I**'ve been** in love with Stella **since 2002**.*
*I**'ve loved** travelling **all my life**.*
*I**'ve disliked** bananas **since I was a child**.*
*We **haven't had** a holiday **this year**.*

21.4 Present perfect continuous

We use the present perfect continuous

1 to talk about a recent activity when the effects of that activity can still be seen.
A: *Why are you out of breath?*
B: *I**'ve been running**.*

2 to emphasise how long an action has been going on for, or that it has been repeated many times.
*I**'ve been replying** to emails all morning.*
*I**'ve been cleaning** the house all day.*

3 to suggest that an activity is temporary.
*I**'ve been living** here for five years but I'm going to move soon.*

4 to suggest that an action is not complete.
*I**'ve been reading** 'Ulysses', but I haven't finished it yet.*

> **Watch out!** We don't use verbs that refer to a state (e.g. *be, know, love*) in the continuous form.

21.5 Narrative forms: past simple

We use the past simple

1 to talk about a finished event that happened at a specific time in the past.
*I **saw** Paul **last night**.*
*I **went** to Brazil five years **ago**.*

2 to describe a sequence of finished events in chronological order.
*I **took** out my key, **opened** the door and **walked** in.*

3 to talk about habits in the past.
***Did** your parents **read** to you when you were younger?*

4 to talk about states in the past.
*When I **was** a child, I didn't enjoy watching TV at all.*
*The house **belonged** to my father from 1990 to 2000.*

5 in reported speech.
*She **said** she **didn't want** to join us.*

21.6 Narrative forms: past continuous

We use the past continuous

1 to describe an action in progress in the past, often to set the scene for a particular event.
*I **was sitting** in the garden, reading a book.*

2 to talk about temporary situations in the past.
*Rodolfo **was living** in South America at the time.*

3 to talk about an event that was in progress in the past and was interrupted.
*I **was going** out of the house when I heard a noise.*

4 to talk about multiple actions in progress at the same time in the past.
*While I **was painting**, you **were watching** TV.*

5 to talk about anticipated events that did not happen.
*We **were going** to Rome for a holiday, but then I broke my leg.*

21.7 Narrative forms: past perfect

We use the past perfect

1 to refer to a time earlier than another past time, when this is needed to make the order of events clear.
*The bird's wings **had been clipped** so it couldn't fly.*
*By the time the fire engine arrived, the house **had** completely **burnt down**.*

> **Watch out!** Be careful not to overuse the past perfect. It is not necessary with *before/after*, which make the sequence of events clear.
> Once we have established the time sequence, we can revert to the past simple.

2 in reported speech.
*They said they **had met** before.*

21.8 Future forms

FORMS   *shall/will* + infinitive without *to*
going to + infinitive without *to*
present continuous (see 21.2)
present simple (see 21.1)
future continuous (*will* + *be* + *-ing* form)
future perfect (*will* + *have* + past participle)

1 We use *will* + infinitive without *to*
- for predicting something based on our belief or our knowledge of characteristic behaviour.
*This medicine **will make** you feel sleepy.*
*You'll **feel** better when you've had a good night's rest.*

> **Watch out!** We cannot use the present continuous in this case.

- for promises, threats, offers and requests.
*If you tell anyone, I'**ll kill** you!*
*I promise I'**ll pay** the money back.*
*I'**ll meet** you at the station if you want.*
***Shall I meet** you at the station?*
***Will you do** the washing-up for me?*

> **Watch out!** We cannot use *going to* in this case.

2 We use *going to* or the present continuous to talk about things that have already been decided.
*She's decided she's **going to lose** ten kilos.*
*Where are you **going to have** the wedding reception?*

> **Watch out!** We cannot use *will/shall* + infinitive in this case.

3 We use *going to* to talk about things that are certain to happen because there is present evidence.
*I've got no sense of direction – I know I'**m going to get** lost.*
*Look out – you'**re going to fall**!*

> **Watch out!** We cannot use *will/shall* + infinitive or the present continuous in this case.

4 We use *will/shall* + infinitive without *to* to talk about future actions decided at the time of speaking.
*I think I'**ll give up** smoking.*
*I'**ll wear** my black dress.*

5 We use the future continuous (*will/shall* + *be* + *-ing*) to say that an action will be in progress at a definite time in the future.
*I'**ll be living** a normal life by this time next year.*

6 We use the future perfect (*will/shall* + *have* + past participle) to describe something that will be completed before a definite time in the future.
*By the end of June I'**ll have been** at this school for a year.*

22 Verb patterns: -ing/ infinitive

2.2.1. Common verbs followed by -ing

admit, appreciate, consider, delay, deny, detest, dislike, enjoy, escape, feel like, finish, give up, imagine, involve, mention, mind, miss, postpone, practise, prefer, put off, recommend, resent, risk, suggest

I **don't recommend going** to that restaurant.

22.2 The infinitive

The infinitive is used

- after some main verbs (see 22.3 and 22.4).

- after some adjectives.
  I was **happy to see** her.
  They were **wrong to refuse**.

- after some nouns.
  She never regretted her **decision to be** a teacher.
  It's **time to leave**.

- to express purpose.
  I **went** to London **to see** my aunt.

22.3 Common verbs followed by infinitive

afford, agree, appear, arrange, ask, attempt, begin, choose, consent, decide, expect, fail, forget, happen, hate, help, hesitate, hope, intend, learn, like, love, manage, mean, offer, prefer, prepare, pretend, promise, refuse, remember, seem, start, swear, try, want, wish

I can't **afford to eat** in that restaurant.

22.4 Common verbs followed by object + infinitive

advise, allow, ask, cause, encourage, expect, forbid, force, get, help, instruct, intend, invite, leave, like, mean, need, order, persuade, prefer, remind, request, teach, tell, tempt, want, warn

He **asked me to help** him.

22.5 The infinitive without *to*

The infinitive without *to* is used

- after some main verbs (see 22.6).

- after modal verbs.
  You **must leave** now.

- after *would rather/had better*.
  You'd **better come** in now.

22.6 Common verbs followed by object + infinitive without *to*

let, make, hear, help, see
He **made me repeat** the exercise.
Her parents **won't let her stay** out late.
I **heard her play** in Milan.

> **Watch out!** In passive sentences *make, hear* and *help* are followed by an infinitive with *to*.
> He was **made to report** to the police.

Let cannot be used in the passive form. Instead, *allowed* must be used.
My parents **let** me **stay out** late.
I **am allowed to stay out** late by my parents.

22.7 Verbs/Expressions followed by -ing or infinitive with a difference in meaning

1. *can't bear/stand, hate, like, love, prefer.* When these verbs are used with the infinitive, they refer to more specific situations. When they are used with -ing, they refer to more general situations.

> **Watch out!** The difference in meaning is very slight.

I *prefer to work* on a computer than to write by hand.
I *can't bear listening* to her complaining all the time.

2. *remember, forget, regret, stop, try*

- *remember/forget* + -ing refers to an action that happened before the moment of remembering/forgetting

- *remember/forget* + infinitive refers to an action after the moment of remembering/forgetting
  I **remember seeing** you somewhere before. (= that I have seen you)
  Did you **remember to lock** the door?
  She had completely **forgotten telling** him about her cat.
  I **forgot to give** Sally the book.

- *regret* + -ing means be sorry about an action that happened in the past

- *regret* + infinitive means be sorry about a present action
  I **regret going** to the party last night.
  I **regret to have to tell** you that your car has been stolen. (= formal)

- *stop* + -ing means stop something you do, e.g. a habit

- *stop* + infinitive with *to* means stop what you are doing in order to do something else
  I **stopped drinking** coffee: it kept me awake at night.
  We **stopped to have** a coffee on the way home.

- *try* + -ing means do an experiment (= doing the action may not be successful)

- *try* + infinitive means make an effort (= the action may be difficult or impossible to do)
  Try studying in the morning – it might suit you better.
  Try to study at regular times.

Writing reference

Checklist

Answering the question

Have you

- answered all parts of the question and included all the necessary information?
- written the required number of words?
- organised your ideas appropriately, using paragraphs where necessary?
- written clearly so that it is easy to read?

Accuracy

Have you checked for mistakes with

- grammar, such as agreement, verb tenses?
- vocabulary, such as incorrect word or wrong word formation?
- spelling or punctuation?

Range

Have you used a variety of grammatical structures, interesting vocabulary and linking words?

Style and layout

Have you

- used a layout appropriate for the type of writing?
- included an appropriate introduction and conclusion?
- used language appropriate for the type of writing?
- made your answer interesting for the reader? Would it have a positive effect?

Gold First by Bell + Thomas
© Pearson.

1 Model answers, with hints and useful phrases

1.1 Essay (Part 1)

For work on essays, see pages 24, 44, 76, 96, and 148.

TASK

In your English class, you have been talking about technology. Now, your English teacher has asked you to write an essay.

Write an essay using **all** the notes and give reasons for your point of view.

> Do people depend too much on technology nowadays?
>
> **Notes**
> Write about:
>
> 1 communication
> 2 education
> 3 _____ (your own idea)

Write your **essay**. (You should write **140–190** words.)

Model answer

DON'T start by saying *I agree with this* – your **essay** should present your own argument.

DO use rhetorical questions to engage the reader with the topic.

DO use linking expressions to introduce points in an **essay**.

DON'T forget to express your opinion in the conclusion.

DO state the topic in your first sentence, but use your own words.

DO include supporting detail for the points in each paragraph.

DO include your own idea.

Nowadays nearly every aspect of life is affected by technology. Computers are used for communication, education and entertainment; but do we depend on them too much?

Some people are afraid that if people spend all their time talking to others on their computers, they become unable to make real relationships. They live through computers or mobile phones, and feel uncomfortable if they are not online. Such people are clearly too dependent on technology, although easy communication has advantages in the business world.

Education has benefited from technology as students can find all the information they need in seconds without needing to spend time going through books. However, if students lose the ability to think for themselves, this is not a good thing.

It is very easy to find entertainment through technology, and it is also used in film-making. We all expect to see special effects in films nowadays and these are produced by technology. But are these films really better than the films of the past?

In my opinion, we have to accept the role of technology nowadays, but we should be aware of the dangers of becoming too dependent on it.

TASK

In your English class, you have been talking about the importance of advertising. Now, your English teacher has asked you to write an essay.

Write an essay using **all** the notes and give reasons for your point of view.

Nowadays there is a great deal of advertising everywhere. Do you think it should be restricted?

Notes

Write about:

1 health
2 information
3 _____ (your own idea)

Write your **essay**. (You should write **140–190** words.)

Useful language

- *Some people claim that* your teenage years are the best years of your life.
- *It is often said that* TV is a bad influence on young people.
- *However, in my view/opinion,* …
- *However, on balance,* …
- *Firstly, it is clear that* money cannot buy happiness.
- *There is a strong argument for* …
- *While it is true/Although it may be said that* computer games are stimulating, they may not be good for you in the long run.
- *To clarify the point,* there is more advertising on TV than ever before …
- *From my point of view/In my view,* job satisfaction is more important than a large salary.
- *It seems clear to me that* …
- *Finally, it is important to remember/must be remembered that* …
- *Lastly, I feel that* …
- *To sum up/In conclusion, it seems to me that* …

Model answer

DO state the topic in your first sentence in general terms in the introduction.

We are surrounded by advertising. It is in shops, on posters, on television, in magazines, online — it is impossible to escape. Is it too much, and should it be restricted?

DO use rhetorical questions to engage the reader with the topic.

DO write in semi-formal style.

There is a strong argument for restricting advertising for unhealthy things like sweets on television because these advertisements can influence the children who see them. The children want to try the products in the advertisements, and this can be bad for their health. Children can't tell the difference between an advertisement and a programme, and of course they have no choice about seeing the advertisement if they are watching the programme.

DO use linking expressions to introduce new points in a new paragraph.

On the other hand, advertisements in magazines give people the chance to see what is available and decide whether to buy a particular product or not. Of course, there is also the point that too many advertisements encourage people to spend money they may not have, which is a bad thing, but people don't have to buy magazines.

DON'T forget that your conclusion should follow your argument clearly.

Some people actually enjoy advertisements because they are often funny and can be entertaining. However, on balance I feel that although advertising has a place in our lives, it should be restricted on television.

DO show that you appreciate the other point of view, even if you don't agree with it.

1.2 Informal letter/email (Part 2)

For work on informal letters and emails, see pages 14 and 138.

TASK

You have received this email from your English-speaking friend Carole.

> When you visit me next month, what would you like to do? You said something about visiting historic places but I know you like sports as well. I've just passed my driving test, so we can get around easily. Have you got any questions for me about your visit?

Write your **email**. (You should write **140–190** words.)

Useful language

Beginning the letter or email

- *Many thanks for your letter/email* – *it was great to hear from you again.*
- *I thought I'd better write* *and give you some more details about …*
- *It's been such a long time since we wrote to each other.*
- *How are things with you?*
- *How was* *your holiday?*

Introducing the topic

- *I know you're keen to hear about* *my holiday.*
- *You remember I told you in my last letter* *that I was going to …*

Ending the letter or email

- *Give my love/regards to* *your family.*
- *Please write soon.*
- *I look forward to* *meeting up again soon.*

Model answer

DO use your friend's name. Don't write *Dear friend*.

DO mention a **letter or email** you have received from the person you are writing to, or refer to a shared experience.

DO use informal language.

DO mention the next time that you will see the person you are writing to.

DO say what you've been doing recently, and give some interesting details.

DO think of some specific details to include in each paragraph – this will make your **letter or email** more interesting.

DO think of some interesting questions to ask.

DO use an appropriate phrase to end your **letter or email**, e.g. *Love, All the best, Best wishes*. DON'T finish your **informal letter or email** with *Yours sincerely/faithfully*.

Hi Carole,

Thanks for your email – it was great to hear from you. I'm sorry I haven't written for a while, but I've been really busy preparing for my exams. It's good news that you've passed your driving test. Congratulations!

I'm really looking forward to my visit - thank you again for inviting me. I know you have a wonderful beach near your house and I'd really enjoy spending some time there. I expect the weather will be hot, so I hope we can go swimming. As you know, I'm also interested in history, so it'd be great if you could drive to the castle in the next town – you told me about it before.

I have a couple of questions. What sort of clothes should I pack? Casual or formal? Would you like me to bring anything for you? I'd like to bring something special for you and your family from my country.

I'd better stop now and get on with my studying. I hope you're enjoying driving your car, and I can't wait to meet up very soon!

All the best,

Irene

1.3 Semi-formal letter (Part 2)

For work on semi-formal letters, see page 86.

TASK

You see this advertisement in a local English language newspaper.

LOOKING FOR PART-TIME WORK?

We need students of English to spend two mornings a week helping in the local tourist office.

Good pay and conditions for the right applicants.

Write to us, giving information about your level of English and explaining why you would be suitable for the job.

Write your **letter**. Do not write any postal addresses.
(You should write **140–190** words.)

Useful language

- *I have always been interested in* using English in my work.
- *One of the main reasons I am applying for this job is that* I want to work in England.
- *I have a lot of experience of* dealing with the public.
- *I am available to start work* at any time/from the end of the month.
- *Thank you for considering my application.*
- *I would be grateful if you would* send me further details of the job.
- *I can be contacted* on 0849 58 48 43 *at any time.*
- *I look forward to hearing from you soon.*

Model answer

Dear Sir/Madam,

I am writing to apply for one of the positions helping in the local tourist office which were advertised in 'Kent Weekly' on 23 August.

> DO say which job you are applying for and where and when you saw it advertised. You can invent a newspaper and date.

I am nineteen years old and come from Switzerland. German is my mother tongue and I have been learning English and French for five years at a comprehensive school. At the moment I'm a student at English International, studying for the Cambridge First Exam.

> DO organise your **letter** so that you mention each of the areas in the advertisement.

> DON'T make mistakes with time expressions and tenses.

I have always been interested in working with people. As I have already spent three months in England, I know the local tourist attractions quite well. I would also say that I have a good knowledge of history and old places because I have read a lot about the subject recently. In the near future, I would like to continue studying English, and so the job in your tourist office would be a great opportunity for me to improve my speaking.

> DON'T forget to mention why you think you are suitable for the job.

I am available for interview at any time. I can be contacted on 0795 51 32 41 after 6p.m. every evening.

> DO say when and how you can be contacted.

Thank you for considering my application. I look forward to hearing from you.

Yours faithfully,

Gabriella Daniels

Gabriella Daniels

> DO begin and end your letter as you would other formal letters.

(Gold first, Pearson 2014)

1.4 Report (Part 2)

For work on reports, see pages 66 and 128.

TASK

The school where you study English has decided to spend some money on **either** buying more computers **or** improving the library. Write a report for the school director describing the benefits to the school of both these options, and recommending which one the school should spend money on.

Write your **report**. (You should write **140–190** words.)

Useful language

Introduction

- *The aim of this report is to* …
- *This report is intended to* …

Reporting results

- *Most people seem to feel that* …
- *Several people said/told me/suggested/thought that* …

Presenting a list

- *They gave/suggested the following reasons:*
- *They made the following points:*
    - *1* …
    - *2* …

Making recommendations

- *I would therefore recommend* that we expand the library/ installing a new coffee machine.
- *It would seem that* banning mobile phones *is the best idea*.

Model answer

DON'T begin and end your **report** with *Dear Sir/ Madam*, like a letter.

DO use headings because this makes it easier for the reader to find the main information.

DO include two or three points under each heading. DO use numbering or bullet points to highlight main points.

DO use formal language in your **report**.

DO say how you collected the information.

DO use a range of specific vocabulary or set phrases e.g. *Some thought this was a good idea* …/*other students said they preferred* …, but DON'T use lots of adjectives and dramatic language as you do in a story. A **report** gives factual information.

DON'T include irrelevant details or description.

DO express opinions impersonally. DON'T express recommendations or opinions until the conclusion.

Use of money for school improvements

Introduction
The aim of this report is to compare the advantages of buying additional computers and of improving the library, and to suggest which would be best. I asked students for their views.

Buying more computers
Some students thought this was a good idea as computers were useful for:

- practising writing
- using the internet
- playing games.

Others said that they preferred to use their own computers at home.

Improving the library
The majority of students preferred this suggestion, for the following reasons:

1 Many do not have a quiet place to work at home. The library could be a good place for private study, but at present there are not enough tables and chairs for everyone.
2 More up-to-date reference books are needed, even though many students use electronic dictionaries.
3 They want to be able to read books written for young people, without having to buy them.

Recommendations
It was felt by most students that improving the library would be more useful and that adding to the workspace and buying reference books would benefit the majority of students. I would therefore recommend spending money in this way.

FCE Gold by Bell & Thomas © Pearson

1.5 Article (Part 2)

For work on articles, see pages 34 and 106.

TASK

You see this advertisement in an English language magazine.

ARTICLES WANTED!

What is the most important celebration in your country?
Why is it so important? What do people do?

Write us an article answering these questions.

The best articles will be published in the magazine.

Write your **article**. (You should write **140–190** words.)

Useful language

Involving the reader
- *Are you thinking of* getting married in the near future?
- *I'm sure you'll agree* it was a great idea.

Developing your points
- *Let's start with* why it is so important to take plenty of exercise.
- *Another advantage* of using a computer is that …
- *On top of that,* …

Giving your own opinion
- *I think that/In my opinion* traditional celebrations are very important.
- *It seems to me that* people are much more aware of the importance of a good diet nowadays.

Model answer

DO think of an interesting title. Use the title given in the task. If there isn't a title given, write one of your own.

DO try to involve your reader directly, e.g. by using a question.

DO use informal language to involve the reader.

DON'T forget to express your opinion.

DO finish your **article** by summarising your main point and giving your opinion or expressing your feelings.

> Olinda's carnival – something for everyone
>
> When most people think of Carnival, they think of Rio de Janeiro. But Rio isn't the only city in Brazil that knows how to have parties. I live in Olinda, a lovely city in the north-east of Brazil. What can we say about the carnival at Olinda? Just that it's the best in the world!
>
> Carnival has its origins in ancient Egyptian and Roman festivals. It was introduced to Brazil by the Portuguese, and was influenced by African rhythms and Indian costumes. Now it's a big national celebration.
>
> Once Carnival starts, the whole town goes crazy! Everyone's singing and dancing. Parades of people wearing costumes typical of our north-eastern folklore dance through the streets. I love the giant street dolls, both the traditional ones such as 'the man of midnight' and the new ones that appear each year.
>
> The best thing about our carnival is that no one has to pay and there are no big stars. Everyone takes part, rich and poor, old and young, residents and tourists. If you come, I promise you'll never forget it!

1.6 Review (Part 2)

For work on reviews, see pages 54 and 118.

TASK

You see this announcement in an English language magazine.

Film reviews wanted

We want your views on films being made today! Write us a review of the last film you saw. Tell us about the story, characters and any special features of the film, and whether you would recommend the film to other people. The best review will be published in the magazine.

Write your **review**. (You should write **140–190** words.)

Useful language

Introduction

- *The film I would like to review is …*
- *The last film I saw / book I read was …*

Summarising the story

- *It's set in …*
- *The story is based on a book …*
- *It's about …*
- *There are many memorable characters including …*
- *The main theme of the film is …*
- *What the film is saying is …*

Recommending the film

- *I would recommend this film to anyone.*
- *Although I enjoyed it, I would not recommend it for …*
- *It's one of the best shows I've ever seen.*
- *Although I am not normally keen on musicals, I'm glad that I decided to go.*
- *The film lifts you out of your everyday life.*

Model answer

The last film I saw was not new; in fact it was *The Lord of the Rings*.

It is based on the well-known book and tells the story of a creature called a hobbit who takes a dangerous magic ring back to the place where it was made in order to destroy it. There are many memorable characters apart from the hobbit and his friends, including a wizard called Gandalf and a suspicious creature called Gollum.

This is a film about friendship and loyalty. However, it is the special effects that make it truly magical. There are vivid battle scenes with fantastic animals and birds, and sets that are so imaginative that you want to believe they are real. But as well as this, the actual locations are beautiful too.

I would recommend this film to anyone, even those who do not usually enjoy fantasy films. What I would say to them is – go and try it! Like me, you might find that the film lifts you out of your everyday life into a world you may not want to leave.

DO say what the film is about, but not in too much detail.

DO try to use a range of interesting vocabulary, to bring the film to life for the reader.

DO remember to mention important or memorable characters, but don't spend too much time describing them.

DO remember to explain your ideas clearly and to link paragraphs together.

*DO remember to give your opinion, as this is the purpose of a **review**, but not until the end.*

2 Sample answers

The following scripts were written by students. Read the general marking guidelines on page 194, and use them to help you assess each answer and decide on its strong and weak points. Then read the comments given and the suggested band score, and compare your ideas.

2.1 Essay (Part 1)

TASK

In your English class you have been talking about what people do in their free time. Now, your teacher has asked you to write an essay.

Write an essay using **all** the notes and give reasons for your point of view.

Many people in a city go shopping in their free time. Do you think this has any value as a leisure activity?

Notes

Write about:

1 relaxation
2 social activity
3 .... (your own idea)

Write your **essay**. (You should write **140–190** words.)

Sample answer

I believe that shopping can be one of the important things people do, like eating and sleeping, and for some, shopping is their chance to do their favourite things like walking and meeting friends.

On the one hand, I think that is true that shopping has no value in some lifestyles. People think of shopping only as a chance to do whatever they want, and then it is an escape from doing things they should do. I mean people go shopping instead of do work. They don't think of going to sightseeing or interesting things. However, others think of it as a chance to meet some friends who you only see from time to time. In addition, it is useful time to discuss every day problems – for example, if you have got some problems, in that shopping time you might listen to others problems and think that yours are nothing compared to theirs. It can make a break from every day work pressure and so it is valuable for some who have a hard job and lifestyle.

In conclusion, it's true that buying things has little value, but people are different, which means that shopping will be priceless for some.

Comments

This answers the question clearly and uses a wide range of vocabulary and some good expressions (e.g. *think that yours are nothing compared to theirs*). The paragraphs are clearly introduced with linking words (e.g. *On the one hand*). However, there are some grammatical mistakes (e.g. *instead of do work*). The style is appropriate, and the writer has included interesting ideas of their own about discussing problems with friends when shopping. The conclusion clearly returns to the question and gives a nice summary of the writer's opinion. A very good communicative achievement. **Band 4**

(Gold First, Pearson 2014)

TASK

In your English class you have been talking about consumerism. Now your English teacher has asked you to write an essay.

Write an essay using **all** the notes and give reasons for your point of view.

Write your **essay**. (You should write **140–190** words.)

Nowadays people buy products that come from all over the world instead of things that come from their local area. Do you think this is a good idea?

Notes

Write about:

1 employment
2 quality of products
3 .... (your own idea)

Sample answers

A

Everything in the world always has advantages and disadvantages. As local products, it doesn't have famous brand, but it can help many people get a good job, and get a high income.

To begin with, it contributes various types of jobs for people. As a country able to educate their citizens to produce their own product, this will bring plenty of careers for these people. Also the products can be more fresher and more healthier because they are home made without any chemical that harmful people's health.

On the other hand if we live in that area and we use that products too, we can know clearly how they made it, because we can go to the company or places where they were made. For example, bread, if we want to know how it was made and what they put in it, we can go to the place where it made. So we can give the people feedback and help them to improve.

So in my opinion it is better to buy local products rather than bought products from other countries.

B

There are many reasons to support domestic products in our country. Firstly, jobless in own country can be reduced because more people will have employment.

Another point is that having local products is more convenient and more reliable. For example, if you get some products that are not related to our country you may get products that don't have our native language on it. This, how can you read the use or the benefit of it? And this will cause you a great deal of problem.

On the other hand there will still have some disadvantages about this point. Some people want to buy product from all over the world because they want to try new thing, for example food they want to try new tasty, or for mobile phone, they want to try if it's better than local product or not.

The conclusion I strongly disagree about the sentence that it is good thing to buy local products imported from all over the world because most of the people, they want to try new things, get new experience.

Comments

A This has a fairly good range of grammar, and the answer is well organised in paragraphs with appropriate linking words. The introduction is a little confusing but the conclusion works well, and it is possible to understand the writer's viewpoint. The writer has used the idea of working with local producers to give feedback as their third point. There are some grammatical mistakes (e.g. *more healthier, harmful people's health*). The style is generally suitable for an essay. A satisfactory communicative achievement. **Band 3**

B This has no introduction to the topic, and the ideas are not clearly expressed. The writer mentions the lack of native language and trying new things as his own ideas, and uses this in his conclusion. There are grammatical mistakes with articles and some sentences are not clear (e.g. *for example food they want to try new tasty*). The conclusion does not seem to follow the argument logically. The essay just about has a reasonably satisfactory communicative effect and would just reach **Band 3.**

2.2 Informal letter (Part 2)

Sample answers

A

Dear Tom,

Hi! How are you? Thank you for your letter! I'm very happy about your plan!

OK! If you let me know your arrival time, I will come to you, at Narita airport. I've thought about our plan in Japan. I know you really like football! So, how about visiting stadiums of the World Cup? You can visit a locker room in Yokohama International Stadium where the final was held, and you can see autographs of Brazilian national team members.

In July, Japan is very hot, but sometimes there is a heavy rain so you have to bring an umbrella. And there are lots of mosquitoes, you must bring a medical cream to protect yourself against them.

Do you have any special requests? If you have any, please let me know. I'll try to do it!

I'm looking forward to your reply and to meeting you in July!

Lots of love,
Yuka

B

Dear Tom,

Nice to hear from you. I'm so surprised that you are on your way to come here this summer. I have to say that you've made a good decision.

First of all, I would like to recommend you some places where you shouldn't miss such as Sentosa island. You can have different activities there. For example, if you would like having sunbathing. I think 'Sun World' is the best choice to relax. Don't forget to bring swimwear. I don't think Bird Park is a good place to visit. It's quite boring I have to be honest to say that. However if you are really interesting in visiting there I could show you around.

Secondly, it's the best time come here if you enjoy the shopping. We have big on sale in July. Therefore, I can arrange the shopping table for you.

I don't think you need to bring any special stuff. That's because you can buy them here. Don't forget to prepare some more empty suitcase for your shopping.

If you have any question just ask me. I'll do my best to solve them.

Best wishes,
Carel

Comments

A All parts of the question are dealt with, in an appropriately informal style. There are some grammatical mistakes (e.g. *there is a heavy rain*) and problems in pronoun use (e.g. *I'll try to do* it) but the student uses tenses accurately and shows a good range of vocabulary, and the paragraphs are clear and well constructed. The letter has a positive effect on the reader. **Band 4**

B This is a full answer to the question, with a fairly good range of grammar, but there are quite a few grammatical problems (e.g. *recommend you some places where you* instead of *recommend some places to you which; interesting in* instead of *interested in*). Vocabulary problems sometimes make the meaning unclear (e.g. *I can arrange the shopping table for you*). Paragraphs and connecting words are well used and the style is generally suitable for a letter from a friend. It has a satisfactory effect on the reader. **Band 3**

2.3 Semi-formal letter (Part 2)

TASK

You have received this letter from the organisers of a competition you entered.

Write your **letter.** Do not write any postal addresses. (You should write **140–190** words.)

> Congratulations! You have won first prize in our competition – a two-week trip to Vancouver OR San Francisco. Your prize includes FREE return flight to the city of your choice, a two-week English course and FREE accommodation with a family.
> Which city would you prefer, and when? Would you like us to make any special arrangements for you?

Sample answers

A

Dear Mrs Thompson,

Thank you very much for the letter. I am very pleased that I've won the prize. I would like to go to San Francisco because I have never been to the USA before. However, there are several questions I would like to ask.

First of all, I would like to know whether the return flight is a direct flight or not. I would like to book a direct flight because it is much more comfortable.

Secondly, I would like to know how long we are being teached every day and if there are classes in the morning or the afternoon. Is there a difference between Vancouver and San Francisco concerning this point?

You wrote about a free accommodation with a family. Are the meals included and/or do I have the opportunity to cook by myself? Please let me also know the distance from the school.

Finally, I would like to ask you if it is possible to stay at school for an extra week. If it is possible please let me know the price I have to pay.

I like to thank you in advance for your assistance and I look forward to hearing from you soon.

Yours sincerely,

Anders Moser

B

Dear Sir or Madam

Thank you very much for your letter which I received yesterday. I would like to go to Vancouver, because I have never been there. As I know that the weather in Canada is very nice in summertime, my preferred month is July.

Furthermore, I would like to enquire whether you could let me have some more information about my prize. First of all, I am interested in my course: how many lessons in a week do we have? And only in the morning, or in the afternoon as well? In addition to this. I would like to know if my flight is a direct one or not. My other questions concern my host family. As I am vegetarian, I would prefer to go in a family who cooks not only meat dishes. Is this possible? And how far do students usually have to walk to school?

I would be grateful if you could reply to these questions as soon as possible.

Yours faithfully

Andrea Larssen

Comments

A There is no irrelevant information and the student answers the question with interesting details. There are some grammatical mistakes (e.g. *we are being teached*; *a free accommodation*), but these don't cause problems in understanding the meaning. He uses quite a wide range of structures, although he tends to repeat *I would like to know*. Ideas are organised in paragraphs with appropriate vocabulary. The style is sometimes too formal (e.g. *concerning this point*) but the letter shows a high level of communicative achievement. **Band 5**

B There is a grammatical mistake in word order (*'who cooks not only meat dishes'*) but she uses a wide range of structures accurately including the present perfect. The vocabulary is appropriate and there is clear paragraphing although the use of *furthermore* is not appropriate. All parts of the task are dealt with. The style is semi-formal and appropriate, and the letter shows a high level of communicative achievement. **Band 5**

2.4 Report (Part 2)

> **TASK**
>
> The principal of your school wants to make some changes to the school classrooms and has asked students for ideas about what should be done to make the classrooms better places to study in. Write a report making suggestions for how the classrooms could be improved.
>
> Write your **report**. (You should write **140–190** words.)

Sample answer

Introduction

This report is to suggest what we need to make the classrooms better in our school. I asked students for their ideas.

Background situation

What it's need to be inside a good school classrooms is that they all have all the equipment students might need starting from the essential things like chair, blackboards, finishing with accessories like televisions.

Suggestions

I certainly believe that two things need to start our plan to improve the school classrooms, they are money and good management. My idea of improving the classrooms is to start with what we have and see what needs to be repared and what has to be thrown away and replaced with a new equipment and some computers that the students might need also having a massive liberrary is one of the more important things that students request. Heating and air conditioning are necessary to make the atmosphere in the classrooms cosy.

Personal opinion

In conclusion, the chance of having a good classrooms looks easy from a distance, in fact it isn't, and that we must try to find the balance between having a very good school and not spending too much.

Comments

This report makes some relevant points, but the style is more suitable for an essay than a report. It is not easy to identify the main suggestions because of problems with sentence linking and punctuation. *My idea of … is to start with what we have* is good. The problem is the sentence is too long and needs splitting up, e.g. *My idea of improving the classrooms is to start with what we have. Then we can see …*. There are some problems with passive forms (e.g. *what it's need* instead of *what is needed*) but also some good expressions (e.g. *to start with what we have; we must try to find the balance between*). The student has a good range of vocabulary although this is not always appropriately used (e.g. *massive, cosy*) and there are some spelling mistakes (e.g. *repared, liberrary*). It has a generally satisfactory level of communicative achievement. **Band 3**

2.5 Article (Part 2)

TASK

You see this advertisement in an English language magazine for young people.

> *I'd love to have …*
>
> Write an article about something you would like to have, saying why you would like to have it and what difference it would make to your life.
>
> **The best article will be published in the magazine.**

Write your **article**. (You should write **140–190** words.)

Sample answers

A

I'd love to have…

Now, I'm living in England to study English. I came from Japan. Have you been there? It takes 13 hours to get there by airplanes. The most thing which I really need is not airplane tickets, it's a computer.

Yes, I know. Most people's opinions are same as me. In my case, the situation is slightly different. In my computer, I could have lots of digital photos. They remind me many memories of my friends in Japan and friends who I make in England. When I get a homesick, they help me. I can feel that I'm not alone. Indeed, I could connect with my parents and friends by emails. The fact that we live in foreign countries is sometimes very stressful, but I could consult to them whenever I want. It's very convenient! And writing to my foreign friends is very good writing practice, isn't it?

If you studied abroad, I would recommend you to have a computer. Trust me! It will make life so much easier for you.

B

Money would be lovely!

I'd love to have a lot of money although I think money is not a perfect solution. Of course not! However, if I had enough money, I could do a plenty of things which I want to do.

Above all, I want to study in other countries, because. It is a good chance to develop my abilities. In this case, I don't need to worry about the fee of education in my life. I can only concentrate on studying as long as I do my best.

Secondly, I would like to prepare a lovely house for my parents. Although they didn't say to me at all, I think the work of electric services is so hard to continue at their ages within 10 years. Therefore, I hope that I could make them relax and enjoy their life.

On the other hand, I can help the other people who are suffering from lack of food, illness and so on. When I saw a TV programme which announced those people's stories, I thought if I were them I would get really depressed.

Sometimes, money can be used in a bad way, but if I am a rich person, I will spend them on not only for me, but I also give an opportunity to others.

Comments

A The language is informal: *Yes, I know*, and *Trust me!* are more like spoken English although the style is also engaging. There are grammar mistakes(e.g. *a homesick, recommend you*). The paragraphing is clear but the introduction is confusing because it includes irrelevant information. The answer has a reasonably satisfactory level of communicative achievement. **Band 3**

B There is a range of structure and vocabulary but there are mistakes (e.g. *If I am a rich person, I will spend them on not only for me*). It is difficult to understand what she says about her parents (*Although they didn't say to me at all, I think …*). Paragraphs are well planned but there are mistakes with punctuation and linking words (e.g. *On the other hand, Secondly*). There is informal and informal language (e.g. *Of course not!/therefore*). It has a satisfactory level of communicative achievement. **Band 3**

2.6 Review (Part 2)

Sample answers

A

I want to tell you about a movie really discussed in Italy, 'L'Ultimo Bacio' (The Last Kiss) directed by Gabriele Muccino in 2001.

It is set in an Italian city in the same time in which actors play, in fact, the director's purpose is take a plausible picture of people's life. The movie tell us about the crisis of two different generations worried by the difficulty of grow up and take their responsibility.

On the one hand, there are thirty years old people who think wedding like an important change of life but sad and serious, therefore they are very frightened of doing it, preferring an affair with someone else to solving their couple's problems.

On the other hand, fifty years old people are frightened of growing old.

I think the story is really topical and show a widespread situation, the actors' performance is really good, the dialogues are fast and accurate. Although is a great film I must admit that it is a bit too shouted, but this is Muccino's style.

A good story, great actors and good dialogues and editing, 'L'Ultimo Bacio' is really interesting, not boring at all.

B

My favourite film is called 'If only'. It's the best romantic film I have ever seen.

It's set in London and about a hard-working businessman and a lovely violinist woman. The man is too busy to take care his love. He thinks work is more important than his girlfriend. On the concert of her graduation he meets a taxi driver and talks with him about their love. He realises something but it's too late because his girlfriend dies by car accident. He regrets everything, but surprisingly there is a great chance of living with her again. Finally he can appreciate her, but sadly he has to die instead of his girlfriend.

I have seen it 5 times. Until I saw it 3-4 times it was just love story with strange situation, but last time, I can feel character's feelings. So it was a really romantic film. The plot and the song of the actress was fantastic. The story could be a bit artificial and far-fetched. But if you focus on character's feelings you can be given a good precept. Don't calculate your love, just appreciate her!

If you fall in love or like romance you'll love this film.

Comments

A This review has some style problems and is not always easy to follow. *On the one hand / On the other hand* does not link well to *two different generations*. There is a good range of vocabulary (*plausible picture, taking responsibility, widespread situation*) but some words are misused, e.g. *too shouted*. There are basic grammatical mistakes, e.g. *-ing* form after prepositions (*difficulty of grow up*). The review only has a satisfactory level of communicative achievement. **Band 3**

B This is clearly organised and easy to follow. The style and paragraphing are both generally appropriate, and the writer has given her opinion. There is some interesting vocabulary although some words are misused, e.g. *precept*. The sentences are simple, but there is a range of structures including present perfect and modals. Mistakes do not usually impede communication. The review generally has a satisfactory level of communicative achievement. **Band 3**

3 Marking guidelines

Both Parts of the Writing paper carry equal marks. Here are some guidelines for assessment

Band	Content	Communicative achievement	Organisation	Language
5	All the content is relevant. The reader has all the information they need.	Communicates both straightforward and complex ideas effectively.	The text is well-organised and coherent, with a variety of connecting words.	Uses a range of vocabulary, including less common words, appropriately. Uses a range of simple and complex grammatical forms with only occasional errors.
4	A mix of bands 3 and 5			
3	Nearly all the content is relevant. In general, the reader has all the information they need.	Communicates straightforward ideas effectively.	The text is generally well-organised and coherent, with a variety of connecting words.	Uses a range of everyday vocabulary appropriately. There may be occasional errors with less common lexis. Uses a range of simple and complex grammatical forms. There may be some errors, but these do not cause difficulty for the reader.
2	A mix of bands 1 and 3			
1	Some of the content is irrelevant. Some information needed by the reader is omitted.	Generally communicates straightforward ideas appropriately.	The text is connected and coherent, using basic linking words.	Uses everyday vocabulary generally appropriately, while occasionally overusing some words. Uses simple grammatical forms with a good degree of control. Errors are noticeable, but the meaning can still be understood.
0	The content is totally irrelevant. The reader does not have the information they need.	Below band 1		

4 Guide to writing genres

The range of task types in Parts 1 and 2 of the Writing Paper give you the chance to write in different styles and for different purposes. This enables you to show a range of language across the paper, and in Part 2 you can choose to write in a style you feel comfortable with.

4.1 Part 1

Essay

An essay is written for a teacher or tutor. The purpose of an essay is to present an argument or point of view that the reader can easily identify and understand. You should answer the question provided in the task by discussing the two content points you are given and adding a new idea of your own. You should organise your essay into clear paragraphs with a new paragraph for each point. There should be an introduction to the topic in the first paragraph and the essay should finish with an appropriate conclusion that rounds off the argument and sets out your point of view. The style will probably be semi-formal and ideas should be linked with appropriate words and phrases.

4.2 Part 2

Email/Letter

An informal or semi-formal letter or email is written as a response to part of a letter or email provided in the task. There may also be a situation you have to respond to, such as an advertisement for a job or course. The letter or email may be written to an English-speaking friend, a possible employer, a college principal or an editor of a newspaper or magazine. It is important that you write in a consistent and appropriate style for the reader of your letter or email, and that you include all the information required so that the reader is fully informed.

Article

An article is usually written for an English language magazine, newsletter or website on a topic of general interest to both the readers and the writer of the article. In an article you may have to give examples to support an idea or comment on a topic. The purpose of an article is to interest, entertain and engage the reader, and so you should try to use techniques to engage the reader such as rhetorical questions as well as a range of interesting language.

Report

A report is usually written for a teacher or principal or a fellow-member of a club or similar organisation. In a report you usually have to give factual information about a given situation and make suggestions or recommendations about that situation. The purpose of a report is to give information to enable the reader to decide on a course of action. This means the information and recommendations in the report should be well-organised and expressed clearly. It may be helpful to use headings and bullet points for recommendations. The introduction should include a summary of the purpose of the report, and the conclusion should highlight the recommended course of action.

Review

A review is usually written for an English language magazine, newspaper or website. Reviews may be about a film a book, a holiday, a product, a website, and so on. The purpose of a review is to inform the reader by describing something and giving a personal opinion about it in an interesting and engaging way. You should give a brief description of the film/book etc., and provide clear reasons for recommending it to others or not. It is important for you to describe well and explain your opinions clearly so the reader understands whether you are recommending the film, etc. or not, and why.

5 Additional tasks with suggested plans

You should always plan your answer before you start to write. In the exam you should allow time for this, and also for checking for mistakes after you have finished. Here are some tasks, and suggested plans. Read them to see how the plan works with the task, then try writing your own plan and answer.

5.1 Essay (Part 1)

TASK

In your English class you have been talking about students doing part-time jobs. Now your English teacher has asked you to write an essay.

Write an essay using **all** the notes and give reasons for your point of view.

> Many students do part-time jobs. Is this a good idea?
>
> **Notes**
> Write about:
>
> 1 disadvantages
> 2 advantages
> 3 .... (your own idea)

Write your **essay.** (You should write **140–190** words.)

Plan

Introduction

Introduce the topic in a general way but don't give your own opinion.

Paragraph 1

Describe possible disadvantages, e.g. time, low pay.

Paragraph 2

Describe possible advantages, e.g. earning money for fees, work experience.

Paragraph 3

Add an extra point, e.g. improved attitude to life.

Conclusion

Give your own opinion about whether a part-time job is a good idea or not.

5.2 Letter (Part 2)

TASK

You receive this letter from a travel company about a recent holiday you have had with them.

> We understand that you were dissatisfied with the holiday you have recently taken with our company, and we would like to find out what happened. Write to us explaining what the problems were, what your experiences were and what you would like us to do.

Write a **letter.** (You should write **140–190** words.)

Plan

Introduction

Say when and where you were on holiday with the company.

Paragraph 1

Describe the problems, e.g. location of hotel, extra costs for meals, evening activities.

Paragraph 2

Explain your experiences e.g. disappointment with holiday, extra expense.

Paragraph 3

Say what you want the company to do.

5.3 Article (Part 2)

TASK

You see this advertisement in a local English language newspaper.

Articles wanted: Life today

Is life better for young people now than it was for our parents? What has improved? What is worse?
Write us an article answering these questions. We will publish the best articles in the newspaper.

Write your **article**. (You should write **140–190** words.)

Plan

Decide on a title

Introduction

Introduce the topic generally – maybe with a rhetorical question.

Paragraph 1

Describe something that is better, e.g. technology, entertainment.

Paragraph 2

Describe something that is worse, e.g. pollution, stress and pressure.

Conclusion

Give your opinion, with an amusing or interesting ending.

5.4 Report (Part 2)

TASK

Your college principal wants to improve the land around the college buildings to make it more attractive for students. He has asked students to write a report on the current situation, and make recommendations for using the land.

Write your **report**. (You should write **140–190** words.)

Plan

Introduction

Explain the purpose of the report and who you interviewed.

Current situation

Explain why the land is not nice now, e.g. it is overgrown.

Suggestions

Make recommendations for the land based on student feedback, e.g. a garden, sports pitches.

Conclusion

Highlight the results of following your suggestions.

5.5 Review (Part 2)

TASK

You see this announcement in an English language magazine.

BOOK REVIEWS WANTED

Have you read a book in which the main character is particularly interesting? Write us a review of the book, explaining what makes the main character so interesting and why you liked them. Tell us whether you would recommend this book to other people or not.

Write your **review**. (You should write **140–190** words.)

Plan

Introduction

Introduce the book and the main character.

Paragraph 1

Explain what makes the main character interesting and why you like them.

Paragraph 2

Sum up the reasons you recommend the book to others.

Conclusion

Finish with an interesting or amusing concluding sentence.

6 Discourse markers and linking words and phrases

6.1 Time sequencers

Examples include *before, after, after a while, eventually, later, then, finally, as soon as, at first, at last, when, while*.

I immediately phoned the police. **While** *I was waiting for them to arrive, I watched the house.*

At first, no one got out of the car, but **after a while** *the driver's door opened.*

And **then** *I* **finally** *found what I was looking for.*

6.2 Listing points

Examples include *first, firstly, first of all, to begin with, secondly, thirdly, finally*.

Our holiday was spoiled, **firstly** *because the hotel was uncomfortable and* **secondly** *because the weather was bad.*

6.3 Adding information/Emphasising points

Examples include *as well as (that), in addition (to), moreover, furthermore, not only … (but also…), what's more, on top of that, to make matters worse, in fact, as a matter of fact*.

The hotel was miles from the beach. **On top of that**, *the view from our bedroom window was terrible.*

Not only *was the hotel miles from the beach,* **but** *the view from our bedroom window was terrible too!*

In fact, *everyone is different when it comes to personal taste.*

6.4 Giving examples

Examples include *for example, for instance, such as*.

I like pop groups **such as** *Take That.*

My town has a lot of things for young people to do. **For example**, *there are three cinemas.*

6.5 Reasons, causes and results

Examples include *as a result, because, because of (this), so, therefore*.

I have visited Britain several times and, **as a result**, *my English is quite good.*

By the end of the day, you haven't managed to find anything that you like. **So**, *you go home frustrated.*

6.6 Contrast

but

But links two contrasting ideas. It is not normally used at the beginning of the sentence.

Many people argue that TV is bad for you, **but** *I disagree with this.*

however

However can come at the beginning or end of a sentence. It must be separated off by commas.

The advert claimed that there were huge discounts for students. **However**, *the discount was only five percent.*

I love travelling. I don't enjoy long flights, **however**.

although, even though, though

These expressions introduce a subordinate clause of contrast. If the subordinate clause comes first, it is separated from the main clause by a comma.

Although *he practised every day, he didn't manage to improve.*

I walked home **even though** *it took me two hours.*

NOTE *though* can be used after a comma at the end of a separate sentence that expresses something surprising.

We lived in the middle of a city. We still had a large garden, **though**.

whereas, while

• *Whereas* and *while* are used to compare two things and show how they are different.

She likes football **whereas** *I prefer tennis.*

My sister is very like my father, **while** *I take after my mother.*

• *While* is also used in the same way as *although*.

While *computers are important, we shouldn't let them rule our lives.*

in spite of (the fact that), despite (the fact that)

These expressions must be followed by a noun or *-ing* form. *Despite* is slightly more formal than *in spite of*.

In spite of *the fact that they are expensive, many people want to buy designer clothes.*

Despite *all the research that has been done, we still haven't found a cure for cancer.*

in fact, the fact of the matter is

This is used when you are saying what the 'real' truth of a situation is.

According to the brochure, the service is free for students. **In fact,** *students are charged at the same rate as everyone else.*

On (the) one hand, … On the other hand, …

These expressions are used to introduce opposite points in a discussion.

(On the one hand,) *if I take the job in Milan, I'll be able to go to the opera.* **On the other hand,** *if I take the job in Barcelona, I'll be able to go to the beach.*

otherwise

This is used to say what will happen if something else does not happen first.

You have to choose your holiday carefully. **Otherwise,** *you could be disappointed.*

7 Academic language

For the Writing paper, it is important to use the correct style. If you are writing an essay or report, it may be appropriate to use language that is academic. Here are some examples of sentences using: **1** non-academic English, and **2** academic English.

7.1 Nouns

function
1 I don't know what they will use the new building for.
2 The **function** of the new building is unclear to me.

area
1 This is something that we don't know much about.
2 This is an **area** that we know little about.

role
1 An important way to improve people's eating habits is by educating them.
2 Education **plays an important role** in improving people's eating habits.

source
1 We don't know where this information comes from.
2 The **source** of this information is not known.

factor
1 If people are poor, they may commit crimes as a result.
2 Poverty seems to be **a key factor** in many crimes.

aspect
1 If you are ill, that can affect different parts of your life.
2 Ill health may affect **different aspects** of your life.

concept
1 Some people find it hard to understand the idea of climate warming.
2 Some people cannot **grasp the concept** of climate warming.

feature
1 The new sports stadium is an important building in our city.
2 The new sports stadium is **a major feature** of our city.

7.2 Adjectives

beneficial
1 The effects of the internet are not all good for people who use it.
2 Not all the effects of the internet are **beneficial** to its users.

varied
1 People replied to our question in lots of different ways.
2 Many **varied** responses were given to our question.

significant
1 Technology is very important in people's lives.
2 The effect of technology on people's lives is very **significant**.

financial
1 Often, young people don't have enough money.
2 Young people often suffer from **financial problems**.

specific
1 The speaker talked about the special problems that people around here have.
2 The speaker **discussed the specific problems affecting** people living in this area.

sufficient
1 I hope there will be enough money from the government to finish the project.
2 I hope to have **sufficient government funding** to complete the project.

7.3 Verbs

establish
1 They started the company in 1978.
2 The company **was established** in 1978.

assess
1 They did research to find out how much long distance runners were affected by diet.
2 **Research was carried out to assess the effects** of diet on long-distance runners.

identify
1 We can see three big problems in the plans for a new car park.
2 Three **major problems can be identified** in the plans for a new car park.

occur
1 Some bad flooding happened in places round the town.
2 Serious flooding **occurred** in areas around the town.

assume
1 The students think they can use the school hall for the event.
2 The students **assume** they can use the school hall for the event.

require
1 The main thing a mountain climber needs is a good head for heights.
2 The main thing **required of** a mountain climber is a good head for heights.

Exam focus

Contents

Reading and Use of English Paper (1 hour 15 minutes)

Part 1 (Multiple-choice cloze)

What is being tested?

Part 1 tests your awareness of vocabulary, including words with similar meanings. It also tests some grammatical features, e.g. phrasal verbs and fixed phrases.

What do you have to do?

- Read a text with eight missing words.
- Choose the correct word or phrase from each set of four options.
- Mark the correct letter A, B, C or D on your answer sheet.

Strategy

1 Read the title and the text quickly to get a general idea of what it is about, without trying to fill any of the gaps.

2 Read the text again. Stop at each gap and try to predict what the missing word or phrase might be.

3 Look at the options for each gap carefully. Try putting each of the options in the gap to see which one fits best.

4 Check the words on either side of the gap to see if the option you have chosen goes with these.

5 Read the whole text again to make sure the options you have chosen make sense. Do not leave a blank; if you are not sure, choose the one which seems most likely.

6 Transfer your answers to the answer sheet.

Part 2 (Open cloze)

What is being tested?

In Part 2, the focus is on grammar and the missing words will be grammatical words like auxiliary verbs, articles, prepositions, pronouns, phrasal verbs, etc. Again, there is also a lexical element.

What do you have to do?

- Read the text with eight missing words.
- Put one word in each of the eight gaps.
- Write the the correct word for each gap clearly on your answer sheet.

Strategy

1 Read the title and text quickly to get a general idea of what it is about, without trying to fill any of the gaps.
2 Think about what kind of word is missing, e.g. preposition, article, pronoun, etc.
3 Write in the missing words in pencil. Only write one word in each gap.
4 When you have finished, read through the whole text again. Check it makes sense, and check the spelling.
5 Transfer your answers to the answer sheet.

Part 3 (Word formation)

What is being tested?

Part 3 focuses on both vocabulary and grammar and tests your knowledge of how words are formed using prefixes and suffixes, etc. You'll have to understand what kind of word is required in each gap (e.g. noun, adjective, adverb), and be able to form it.

What do you have to do?

- Read a paragraph with eight gaps.
- Use the word in capital letters at the end of each line with a gap to form a word which fits each gap.
- Write your answers on your answer sheet.

Strategy

1 Read the title and the text quickly to get a general idea of what it is about.
2 Read the text again. This time stop at each gap. Think about whether the missing word is positive or negative, plural or singular, a noun, verb, adjective or adverb. Use the words before and after each gap to help you decide.
3 Write the correct form of the word in the gap.
4 Read the text again to make sure your answers make sense and the words are spelt correctly.
5 Transfer your answers to the answer sheet.

Part 4 (Key word transformations)

What is being tested?

Part 4 tests a range of grammatical structures as well as vocabulary, and shows examiners that you can express yourself in different ways.

What do you have to do?

- Complete six sentences using two to five words, including a key word which is provided. Your completed sentence must have a similar meaning to the lead-in sentence. You will usually have to change two things.
- Write your answers on the answer sheet.

Strategy

1 Read the first sentence and the key word. Work out what is being tested, e.g. you may need a passive form in the future.
2 Identify what is missing from the second sentence.
3 Think about what kind of words need to be used with the key word.
4 Write down the missing words. Do not change the key words in any way.
5 Make sure you have not written more than five words (contractions, e.g. *don't*, count as two words) and that you have not changed the meaning at all.
6 Check your spelling and that the sentences make sense.
7 Transfer your answers to your answer sheet.

Part 5 (Multiple choice)

What is being tested?

Part 5 focuses on your ability to understand a text in detail. Questions will focus on different things such as the main idea of a text, specific details in a text, the writer's opinion, attitude or purpose, your ability to understand the meaning of words or phrases from the context, and to follow features of text organisation such as examples and references.

What do you have to do?

- Read the text and answer six questions. Each question has four possible answers (A, B, C or D) and the questions follow the order of the text.
- Choose the correct option for each question, based on the information in the text.
- Mark the correct letter A, B, C or D for each answer on your answer sheet.

Strategy

1 Read the instructions, title and sub-heading of the text.
2 Skim the text to get a general idea of what it is about.
3 Read each question and highlight the key words (don't worry about the four options yet).
4 For each question, highlight the part of the text that the question relates to.
5 Read the text again carefully. When you find a part of the text you have highlighted, look at the question and the four options and decide on the answer. The meaning will be the same but the language will be different.
6 Check all the options again carefully, crossing out ones that are obviously wrong.
7 Make your decision. If you are not sure, choose the option that seems most likely.
8 When you have completed all the questions, transfer your answers to the answer sheet.

Part 6 (Gapped text)

What is being tested?

In Part 6, you will be tested on your understanding of how a text is structured.

What do you have to do?

- Read through the text, from which six sentences have been removed.
- Read the seven sentences (there is an extra one which doesn't fit anywhere) and decide which sentence best fits each gap.
- Mark your answers on your answer sheet.

Strategy

1 Read the title and sub-heading to get an idea about the topic of the text.
2 Read the main text carefully to make sure you understand what it is about.
3 Read the section before and after each gap and predict what information is missing from each gap.
4 Underline any nouns, pronouns, linkers etc. which will help you to find a link.
5 Read the seven sentences and look for clues that will connect them to the gaps. Look for topic words, synonyms and reference words.
6 If you are not sure about what goes in a gap, go on to the next question and return to it later.
7 When you have finished, read through the completed text to check that it makes sense. Make sure you have filled in all the gaps and not used any sentences more than once.
8 Try the extra sentence in each gap again to make sure that it doesn't fit anywhere.
9 Transfer your answers to the answer sheet.

Part 7 (Multiple matching)

What is being tested?

Part 7 focuses on your ability to search through a text (or texts) to find specific information, and on understanding writers' opinions and attitudes.

What do you have to do?

- Read four to six short texts around the same theme, or one longer text divided into four to six paragraphs. To answer the questions, you will have to read quickly to find specific information.
- Match ten questions or statements to the text or paragraph that it relates to. The text does not follow the same order as the questions.
- Write the correct letter for each answer clearly on your answer sheet.

Strategy

1 Read the title of each text and any subheadings.

2 Skim each text quickly to get an idea of what it is about.

3 Read the questions carefully and highlight key words.

4 Scan each section of the text to find the information in the questions. You do not need to read in detail. Look for words or phrases which are similar in meaning to the words or phrases in the questions.

5 Underline or highlight possible answers. Do not mark them on your answer sheet yet: you may find similar – but not exactly the same – information in other sections.

6 Read the information carefully to check which one is an exact answer to the question.

7 Leave any questions that you are not sure about; but always go back and answer them at the end as you will not lose marks for a wrong answer. Choose the most likely answer.

8 When you have finished, transfer your answers to the answer sheet.

Writing Paper (1 hour 20 minutes)

Part 1 (essay)

What is being tested?

Part 1 tests your ability to write an essay outlining and discussing issues on a particular topic.

What do you have to do?

- Write an essay based on a title and notes to guide your writing.
- Write in an appropriate style (formal or informal).
- Write 140–190 words.

Strategy

See Writing reference page 179.

Part 2 (choice of task)

What is being tested?

There is a choice of tasks in Part 2, and the testing focus depends on the task. You will have to communicate clearly in a style appropriate to the task. You may also have to advise, compare, describe, explain, or recommend.

What do you have to do?

- Choose one task out of the three tasks you are given.
- Write an answer to the task using an appropriate format and style. The three options could be from the following: an article, a review, a report, a letter or email.
- Write 140–190 words.

Strategy

See Writing reference page 179.

Listening Paper
(approx. 40 minutes)
Part 1 (Multiple choice: short extracts)
What is being tested?

Part 1 tests a range of listening skills. You may be asked about the main idea, the attitude or opinion of the speakers, their relationship, etc.

What do you have to do?

- Listen twice to eight short extracts which last about thirty seconds each on different topics. These may be monologues or dialogues.
- Answer one multiple-choice question about each of the eight extracts.
- Write the correct letter A, B or C on your answer sheet. (You are given five minutes at the end of the test to transfer your answers from the question paper to the answer sheet.)

Strategy

1 Read the questions and options and highlight the key words before you listen (you are given some time for this).
2 The first time you listen, mark the answer you think is best on your answer sheet.
3 Check your answers the second time you listen and make sure the options you have chosen answer the questions correctly.
4 If you aren't sure, choose the answer you think is most likely – you don't lose marks for wrong answers.

Part 2 (Sentence completion)
What is being tested?

In Part 2, the focus is on listening for detail, specific information and opinion in a longer text.

What do you have to do?

- Read the ten sentences with gaps about the recording.
- Listen twice to a monologue which lasts about three minutes on a particular topic.
- Complete the ten sentences with a word or words from the recording.
- Write your answers on your answer sheet.

Strategy

1 Before you listen, read the sentences carefully. Highlight key words and think about the kind of information that's missing. You have some time for this.
2 As you listen, try to complete the sentences. The sentences are in the same order as the information on the recording. Write one to three words to complete each sentence. You should write the words you hear; you do not need to change these words.
3 If you can't complete a sentence the first time you listen, leave it blank.
4 The second time you listen, complete any remaining sentences and check your answers. Don't leave any of the gaps blank – you don't lose marks for a wrong answer.
5 Check that your spelling and grammar (e.g. singular/plural) is correct and that the sentences make sense.
6 Be careful not to make any mistakes when you copy your answers on to the answer sheet at the end of the test.

Part 3 (Multiple matching)

What is being tested?

In Part 3, the focus is on your ability to understand the main idea. You may also have to listen for specific details, understand a speaker's attitude or opinion, etc.

What do you have to do?

- Listen twice to five short monologues which last about thirty seconds each on a related topic.
- Match one of eight options to each monologue. There are three extra options which do not match any of the monologues.
- Write the correct letter A–H for each answer on your answer sheet.

Strategy

1 Read the rubric carefully. This tells you what topic the speakers will talk about.

2 Read each option. Highlight key words/phrases and think of synonyms/paraphrases for these words.

3 The first time you listen, try to identify the main idea of what the speaker is talking about, and mark the option which you think matches most closely.

4 During the second listening, check that the options match exactly what the speaker says. Don't choose an option just because it contains a word from the monologue.

Part 4 (Multiple choice: longer text)

What is being tested?

Part 4 focuses on your ability to follow a longer text and listen for the main idea, for a speaker's attitude or opinion, or for specific information.

What do you have to do?

- Listen twice to an interview or a conversation which lasts about three minutes a topic.
- Answer seven multiple-choice questions.
- Write the correct letter A, B or C for each answer on your answer sheet.

Strategy

1 Before you listen, read the introduction to the task to get information about who the speakers are and what they will talk about.

2 Read the questions and options and highlight key words/phrases. Think about the kind of information you need to listen for.

3 Listen for paraphrases of the words and phrases on the recording and choose one of the options A, B or C. If you are not sure of an answer, continue answering the other questions and come back to it in the second listening.

4 During the second listening, check the options you have chosen. If you aren't sure, choose the one that seems most likely.

Speaking Paper
(approx. 14 minutes)
Part 1 (Interview)
What is being tested?

Part 1 focuses on your general interaction and on social language skills.

What do you have to do?

- The examiner will ask you and the other candidate for some personal information.
- You will be asked different questions about things such as where you live, your family, what you do in your spare time, your work/studies, future plans.
- This will take around two minutes.

Strategy

1 Speak clearly. Try to relax and speak confidently.
2 Try to sound interested and interesting. Try not to speak in a monotone.
3 If you don't know a word, say it in another way. Don't leave long pauses.
4 Listen carefully both to the examiner and to your partner.
5 If you don't understand the question, ask for it to be repeated.
6 Give relevant, personal answers. Avoid giving one-word answers, but don't speak for too long.

Part 2 (Individual long turn)
What is being tested?

In Part 2, the focus is on your ability to organise your ideas and express yourself clearly. You will have to compare, describe and express your opinions.

What do you have to do?

- The examiner gives you two photographs on the same topic.
- Listen to the examiner explaining the task, which is also printed on the page with the photographs.
- The task has two parts; first you compare the photos, then you give a personal reaction to them. You have one minute.
- You then listen to the other candidate speaking, and look at their photos.
- When they have finished, you will be asked to give a short 30-second answer to a question related to the topic.

Strategy

1 Listen carefully to the instructions. It's important that you understand exactly what you need to talk about. Ask the examiner to repeat the instructions if necessary but remember that the question is also written above the photographs.
2 Summarise the main similarity and any differences between the two photos. Talk about the general ideas and don't be tempted just to describe the photos or go 'off topic'.
3 You may need to speculate about the photos if you are not sure what they show.
4 Make sure you save enough time to do the second part of the task, in which you give your opinion on something.
5 Keep talking for the whole minute. Use paraphrases and 'fillers' if necessary. The examiner will say 'thank you' when the minute is finished.
6 Listen carefully while the other candidate is speaking. Look at their photos, but don't interrupt. When the examiner asks you a question related to the photos, give a short answer (about 30 seconds).

Part 3 (Collaborative task)

What is being tested?

In Part 3, you'll be tested on your range of language and your ability to interact with another person. You'll be expected to exchange and discuss ideas and opinions, and invite and respond to your partner's contributions.

What do you have to do?

- In this part of the test, you work with a partner to discuss something together.
- The examiner gives you written instructions and prompts to look at.
- The task has two parts. The first part will usually involve talking about each of the prompts in turn. The second part may involve solving a problem, making a decision, choosing the two most important factors, etc.
- Discuss the task with a partner for about two minutes. You are then given a minute to reach a decision, although you do not have to agree.

Strategy

1 Read and listen carefully to the instructions. Ask for clarification if you do not understand.

2 In the first part of the task you should discuss each of the prompts in some detail (but don't spend too long on any one prompt – you only have two minutes to do this).

3 One of you should start the discussion. Then take turns to give your opinions, agree, disagree, etc. You are tested on the language you use to work together.

4 Turn-taking skills are important. Avoid dominating the discussion or interrupting rudely. It is important to involve and encourage your partner and follow up on what they say.

5 Explain things in a different way if you can't think of a word or phrase and don't leave long pauses. Use words such as *right* or *OK* to 'fill the gaps'.

6 Try to use a range of functional language, such as asking for and reacting to opinions, agreeing and disagreeing, suggesting, speculating, opening and summarising the discussion.

7 You will be given a minute to reach a decision. You don't have to agree.

Part 4 (Discussion)

What is being tested?

Part 4 focuses on your ability to discuss issues in more depth by giving and justifying opinions, agreeing and disagreeing, etc.

What do you have to do?

- In this part, the examiner asks you both questions which develop the topic in Part 3 and may lead to a more general discussion.
- You may add to what your partner has said or agree/ disagree with their ideas.
- The discussion will last for around four minutes.

Strategy

1 If you don't understand the question, ask the examiner to repeat it.

2 Give opinions and express your feelings about issues. Give reasons or examples.

3 Listen to what your partner says and ask them questions or give follow-up comments.

4 Use a wide range of language, but don't dominate the discussion.

Pearson Education Limited
Edinburgh Gate
Harlow
Essex CM20 2JE
England
and Associated Companies throughout the world.

www.pearsonELT.com/examsplace

Main Coursebook: Jan Bell and Amanda Thomas
Writing reference and Grammar reference: Jacky Newbrook and Judith Wilson

New Edition first published 2014

ISBN: 978-1-4479-0714-5 (Gold First NE Coursebook)
ISBN: 978-1-4082-9792-6 (Gold First NE Coursebook with MyEnglishLab:
                Cambridge First)

Set in Myriad Pro
Printed in Slovakia by Neografia

Acknowledgements
The publishers and author(s) would like to thank the following people and institutions for their feedback and comments during the development of the material: Nora Brussolo, Adriana Lado (Argentina); Henrick Oprea, Atlantic Idiomas (Brazil); Anna Kraśko, Katarzyna Machala (Poland); Eleonora Olaru (Romania); Idiomas O'Clock team, Kamal K Sirra (Spain); Tina Casura-Risch, Riana Paola (Switzerland); Pauline Bokhari, Fiona Johnston, Jacky Newbrook, Judith Wilson (UK)

Author Acknowledgements
The authors would like to thank Nick Kenny for his very helpful suggestions, our families for their patience and all the team at Pearson for their hard work.

Text
Extract in unit 1 adapted from "From mod to emo: why pop tribes are still making a scene", *The Guardian*, 26/02/2010 (Rogers, J.), copyright © Guardian News & Media Ltd 2010; Extracts in units 2 and 3 adapted from "Relative Values: Colin Firth and his sister Kate", *The Sunday Times*, 21/08/1994 (Fox, S.); "Relative Values: Jonathan Self and his brother Will", *The Times*, 18/10/2007 (Neustatter, A.); "Relative Values: Zoë Heller and her sister Emily", *The Sunday Times*, 27/09/2009; "Relative Values: Will Young and his twin brother, Rupert", *The Sunday Times*, 28/09/2009; "Relative Values", *Sunday Times Magazine*, 15/03/1998 (Williamson, N.); and "All you need is love (and a scarf)", *The Times*, 25/05/2005 (Rudd, A.), copyright © The Times, 1994, 1998, 2005, 2007, 2009, www.nisyndication.com; Extract in unit 4 adapted from *Esquire presents: What it feels like* (Jacobs, A.J. (Eds) copyright © 2003 by A.J. Jacobs and Esquire Magazine. Reprinted by permission of Three Rivers Press, a division of Random House, Inc. and International Creative Management, Inc.; Extract in unit 5 adapted from "12-Year-Old's a Food Critic, and the Chef Loves It", *New York Times*, 16/11/2008 (Dominus, S.), copyright © 2008, The New York Times. All rights reserved. Used by permission and protected by the Copyright Laws of the United States. The printing, copying, redistribution, or retransmission of this Content without express written permission is prohibited; Extract in unit 5 adapted from Hard Rock Cafe London, http://golondon.about.com, copyright © 2011, Laura Porter. Used with permission of About Inc., which can be found online at www.about.com. All rights reserved; Extract in unit 6 adapted from "The future of entertainment Middle-class struggle", *The Economist*, 26/11/2009, copyright © The Economist Newspaper Limited, London 2009; Extract in unit 7 from *Brooklyn*, Viking (Colm Tóibín 2009) pp.27-31, copyright © Colm Tóibín, 2009. Emblem edition first published 2010. Published by McClelland & Stewart Ltd. Used with permission of the publisher, Penguin Group (UK) Ltd and The Free Press, a Division of Simon & Schuster, Inc., All rights reserved; Extract in unit 9 adapted from "How a suburban street in Reading became a wellspring of champions", *The Week*, 08/05/2010, copyright © Dennis Publishing Ltd; Extract in unit 9 adapted from "Mental Imagery" by Brian Mackenzie, 2002, www.brianmac.co.uk/mental.htm, copyright © Sports Coach, reproduced by permission; Extracts in unit 10 adapted from "Would you rent a friend?", *The Guardian*, 21/07/2010 (Dowling, T.); and "Virtual people, real friends", *The Guardian*, 02/01/2009 (Pickard, A.), copyright © Guardian News & Media Ltd 2009,2010; Extract in unit 10 adapted from *Long Way Round*, Time Warner Books (Charley Boorman and Ewan McGregor, 2004). Reproduced with permission by Little, Brown Book Group Limited; Extracts in units 11 and 13 adapted from "The kid who climbed Everest (It was his dad's idea)", *The Times Magazine*, 16/10/2010 (Watters, E.); "They all look the same to me", *The Sunday Times*, 17/12/2006 (Maltby, A.); and "Who are you again?", *The Times*, 11/08/2006 (Sieghart, M.A.), copyright © The Times, 2006, 2010, www.nisyndication.com; Extract in unit 12 from *One Good Turn: A Jolly Murder Mystery* (Kate Atkinson, 2010) pp.22-23,38. **Published by Doubleday.** Reprinted with permission from The Random House Group Limited; Extract in unit 13 adapted from "The art of digital forgetting", 20/10/2010 (Peter Haber, translated by Ulrike Anderson), first published in German at http://weblog.hist.net/archives/4610, English translation published on http://weblog.hist.net/

archives/4681. Republished under the Open Licence CC BY-NC-SA and by permission of Dr Peter Haber; Extract in unit 14 adapted from "Watch your (body) language", *The Guardian*, 07/03/2009 (Wilson, S.), copyright © Guardian News & Media Ltd 2009; Extracts in Progress Test 1 adapted from "Yakutsk: Journey to the coldest city on earth", *The Independent*, 21/01/2008 (Walker, S.); and "Dining on insects: Anyone for crickets...?", *The Independent*, 21/10/2010 (Taylor, J.), copyright © The Independent www.independent.co.uk.

The Financial Times
Extracts in unit 3 and Progress Test 2 adapted from "The seven secrets of a happy life", *The Financial Times*, 28/08/2010 (Powdthavee, N., and Wilkinson, C.); and "France: Claudie Haigneré", *The Financial Times Weekend*, 02/04/2011, p.35 (Kuper, S.), copyright © The Financial Times Limited 2010. All rights reserved.

The publisher would like to thank the following for their kind permission to reproduce their photographs:

(Key: b-bottom; c-centre; l-left; r-right; t-top)

Alamy Images: Pablo Scapinachis Armstrong 38, Asiaselects 33t, Hans Blossey / imagebroker 71l, Marvin Dembinsky Photo Associate 155tr, Gavin Hellier / Jon Arnold Images Ltd 153br, D. Hurst 12, IS2008-10 / Image Source 130bl, IS797 / Image Source 130tc, Jaubert Images 133t, Tiffany Jones 143r, LOOK Die Bildagentur der Fotografen GmbH 39, Corinne Malet / PhotoAlto 154br, Nicosan 138, Oberhaeuser / Caro 153bl, David Pearson 15, Radius Images 23b, 143l, John Rensten / Cultura Creative 101, Maurice Savage 54, Dmitriy Shironosov 132, Stockbroker / MBI 105l, studiomode 32, Jochen Tack 133b; **Bridgeman Art Library Ltd:** Fire, Full Moon, 1933 (oil on canvas), Klee, Paul (1879-1940) / Museum Folkwang, Essen, Germany 59/5, Confidences (oil on board), Potthast, Edward Henry (1857-1927) / Private Collection / Photo © Christie's Images 98; **Corbis:** Alloy 114b, Stephane Cardinale / People Avenue 58t, Cezanne / Barney Burstein 59/3, Sean De Burca / Ivy 105r, Kevin Dodge / Comet 64, Nicolas Ferrando / Fancy 155bl, Frank Hurley / Bettmann 36t, Image Source 35, Andreas Kindler / Johnér Images / Alloy 28, Bob Krist / Terra 127, Frans Lanting / Terra 147, David Leahy / cultura 80, moodboard 62t, Ocean 30bc, 53r, 106, Jose Luis Pelaez, Inc. / Flirt 23t, PoodlesRock / Corbis Art 36b, Radius Images 43, Rembrandt van Rijn 59/1, Patrick Robert / Sygma 153tr, Paul A. Souders / Encyclopedia 117r, Shin Suzuki / Anyone / amanaimages 140; **Fotolia.com:** axway 128; **Getty Images:** Banana Pancake / Photographer's Choice 155tl, Banksy / Marco Di Lauro 59/2, Neil Beckerman / Taxi 33b, Paul Burns / Blend Images 116, Cavan Images / The Image Bank 114c, Chabruken / Photodisc 18r, Martin Child / Digital Vision 16, Robert Churchill / the Agency Collection 82, Compassionate Eye Foundation / Rennie Solis / Digital Vision 18l, Daly and Newton / OJO Images 152bl, Jonathan Daniel 97, Peter Dazeley / The Image Bank 122, Digital Vision 13, George Doyle / Stockbyte 94, Alexey Dudoladov / the Agency Collection 79r, Mark Evans / the Agency Collection 30tr, Steve Fitchett / Taxi 114t, Floresco Productions / Cultura 19, Frank and Helena / Cultura 62b, Ron Galella / WireImage 22, Ron Gaunt / Getty Images for Long Way Down 104, Claire Greenway 6, Juan Gris / The Bridgeman Art Library 30br, Martin Harvey / Gallo Images 49, Jakob Helbig / Photodisc 155br, Dan Higham / Flickr 61, Andrew Holt / Photographer's Choice 115, Roy Hsu / Photographer's Choice 85, Huntstock 156br, IIC / Axiom / Perspectives 120, Ikonica / Radius Images 30l, Image Source 48, Les and Dave Jacobs / Cultura 87, Nico Kai / Iconica 53l, Jonathan Kantor / Lifesize 30tc, Howard Kingsnorth / Photographer's Choice 137, Jonathan Kitchen / Photographer's Choice RF 11, John Knill / Stockbyte 126, Bob Langrish / Dorling Kindersley 154tr, Latitudestock / Gallo Images 84, Manchester Daily Express / SSPL 9b, Ryan McVay / Photodisc 42, Jason Merritt 90t, Anik Messier / Flickr Select 74, Ty Milford / Aurora 113, Heath Patterson / Photographer's Choice 123, Justin Pumfrey / Taxi 153tl, Shelby Ross / Taxi 117l, Design Pics / Dan Sherwood / Perspectives 136, Smith Collection / Iconica 31, Howard Sochurek / Time & Life Pictures 69 (photo on cover), Stockbyte 112, Patrick Strattner 135, Paul Sutherland 141, Tetra Images 152tr, Vincent van Gogh / The Bridgeman Art Library 59/4, Klaus Vedfelt / The Image Bank 154bl, Frank Whitney / The Image Bank 67, WIN-Initiative 9t, Michael S. Yamashita / National Geographic 72, How Heww Young-Pool 156bl; **iStockphoto:** ilbusca 58b, Matt Kunz 68; **Keith Ducatel:** 45; **Mirrorpix:** Mike Moore 95 (inset); **Pam Fishman:** 51; **Pearson Education Ltd:** 81, 206; **Penguin Books Ltd:** BROOKLYN by Colm Toibin (Penguin 2009). Copyright Penguin Books 2009. 69; **Photolibrary.com:** Tom Murphy / Still Pictures 41, Purestock / Jupiter Images 152tl, Urs Schweitzer / Photolibrary 146, VisitBritain / Pawel Libera 152br; **Photostage Ltd:** Donald Cooper 60; **Press Association Images:** Anthony Devlin / PA Wire 29, Jeff Gentner / AP 77, Tony Marshall / EMPICS Sport 92, Fredrik von Erichsen / DPA 121; **Rex Features:** 71r, 95, Graham Chadwick / Daily Mail 90b, Everett Collection 91, David Hartley 154tl, Genoveva Kriechbaum 70, Lehtikuva OY 88, Ken McKay / ITV 10, Offside 26, Tom Oldham 14, Sipa Press 78, 110; **Science Photo Library Ltd:** Peter Menzel 46, 47l, 47r, 79l; **Summersdale Publishers Ltd:** Cover of James Hilton's Lost Horizon: The Classic Tale of Shangri-La 72 (book cover); **The Kobal Collection:** BBC Films / Kudos / Optimum 8, The Social Network / Columbia Pictures 102, ITV Global 65, See-Saw Films 20; **The Random House Group Ltd.:** from One Good Turn: A Jolly Murder Mystery by Kate Atkinson, published by Black Swan. Reprinted by permission of The Random House Group Ltd 125; **www.CartoonStock.com:** Glenn & Gary McCoy 144

All other images © Pearson Education

Illustrated by Oxford Designers and Illustrators